# Python Mastery BIBLE

## A Comprehensive Guide from Novice to Expert

By

Dr. Hesham Mohamed Elsherif

# ABOUT THE AUTHOR

Dr. Hesham Mohamed Elsherif stands at the forefront of library management, research, and the practical implementation of Artificial Intelligence (AI) in educational and library systems. With over 22 years of dedicated service in the field, he brings a wealth of expertise that bridges the worlds of technology, organizational leadership, and scholarship.

Dr. Elsherif's academic credentials are as diverse as they are impressive. He holds two doctoral degrees—one in **Management and Organizational Leadership** and the other in **Information Systems and Technology**. This dual specialization has equipped him with a holistic perspective on how institutions can effectively integrate emerging technologies, particularly AI, to optimize resource allocation, streamline operational processes, and enrich learning experiences.

A recognized authority in **empirical research methodology**, Dr. Elsherif specializes in **qualitative approaches** and **action research**. His mastery of these methodologies has not only bolstered his own scholarly work but has also allowed him to pioneer new ways of investigating and implementing AI-driven solutions in school, academic, and public libraries. Whether he is designing user-centric AI tools or conducting in-depth studies on technology adoption, Dr.

Elsherif's methodical and data-driven approach consistently yields impactful, real-world results.

Over the years, he has made significant strides in shaping the academic community - not just as a **professional researcher**, but also as an **Adjunct Professor**. In the classroom, Dr. Elsherif has a remarkable ability to translate complex theories into accessible insights, thereby training a new generation of thought leaders and specialists in both library science and technology. This multifaceted role, spanning teaching, research, and practice, has cemented his status as a **pioneer** whose influence extends well beyond traditional academic boundaries.

Dr. Elsherif's expertise and passion are truly global in scope. He has served as a **consultant to numerous educational institutions worldwide**, offering guidance on best practices, AI integration strategies, and effective management models. His international collaborations speak to the versatility of his knowledge, which is informed by a deep understanding of how AI can enhance resource discovery, user engagement, and scholarly communication across cultural and institutional contexts.

Central to Dr. Elsherif's mission is the belief that **innovative technologies**, including AI, must be harnessed responsibly and ethically. This commitment is evident in his approach to library management and educational technology, where he advocates for solutions that are inclusive, data-secure, and aligned with the core values of academic freedom and public service. By focusing on ethical implementation, he ensures that advancements in AI serve learners, educators, and researchers effectively and fairly.

Today, Dr. Elsherif continues to break new ground in **library innovation**, **academic research**, and **technology leadership**. Combining a passion for education with an unparalleled depth of knowledge, he remains a guiding force - **inspiring, educating, and leading** in library systems, educational institutions, and beyond.

Through his work, he illuminates the path toward a future where AI seamlessly complements human expertise, thereby enriching the academic and public spheres for generations to come.

# Table of Contents

# PREFACE

Welcome to *Python Mastery Bible: A Comprehensive Guide from Novice to Expert.* Whether you are stepping into the world of programming for the first time or already have experience with other languages, this book is designed to be your complete roadmap to Python proficiency. Python continues to grow in popularity for its simplicity, readability, and versatility—qualities that empower both novices and seasoned developers to build robust solutions in web development, data science, automation, machine learning, and beyond.

## Why This Book?

The digital age has made programming an essential skill in countless fields, from scientific research to marketing analytics. Python has emerged as a preferred language due to its clear syntax and powerful ecosystem of libraries and frameworks. This book was conceived to help readers harness the power of Python in a structured, hands-on manner, focusing not just on theory but also on practical application.

**Key motivations behind this guide include**:

**Accessibility**: Python is a language that prioritizes human-friendly code, making it more accessible for beginners while remaining indispensable for experts.

**Comprehensive Depth**: While beginner tutorials exist in abundance, many of them skip advanced or specialized areas. This guide aims to provide a *complete* learning path—from fundamental building blocks to sophisticated features and real-world applications.

**Practice-Focused Learning**: True mastery comes from doing, not just reading. You will find a variety of example-driven lessons, exercises, and project ideas that reinforce each chapter's concepts.

### Who Should Read This Book?

1. **Absolute Beginners**: Individuals new to programming who want a clear, methodical introduction to Python.
2. **Intermediate Programmers**: Those who have dabbled in Python or other languages and want to deepen their understanding of core and advanced concepts.
3. **Professional Developers**: Software engineers, web developers, and data scientists who aim to refine their Python skills or expand into new Python-based domains (such as asynchronous programming, data analysis, or web development).
4. **Students and Researchers**: Academics looking to utilize Python for prototyping, data processing, and building research tools.

Regardless of your background, this book provides a structured path to becoming confident and efficient in Python programming.

### How This Book Is Organized

The book is divided into **twelve major sections**, each containing multiple chapters that advance your skills step by step:

1. **Getting Started**: An overview of Python's ecosystem, installation, environment setup, and the first "Hello, World!" program.
2. **Core Python Fundamentals**: Exploration of basic syntax, data types, variables, and operators.
3. **Flow Control and Structured Programming**: Learning essential constructs like conditionals and loops.
4. **Data Structures and Collections**: Mastering Python's built-in containers - lists, tuples, sets, and dictionaries - and their practical uses.

5. **Functions, Modules, and Packages**: Understanding the foundations of code reuse and organization in Python.
6. **Object-Oriented Programming (OOP)**: Diving into classes, inheritance, polymorphism, and advanced OOP concepts like metaclasses.
7. **Error Handling, Testing, and Debugging**: Ensuring your programs are robust, well-tested, and easy to debug.
8. **Working with Files, Data, and the Web**: Handling file I/O, data serialization, and communicating with web services.
9. **Advanced Topics**: Covering concurrency, functional programming techniques, and decorators.
10. **Specialized Libraries and Frameworks**: Introducing popular Python libraries for data science, web development, and automation.
11. **Project Deployment and Best Practices**: Packaging your projects, following coding standards, and implementing security and performance optimizations.
12. **Putting It All Together**: Capstone projects that integrate everything you've learned into real-world applications.

Each chapter includes **practical code examples** and **exercises** to help you apply what you've learned immediately. By the time you complete the final section, you will have the foundation to tackle personal projects, collaborate on professional codebases, or continue to more specialized fields in Python.

### A Hands-On Approach

Learning to code effectively involves more than memorizing syntax. As you progress through these chapters, you will:

- Write and run small code snippets that reinforce fundamental concepts.
- Work through mini-projects designed to illustrate how different parts of the language come together.
- Solve practice exercises that challenge your understanding and encourage problem-solving skills.
- Build and deploy larger capstone projects that simulate real-world software development workflows.

This **learn-by-doing** philosophy underpins each section of the book, ensuring that you not only grasp the theory but also gain practical experience.

### Tips for Maximizing Your Learning

1. **Experiment with Examples**: Every example and exercise is an opportunity to expand and experiment. Modify the code, introduce new features, or challenge yourself to optimize it.
2. **Take Notes**: Keep track of important concepts, tricky syntax, and best practices. You'll find it easier to revisit them later.
3. **Stay Curious**: If you encounter terms or techniques you're unfamiliar with, don't hesitate to look them up or explore additional resources. Learning programming is a continuous journey.
4. **Build Projects**: Whenever you can, start mini-projects of your own - automation scripts, small data analysis tasks, or simple web apps. Applying your skills in new contexts is one of the best ways to retain knowledge.
5. **Collaborate and Seek Feedback**: Share your code with peers, participate in coding forums, or join study groups. Feedback from others often reveals insights you might have missed.

## Looking Ahead

By the end of this book, you will have a firm grounding in Python's core principles, practical knowledge of its broad ecosystem, and a portfolio of code samples and projects to showcase your newfound skills. You'll be equipped to delve into Python-based careers - whether that's data analysis, machine learning, web development, or an entirely new area of expertise.

Thank you for embarking on this journey with *Python Mastery Bible: A Comprehensive Guide from Novice to Expert.* Let's begin by setting up your development environment and writing your very first Python program. From there, the world of Python awaits!

*Let's get started on your path to Python mastery!*

# Section 1: Getting Started

# Chapter 1: Introduction to Python and Its Ecosystem

## Why Python?

### Simplicity and Readability

- **Clean Syntax**: Python's syntax is designed to be intuitive and its code highly readable. This clarity means that even someone new to programming can write and understand Python code with ease. Instead of getting bogged down by complex punctuation or boilerplate code, you can focus on solving problems.
- **Minimalist Structure**: Python uses indentation to define code blocks rather than braces or keywords, leading to fewer distractions and a consistent coding style. This natural structure encourages good coding habits from the outset.

### Versatility Across Domains

Python is a true multi-purpose language that can be used in various fields:

- **Web Development**: With popular frameworks like Django and Flask, Python simplifies the process of building and deploying robust web applications.
- **Data Science & Machine Learning**: Python's powerful libraries such as NumPy, pandas, scikit-learn, and TensorFlow have made it a staple in the data science community, enabling everything from data analysis to complex machine learning tasks.
- **Automation & Scripting**: Its simplicity and strong standard library make Python a favorite for writing automation scripts, allowing developers to quickly automate repetitive tasks.

- **Scientific Computing & Research**: Python's role in scientific research continues to expand thanks to libraries like SciPy and Matplotlib, making it a popular choice for simulations, modeling, and data visualization.
- **Game Development and More**: With frameworks like Pygame, Python is also used for developing simple games and interactive applications.

**A Rich Ecosystem of Libraries and Frameworks**

- **Extensive Standard Library**: Python's "batteries-included" philosophy means that many essential tasks, from file I/O to network communication, can be handled with built-in modules. This reduces the need for external dependencies and speeds up development.
- **Thriving Community-Contributed Libraries**: Beyond the standard library, Python boasts an enormous range of third-party libraries and frameworks available via the Python Package Index (PyPI). Whether you're interested in web development, data analysis, or automation, there's a library that can help.
- **Interoperability**: Python easily integrates with other languages and tools. Whether you need to interface with C/C++ libraries or incorporate legacy code, Python's interoperability ensures that it can fit into your existing workflow seamlessly.

**Strong Community and Learning Resources**

- **Global Community**: Python's widespread adoption means there's a vibrant and welcoming community of developers and enthusiasts ready to help, share knowledge, and collaborate. Online forums, local meetups, and international conferences provide ample opportunity for learning and networking.
- **Abundant Learning Materials**: There's no shortage of tutorials, documentation, and courses available to help you learn Python.

From interactive coding platforms to comprehensive books and video courses, resources are readily available for every learning style.

- **Open Source Philosophy**: Python's development is community-driven, and its source code is open for anyone to inspect, modify, and improve. This transparency builds trust and fosters a culture of continuous improvement and innovation.

**Career and Industry Relevance**

- **High Demand in the Job Market**: Python's versatility and ease of use have led to a surge in demand for Python developers across various industries. Whether you're aiming for a career in web development, data science, or automation, Python skills are highly valued.
- **Innovative and Future-Proof**: As technology evolves, Python continues to adapt and grow. Its role in emerging fields like artificial intelligence, robotics, and cloud computing positions it as a language that will remain relevant for years to come.
- **Cross-Platform Compatibility**: Python runs on all major operating systems, including Windows, macOS, and Linux. This cross-platform nature ensures that you can develop and deploy applications on multiple platforms without major modifications.

**The Philosophy Behind Python**

Python is more than just a tool; it embodies a philosophy that emphasizes simplicity, clarity, and the beauty of well-structured code. The "Zen of Python," a collection of guiding principles for writing computer programs in Python, includes aphorisms such as:

- **"Beautiful is better than ugly."**
  Python encourages the creation of aesthetically pleasing code that is not only functional but also easy to understand and maintain.

- **"Simple is better than complex."**
  By prioritizing simplicity, Python ensures that solutions are straightforward and problems are easier to debug and extend.
- **"Readability counts."**
  A core tenet of Python is that code should be written with readability in mind, making it easier for developers to collaborate and maintain projects over time.

These principles underpin every aspect of Python, from its design to its extensive standard library, making it a joy to learn and work with.

***The Ecosystem: Tools and Resources***

**Development Environments**

- **IDEs and Code Editors**: Whether you prefer the simplicity of a lightweight editor like Sublime Text or the robust features of an Integrated Development Environment (IDE) like PyCharm or VSCode, the Python ecosystem supports a wide range of tools to suit your workflow.
- **Interactive Environments**: Tools like Jupyter Notebooks provide interactive computing environments that are particularly useful for data analysis, scientific research, and educational purposes.

**Version Control and Collaboration**

- **Git and GitHub**: Python projects are often managed using version control systems like Git, with platforms such as GitHub facilitating collaboration, code sharing, and project management.
- **Virtual Environments**: Tools like venv and conda help you manage dependencies and create isolated environments for your projects, ensuring that your development setup remains clean and reproducible.

### Documentation and Learning Platforms

- **Official Documentation**: Python's official documentation is comprehensive and serves as a critical resource for developers at all levels. It covers everything from language syntax to standard libraries.
- **Community Resources**: Websites like Stack Overflow, Reddit's r/learnpython, and countless blogs and tutorials provide real-time assistance and insights into Python programming challenges.

### The Impact of Python Today

Python's rise in popularity is no coincidence. Its design philosophy, coupled with a vast ecosystem and supportive community, has transformed it into a language that empowers developers to solve real-world problems efficiently. Today, Python is used in startups and tech giants alike, serving as a bridge between rapid prototyping and production-level applications.

### Real-World Success Stories

- **Web Applications**: Major websites and web services, including Instagram and Pinterest, leverage Python for their backend development.
- **Data Science and AI**: Companies like Google, Facebook, and Netflix harness Python for data analysis, machine learning, and artificial intelligence, driving innovation in these fields.
- **Automation**: Python scripts are widely used in automating system tasks, data scraping, and testing, saving countless hours in both personal and professional contexts.

In summary, python is a language that excels in simplicity, readability, and versatility. Its design philosophy encourages clear, maintainable code, while its rich ecosystem provides tools and libraries that span virtually every area of modern computing. Whether you are a beginner looking to learn programming or an experienced developer aiming to expand your skillset, Python offers a welcoming and powerful platform to achieve your goals.

As you move forward in this book, you will not only learn Python's syntax and core concepts but also how to leverage its extensive ecosystem to build real-world applications. The journey from novice to expert begins here - welcome to the world of Python!

## Real-World Uses of Python

Python's widespread adoption is fueled not only by its elegant syntax and powerful libraries but also by its versatility across a range of real-world applications. In this section, we explore the major domains where Python is making a significant impact - from web development and data science to automation, scientific research, and beyond.

### 1. Web Development

Python has become a major player in the web development landscape due to its simplicity, rapid development cycle, and robust frameworks. Here's how Python is used to build modern web applications:

- **Frameworks and Tools**:
  - **Django**: A high-level web framework that encourages rapid development and clean, pragmatic design. It comes with an ORM (Object-Relational Mapper), templating engine, and built-in security features, making it ideal for large-scale applications.
  - **Flask**: A lightweight and flexible micro-framework that allows developers to build small to medium-sized applications quickly. Flask provides the essentials without too much overhead, making it highly customizable.

- **FastAPI**: An emerging framework that leverages Python type hints to build APIs quickly, with automatic interactive API documentation and high performance.

- **Real-World Examples**:
  - **Social Media Platforms**: Websites like Instagram have used Python and Django to handle millions of active users and large amounts of content seamlessly.
  - **Content Management Systems (CMS)**: Python-powered CMS platforms enable developers to create, manage, and deploy content-driven websites efficiently.
  - **E-commerce**: Python's frameworks support secure, scalable, and customizable e-commerce solutions that can handle complex transactional workflows.

- **Benefits**:
  - **Rapid Prototyping**: Python's clear syntax allows developers to prototype and iterate on ideas quickly.
  - **Scalability and Maintainability**: Frameworks like Django emphasize clean design and reusable code, making it easier to scale applications as they grow.
  - **Community and Support**: A vibrant community ensures continuous improvements, a plethora of plugins, and third-party extensions to extend functionality.

### 2. Data Science and Machine Learning

Python's role in data science and machine learning has exploded in recent years, primarily due to its readability and the powerful libraries available for data manipulation and statistical analysis.

- **Key Libraries and Tools**:

- **NumPy**: Provides support for large, multi-dimensional arrays and matrices, along with a collection of mathematical functions to operate on these arrays.
- **pandas**: A data manipulation library that offers data structures like DataFrames, making it easier to handle and analyze structured data.
- **Matplotlib & Seaborn**: Visualization libraries that help in creating a wide range of static, animated, and interactive plots.
- **scikit-learn**: A comprehensive library for machine learning that offers tools for data mining and data analysis, including algorithms for classification, regression, clustering, and dimensionality reduction.
- **TensorFlow & PyTorch**: Advanced libraries for deep learning, enabling the development and training of complex neural networks.

- **Real-World Examples**:

- **Predictive Analytics**: Companies use Python to analyze historical data, build predictive models, and make data-driven decisions.
- **Natural Language Processing (NLP)**: Python libraries facilitate the analysis and generation of human language, powering applications such as chatbots, translation services, and sentiment analysis.
- **Recommendation Systems**: Retail and media companies leverage machine learning models to recommend products and content based on user behavior.

- **Benefits**:

- **Efficiency in Data Handling**: Python's data libraries allow for efficient processing and analysis of large datasets.

- **Ease of Integration**: Python integrates smoothly with other languages and systems, making it easy to deploy machine learning models in production.
- **Rapid Experimentation**: The interactive nature of Python (e.g., Jupyter Notebooks) fosters an environment where data scientists can quickly test and iterate on new ideas.

**3. Automation and Scripting**

Python's design makes it an excellent choice for automating repetitive tasks, managing systems, and orchestrating complex workflows.

- **Use Cases**:
  - **File Management and Data Processing**: Automate tasks such as file organization, data extraction, and report generation.
  - **System Administration**: Write scripts to manage system resources, monitor servers, and automate backups.
  - **Web Scraping**: Use libraries like BeautifulSoup, Scrapy, or Selenium to extract data from websites automatically.
  - **Task Scheduling**: Automate routine tasks like sending emails, updating databases, or performing regular system checks.
- **Real-World Examples**:
  - **DevOps**: Python scripts are integral in continuous integration/continuous deployment (CI/CD) pipelines to automate testing, deployment, and monitoring of applications.
  - **Business Processes**: Automating invoice processing, customer relationship management (CRM) tasks, and other routine business operations.
  - **Data Aggregation**: Automatically pull data from multiple sources to create consolidated reports and dashboards.

- **Benefits**:
  - **Time and Cost Savings**: Automating routine tasks reduces manual labor, minimizes errors, and increases efficiency.
  - **Flexibility**: Python's extensive standard library and external modules provide tools for virtually any automation requirement.
  - **Rapid Development**: Python's ease of use accelerates the development of scripts, making it possible to quickly implement and test automation workflows.

**4. Scientific Computing and Research**

Python is increasingly used in academic and industrial research for its powerful computational capabilities and ease of use.

- **Key Libraries and Tools**:
  - **SciPy**: A library for scientific and technical computing that builds on NumPy, offering modules for optimization, integration, interpolation, eigenvalue problems, and more.
  - **Sympy**: A library for symbolic mathematics, enabling algebraic computations, solving equations, and performing calculus operations symbolically.
  - **Jupyter Notebooks**: Provide an interactive environment where researchers can combine code, visualizations, and narrative text in a single document.
- **Real-World Examples**:
  - **Simulations and Modeling**: Python is used to simulate physical systems, from fluid dynamics to climate models, due to its ability to handle complex mathematical computations.
  - **Genomics and Bioinformatics**: Python aids in processing large genomic datasets, analyzing genetic sequences, and modeling biological processes.

- **Physics and Engineering**: Researchers leverage Python to solve differential equations, perform statistical analysis, and visualize complex data sets.

- **Benefits**:
  - **Interdisciplinary Use**: Python bridges the gap between different scientific domains, facilitating collaboration across disciplines.
  - **Open Source and Community-Driven**: The academic community's strong support for Python ensures continuous development of specialized libraries and tools.
  - **Reproducibility**: Tools like Jupyter Notebooks enhance the reproducibility of experiments and simulations by integrating code, results, and documentation.

### 5. Beyond the Core: Other Domains Where Python Excels

While web development, data science, automation, and scientific computing are among the most prominent fields, Python's versatility extends further:

- **Game Development**: Libraries like Pygame and frameworks such as Panda3D enable the creation of simple games and prototypes.
- **Internet of Things (IoT)**: Python is used on microcontrollers and Raspberry Pi devices to develop IoT applications, from home automation to industrial monitoring.
- **Desktop Applications**: Frameworks like PyQt and Tkinter allow developers to build cross-platform GUI applications.
- **Cybersecurity**: Python scripts are commonly used in penetration testing, vulnerability scanning, and cybersecurity research due to their ease of use and rapid prototyping capabilities.

In summary, python's extensive real-world applications are a testament to its versatility and effectiveness as a programming language. Whether you are interested in building dynamic web applications, analyzing vast datasets, automating everyday tasks, or pushing the boundaries of scientific research, Python provides the tools and community support to help you succeed.

### The Python Philosophy and the "Zen of Python"

One of the distinctive qualities of Python is not just its syntax or vast ecosystem, but also the guiding philosophy that shapes its design and community culture. The "Zen of Python" is a collection of aphorisms that capture the essence of what Python is all about. This section explores the Python philosophy, why it matters, and how it influences everyday coding practices.

### What Is the Zen of Python?

The Zen of Python is a set of 19 aphorisms that articulate the core values and principles that guide Python's design. Written by Tim Peters, these aphorisms were never meant to be strict rules but rather gentle guidelines that encourage clean, readable, and maintainable code. You can view the Zen of Python by running:

```
import this
```

This command prints out the aphorisms, which serve as a mantra for Python developers worldwide.

### Key Aphorisms and Their Meanings

Let's explore some of the most influential lines from the Zen of Python and understand their significance:

- **"Beautiful is better than ugly."**
  **Meaning:** Code should be aesthetically pleasing. When code is clear and elegant, it is easier to read and maintain. A beautiful

design is a sign of thoughtful problem-solving and attention to detail.

- **"Explicit is better than implicit."**
  **Meaning:** Clarity is paramount. Writing code that explicitly states its intentions makes it easier for others (and your future self) to understand what is happening. This reduces ambiguity and potential errors.

- **"Simple is better than complex."**
  **Meaning:** Whenever possible, choose a straightforward solution over an elaborate one. Complexity can lead to bugs and maintenance challenges. Strive for simplicity to make your code more robust and accessible.

- **"Complex is better than complicated."**
  **Meaning:** While some problems inherently require complex solutions, it is important to avoid unnecessary complications. Complex solutions are acceptable if they are well-structured, but they should never be convoluted.

- **"Readability counts."**
  **Meaning:** Code is read more often than it is written. Prioritizing readability ensures that your code can be easily understood by collaborators, facilitating teamwork and long-term maintenance.

- **"Special cases aren't special enough to break the rules."**
  **Meaning:** Consistency in coding style and design is crucial. Avoid creating exceptions or shortcuts that deviate from the established practices unless absolutely necessary.

- **"Errors should never pass silently."**
  **Meaning:** If an error occurs, it should be acknowledged and handled appropriately. Suppressing errors can lead to hidden issues that become difficult to diagnose later.

- **"In the face of ambiguity, refuse the temptation to guess."**
  **Meaning:** When dealing with uncertain or ambiguous situations in code, choose clarity and explicitness over assumptions. This leads to more predictable and reliable behavior.

- **"There should be one—and preferably only one—obvious way to do it."**
  **Meaning:** Python favors convention over configuration. By promoting a single, clear method to solve problems, Python reduces the cognitive load and prevents fragmentation in coding practices.

- **"If the implementation is hard to explain, it's a bad idea."**
  **Meaning:** Good code should be simple enough that you can easily describe its functionality. If you struggle to explain your implementation, it might be time to reconsider your approach.

**Why the Zen of Python Matters**

**1. Encourages Consistency and Quality**

- **Unified Coding Style:** The Zen of Python provides a shared set of expectations for how Python code should be written. This consistency is essential in collaborative projects and open-source communities.

- **Quality Over Cleverness:** By emphasizing simplicity and readability, the Zen helps steer developers away from overly complex "clever" solutions that might be hard to maintain.

**2. Fosters a Positive Community Culture**

- **Shared Values:** The Zen of Python acts as a common language among Python developers. It promotes a culture of mutual respect, clarity, and continuous improvement.

- **Learning and Mentorship:** For beginners, these aphorisms serve as a set of principles to guide their learning and development. They provide a foundation for building good habits from the start.

### 3. Improves Code Maintainability

- **Ease of Understanding:** Clear and explicit code is easier to debug, refactor, and extend. Following the Zen's guidance results in codebases that can be maintained over time, even as teams change.
- **Reduced Technical Debt:** By avoiding unnecessary complexity, developers can write code that is more resilient to changes and less prone to accumulating technical debt.

### Applying the Zen in Your Daily Coding Practice

- **Before Coding:** Reflect on the problem and consider the simplest, most explicit way to solve it.
- **During Development:** Write code that is clear, well-commented, and adheres to established conventions. Regularly revisit the Zen principles to ensure your solutions align with Python's philosophy.
- **Code Reviews:** Use the Zen as a checklist during code reviews. Ask questions like, "Is this code explicit and simple?" and "Would another developer easily understand this implementation?"
- **Continuous Learning:** As you gain experience, you'll find that the Zen of Python not only influences how you write code but also how you think about problem-solving. Let these principles guide your approach to new challenges.

In summary, the Zen of Python is more than just a set of guidelines - it is a reflection of the values that have helped shape Python into one of the most beloved programming languages in the world. By embracing these aphorisms, you can write code that is not only functional but also beautiful and maintainable. As you continue your journey in this book, remember that the Python philosophy is always there to guide you toward clarity, simplicity, and excellence in your coding endeavors.

# Chapter 2: Installing and Setting Up Your Environment

Before you begin writing Python code, you need to install the Python interpreter and set up your environment. Python is available for Windows, macOS, and Linux. This section provides step-by-step instructions for installing Python on each platform and verifying your installation.

## Installing Python

### 1. Installing Python on Windows

#### Step 1: Download the Installer

1. Visit the official Python website: python.org/downloads.
2. The site usually auto-detects your operating system. Click the **"Download Python 3.x.x"** button (where "3.x.x" is the latest version).

#### Step 2: Run the Installer

1. Locate the downloaded installer (.exe file) and double-click to run it.
2. **Important:** At the bottom of the first installation window, check the box labeled **"Add Python 3.x to PATH"**. This step ensures that Python and its package manager, pip, are available from the command line.
3. Click **"Install Now"**. The installer will set up Python, pip, and the necessary libraries.

#### Step 3: Verify the Installation

Open **Command Prompt** (you can search for cmd in the Start menu).

Type the following command and press Enter:

```
python –version
```

You should see output similar to:

```
Python 3.x.x
```

To check that pip is installed, run:

```
pip –version
```

**2. Installing Python on macOS**

**Option A: Download from Python.org**

1. Visit python.org/downloads.
2. Download the macOS installer by clicking on the **"Download Python 3.x.x"** button.
3. Open the downloaded .pkg file and follow the installation instructions.

**Option B: Using Homebrew (Recommended for Developers)**

If you prefer using a package manager, Homebrew is a popular choice.

1. **Install Homebrew** (if you haven't already):

Open **Terminal** and paste the following command:

```
/bin/bash -c "$(curl -fsSL
https://raw.githubusercontent.com/Homebrew/install/HEAD/inst
all.sh)"
```

2. **Install Python** with Homebrew:

```
brew install python
```

**Step 3: Verify the Installation**

1. Open **Terminal**.

2. Type the following command and press Enter:

```
python3 –version
```

You should see output such as:

```
Python 3.x.x
```

3. To verify that pip is installed, run:

```
pip3 –version
```

**3. Installing Python on Linux**

Python typically comes pre-installed on many Linux distributions. However, you might want to install or upgrade to the latest version.

**Debian/Ubuntu-based Distributions**

1. **Update the Package List:**

Open **Terminal** and run:

```
sudo apt update
```

2. Install Python 3:

```
sudo apt install python3 python3-pip
```

3. Verify the Installation:

```
python3 --version
```

```
pip3 –version
```

**Fedora**

1. **Install Python 3:**

```
sudo dnf install python3 python3-pip
```

2. Verify the Installation:

```
python3 --version
```

```
pip3 –version
```

**Arch Linux**

1. **Install Python 3:**

```
sudo pacman -S python python-pip
```

2. Verify the Installation:

```
python --version
pip --version
```

**Additional Tips and Troubleshooting**

- **Multiple Python Versions:**
  Some systems may have both Python 2.x and Python 3.x installed. Use the command python3 (instead of python) to ensure you're running Python 3.x.
- **Environment Variables:**
  If you encounter issues with the command not being recognized, ensure that Python's installation directory is added to your system's PATH environment variable. On Windows, this can be set during installation or manually in the system settings. On macOS and Linux, you can add the installation path to your shell profile (e.g., .bash_profile, .zshrc).
- **Updating Python:**
  Check python.org regularly or use your package manager's update command (brew upgrade python for Homebrew, sudo apt update && sudo apt upgrade for Debian/Ubuntu) to keep Python up to date.
- **Using Virtual Environments:**
  Once Python is installed, consider using virtual environments (via the built-in venv module or tools like virtualenv) to manage dependencies and isolate projects.

```
# Create a new virtual environment
python3 -m venv myenv
# Activate the virtual environment
# On Windows:
myenv\Scripts\activate
# On macOS/Linux:
source myenv/bin/activate
```

By following these detailed instructions, you'll have Python installed and ready on your chosen operating system. With the interpreter set up, you're now prepared to write and execute Python scripts, explore libraries, and start your journey into Python programming. Next, we'll explore selecting and setting up your integrated development environment (IDE) to further enhance your coding experience.

## Choosing an IDE or Text Editor

Once Python is installed on your system, the next step is choosing an Integrated Development Environment (IDE) or a text editor. Your choice can significantly affect your productivity and overall programming experience. An IDE typically offers a comprehensive suite of tools - including code completion, debugging, and integrated terminal support - while a text editor might be lighter, more customizable, and better suited for quick edits. Below are some popular options along with guidance on how to get started with each.

### 1. IDLE: The Built-in Python IDE

**Overview:**
IDLE is the default IDE that comes bundled with Python. It is simple, lightweight, and excellent for beginners. Its integrated interactive shell and editor make it easy to write, run, and debug Python scripts without additional configuration.

**Features:**

- **Interactive Shell:** Immediately execute code and see output.
- **Syntax Highlighting:** Helps differentiate keywords, variables, and strings.
- **Debugger:** Basic step-through debugging for learning purposes.

**How to Start:**

1. **Launch IDLE:**

   - **Windows/macOS/Linux:** Search for "IDLE" in your applications or start menu.

2. **Write Your First Script:**

   - Open a new file: File > New File
   - Enter your code:

```
print("Hello, Python!")
```

   - Save the file and run it using Run > Run Module (or press F5).

**When to Use IDLE:**
Use IDLE if you are just starting with Python and need a simple environment without the overhead of additional configuration or plugins.

### 2. Visual Studio Code (VSCode)

**Overview:**
VSCode is a free, open-source code editor developed by Microsoft. It is highly customizable with a rich ecosystem of extensions that support Python development. Its powerful features and integrated terminal make it a favorite among both beginners and professional developers.

**Features:**

- **Extensions:** Install the Python extension for code completion, linting, and debugging.
- **Integrated Terminal:** Run your Python scripts directly from VSCode.
- **IntelliSense:** Offers intelligent code suggestions and auto-completion.
- **Version Control:** Seamless integration with Git and other version control systems.

**How to Set Up VSCode for Python:**

1. **Download and Install VSCode:**

   - Visit code.visualstudio.com to download the installer for your operating system.

2. **Install the Python Extension:**

   - Open VSCode.
   - Click on the **Extensions** icon in the sidebar or press Ctrl+Shift+X (Cmd+Shift+X on macOS).
   - Search for "Python" by Microsoft and install it.

3. **Configure the Python Interpreter:**

   - Open the Command Palette by pressing Ctrl+Shift+P (Cmd+Shift+P on macOS).
   - Type and select **"Python: Select Interpreter"**.
   - Choose the correct Python interpreter (e.g., Python 3.x.x) from the list.

4. **Create and Run a Python Script:**

- Open a new file, save it with a .py extension (e.g., hello.py), and type

```
print("Hello, VSCode!")
```

Run the script by clicking the **Run** button or using the integrated terminal:

```
python hello.py
```

**When to Use VSCode:**
VSCode is ideal if you desire a modern, customizable development environment that supports multiple programming languages and offers advanced debugging and version control features.

### 3. PyCharm

**Overview:**
PyCharm is a full-featured IDE developed by JetBrains specifically for Python. It comes in two editions: Community (free) and Professional (paid, with additional features for web development and scientific tools). PyCharm provides robust code analysis, debugging tools, and integration with popular frameworks.

**Features:**

- **Smart Code Navigation:** Quickly jump between definitions, usages, and classes.
- **Refactoring Tools:** Efficiently refactor your code with built-in tools.
- **Integrated Debugger and Test Runner:** Debug your code and run tests seamlessly.
- **Project Management:** Organize your projects and virtual environments easily.

**How to Set Up PyCharm:**

1. **Download and Install PyCharm:**

   - Visit jetbrains.com/pycharm and download the Community edition (or Professional if you need advanced features).

2. **Create a New Project:**

   - Open PyCharm and select **"New Project"**.
   - Choose a location for your project.
   - Configure the Python interpreter (PyCharm often auto-detects your installed Python version, or you can configure a new virtual environment).

3. **Write and Run Your Code:**

   - Create a new Python file within your project: Right-click on the project > New > Python File.
   - Enter your code:

```
print("Hello, PyCharm!")
```

   - Run your script by right-clicking the editor and selecting **"Run"**, or by clicking the green arrow in the toolbar.

**When to Use PyCharm:**
Choose PyCharm if you prefer an IDE with advanced features tailored specifically for Python development, especially if you work on larger projects or require sophisticated debugging and refactoring tools.

**4. Other Text Editors**

While IDLE, VSCode, and PyCharm are among the most popular, there are several other text editors you might consider:

- **Sublime Text:**
  A lightweight, fast editor known for its speed and powerful plugin ecosystem. Ideal for users who want a simple yet customizable coding environment.

- **Atom:**
  An open-source editor developed by GitHub with a modern interface and numerous packages to enhance Python development.

- **Vim/Neovim:**
  For developers who prefer a terminal-based, highly customizable text editor, Vim offers powerful editing capabilities and extensive community support.

**When to Use Other Text Editors:**
If you prefer minimalistic editors or work primarily in a terminal environment, these text editors can provide a streamlined experience with a lower system resource footprint.

**Summary**

Choosing the right IDE or text editor depends on your personal preferences and project requirements:

- **IDLE** is great for beginners and quick experiments.
- **VSCode** offers a modern, extensible environment with strong community support.
- **PyCharm** provides a comprehensive set of tools designed specifically for Python development.
- **Other Text Editors** like Sublime Text, Atom, or Vim can be excellent choices if you prefer a lighter or more customizable setup.

Each tool has its strengths, and as you gain experience, you might find yourself switching between them based on the task at hand.

Experiment with different environments to discover which one best suits your workflow and enhances your coding productivity.

Happy coding!

## Virtual Environments: venv and conda

Virtual environments are a critical component of Python development. They allow you to create isolated spaces for your projects, ensuring that each project has its own set of dependencies and that changes in one environment do not affect another. This is especially important when working on multiple projects with differing package requirements or when you want to avoid conflicts with system-wide packages.

Below, we'll explore two popular methods for creating virtual environments in Python: the built-in venv module and the conda package manager.

### 1. Using the Built-in venv Module

Python 3.3 and later includes the venv module, which provides support for creating lightweight virtual environments directly from the command line.

#### Creating a Virtual Environment with venv

1. **Open Your Terminal or Command Prompt.**
2. **Navigate to Your Project Directory:**
   Change into the directory where you want to create your project (or create a new directory):

```
mkdir my_project
```

```
cd my_project
```

3. **Create the Virtual Environment:**
   Use the following command to create a virtual environment named env (you can choose any name):

```
python3 -m venv env
```

On Windows, you might need to use python instead of python3:

```
python -m venv env
```

4. **Activate the Virtual Environment:**

- **On macOS and Linux:**

```
source env/bin/activate
```

- On Windows

```
env\Scripts\activate
```

Once activated, you'll see the virtual environment's name in your command prompt, indicating that any Python packages you install will be confined to this environment.

5. **Installing Packages within the Virtual Environment:** With the environment activated, you can use pip to install packages:

pip install requests

This package will be available only in the current virtual environment.

6. **Deactivating the Virtual Environment:**

When you're done working, simply run:

```
deactivate
```

1. This command returns you to your system's default Python interpreter.

**Benefits of Using venv**

- **Isolation:** Each virtual environment is independent, preventing version conflicts between projects.

- **Simplicity:** The venv module is included with Python, so there's no need for additional installations.
- **Lightweight:** It creates a minimal copy of the Python interpreter and required libraries.

**2. Using conda Environments**

conda is an open-source package and environment management system that comes with Anaconda or Miniconda. It supports not only Python packages but also packages from other languages, making it a powerful tool for data science and scientific computing.

**Creating a Virtual Environment with conda**

1. **Install conda:**
   If you haven't already, download and install Miniconda or Anaconda.
2. **Open Your Terminal or Anaconda Prompt.**
3. **Create a New Environment:**
   Use the following command to create a new environment named myenv with a specific version of Python (e.g., Python 3.9):

```
conda create -n myenv python=3.9
```

4. Activate the Environment:

```
conda activate myenv
```

The prompt will change to reflect that you are now working within the myenv environment.

5. **Installing Packages within the conda Environment:**
   With the environment activated, install packages using conda:

```
conda install numpy pandas
```

Or you can use pip if a package is not available via conda:

```
pip install requests
```

6. **Deactivating the conda Environment:**

When finished, deactivate the environment by running:

```
conda deactivate
```

**Benefits of Using conda**

- **Cross-Language Package Management:** In addition to Python, conda can manage packages from other programming languages.
- **Precompiled Binaries:** Conda often provides precompiled packages, which simplifies installation of complex libraries.
- **Environment Reproducibility:** Conda environments can be exported to a YAML file, making it easier to replicate the setup on other systems:

```
conda env export > environment.yaml
```

And to recreate the environment on another machine:

```
conda env create -f environment.yaml
```

**Choosing Between venv and conda**

Both venv and conda are excellent tools for managing Python environments. Your choice might depend on:

- **Simplicity and Integration:**
  - Use **venv** if you prefer a built-in, lightweight solution that comes with Python.
- **Advanced Package Management:**

- Use **conda** if you require a broader package management system, especially when working in data science, where managing non-Python dependencies can be crucial.

Virtual environments are essential for creating isolated Python development spaces that prevent dependency conflicts and make your projects more reproducible. Whether you choose the built-in venv module or the more robust conda system, both approaches help ensure that your projects remain organized and manageable.

## Command-Line Basics

Working with the command line (also called the terminal or shell) is fundamental to Python development. Whether you're managing virtual environments, installing packages, or running scripts, understanding the basics of command-line operations will make your workflow smoother and more efficient. In this section, we'll cover common commands, navigation, and how to execute Python scripts from the command line.

### 1. Accessing the Command Line

**Windows**

- **Command Prompt (cmd.exe)**:
  - Type "cmd" in the Windows search bar or press Windows + R, type cmd, and hit Enter.
- **PowerShell**:
  - Type "PowerShell" in the Windows search bar and open the application.
- **Windows Terminal** (on newer versions of Windows):
  - Provides tabs for Command Prompt, PowerShell, and other shells.

## macOS

- **Terminal**:
  - Press Command + Space to open Spotlight, type "Terminal," and press Enter.

## Linux

- **Terminal**:
  - Different desktop environments may label it differently (e.g., "Terminal," "Konsole," or "xterm"), but typically you can search your application menu for "Terminal."

2. Navigation and Basic Commands

Regardless of operating system, a few fundamental commands will help you navigate and manage files and folders (directories).

| Action | Windows (cmd / PowerShell) | macOS / Linux |
|---|---|---|
| Print Current Directory | cd (without arguments) | pwd |
| Change Directory | cd <directory> | cd <directory> |
| List Files and Folders | dir | ls |
| Create a New Directory | mkdir <foldername> | mkdir <foldername> |
| Remove a Directory | rmdir <foldername> | rm -r <foldername> |
| Remove a File | del <filename> | rm <filename> |

## Examples

1. **Viewing Your Current Directory**

```
# Windows

cd

# macOS/Linux

Pwd
```

You'll see the path of your current working directory.

2. Creating and Entering a Folder

```
# Windows / macOS / Linux
mkdir my_python_projects
cd my_python_projects
```

Now you are inside the newly created my_python_projects folder.

3. Running Python Code from the Command Line

Running the Python Interpreter (Interactive Mode)

1. Open the Interpreter:

```
Python
```

(or python3 on macOS/Linux if python maps to Python 2)

2. Test a Simple Command:

```
>>> print("Hello, Python!")
Hello, Python!
```

3. Exit the Interpreter:

```
>>> exit()
```

**Running a Python Script**

1. **Create a Python script** named hello.py with the following content

```
print("Hello from my script!")
```

2. Run the script in the terminal:

```
python hello.py
```

You should see the output:

```
Hello from my script!
```

**Tip:** If you have multiple Python versions installed, you might need to specify python3 or the full path (e.g., C:\Path\to\python.exe hello.py).

### 4. Installing and Managing Python Packages

Python uses pip (or pip3 on some systems) as its primary package manager. You'll often install packages directly from the command line.

#### Installing a Package

```
pip install requests
```

This downloads and installs the requests library into your current Python environment. If you are using a virtual environment, packages will be installed there rather than system-wide.

#### Upgrading a Package

```
pip install --upgrade requests
```

#### Uninstalling a Package

```
pip uninstall requests
```

**Note:** When working in a **conda** environment, use conda install or conda remove for package management in place of pip, unless the package isn't available via conda, in which case you'd still use pip.

### 5. Tips for Command-Line Efficiency

1. **Auto-Completion**:
   Many shells provide auto-completion features. Try pressing Tab while typing a command or filename to see if it completes automatically.

2. **Command History**:
   Use the ↑ and ↓ arrow keys to cycle through previous commands. This is a quick way to run frequent or repetitive commands without retyping.

3. **Shortcuts**:

   - **Ctrl + C**: Cancel the current command or script in most shells.
   - **Ctrl + D** (macOS/Linux) or **Ctrl + Z** (Windows in cmd.exe): Exit the Python interpreter or end-of-file (EOF) signal.

4. **Aliases and Environment Customization**:

   - **Bash (Linux/macOS)**: You can add aliases or custom exports in files like ~/.bashrc or ~/.zshrc.
   - **Windows PowerShell**: You can create profiles for command shortcuts.

5. **Scripting**:

   - Place frequently used commands in a script (.sh file on macOS/Linux, .ps1 on PowerShell) and run them to automate repetitive tasks.

In summary, mastering basic command-line operations is essential for a seamless Python development experience. The command line allows you to:

- Navigate and manage files in your project directories.
- Run Python scripts directly or enter the interactive interpreter for quick testing.
- Install, upgrade, or remove Python packages with pip or other package managers.
- Integrate automation and scripting into your workflow, boosting efficiency.

By understanding these fundamentals, you're well-equipped to set up your Python projects in any environment - be it Windows, macOS, or Linux - and can easily leverage the powerful tools the command line offers. Next, you'll be ready to write and execute your first "Hello, World!" program and embark on your Python journey in earnest!

## Your First "Hello, World!" Script

Once you've installed Python and set up your development environment, it's time to write your first Python script - a simple "Hello, World!" program. This classic example introduces you to Python's syntax, how to create and run a script, and serves as a stepping stone toward more complex projects. Below, we'll walk through the process step by step, using both a text editor (or IDE) and the command line.

### 1. Understanding the "Hello, World!" Program

The "Hello, World!" program is traditionally the first program written when learning a new language. In Python, it's as simple as printing a message to the screen. The basic command is:

```
print("Hello, World!")
```

Here's what happens in this command:

- **print**: This is a built-in Python function used to display the specified message on the screen.
- **"Hello, World!"**: The message enclosed in quotation marks is a string that will be output to the console.

### 2. Writing the Script

*Step-by-Step Process*

#### Using a Text Editor or IDE

1. Open Your Editor or IDE:

Launch your preferred text editor or IDE (e.g., VSCode, PyCharm, IDLE).

2. Create a New Python File:

Create a new file and save it with a .py extension. For example, name it hello_world.py.

3. Write the Code:

Type the following code into your new file:

```
# hello_world.py

print("Hello, World!")
```

4. **Save the File:**

Save your changes. Make sure your file is saved in a directory you can easily access from the command line.

**Using the Command Line (Interactive Mode)**

1. **Open the Python Interpreter:**

- Open your terminal or command prompt.
- Type python (or python3 on some systems) and press Enter to start the interactive Python shell:

```
Python
```

2. **Type the Code Directly:**

In the interactive shell, type:

```
print("Hello, World!")
```

Press Enter to see the output immediately:

```
Hello, World!
```

Exit the interactive shell by typing:

```
exit()
```

### 3. Running the Script from the Command Line

After saving your script, you can run it from the command line to see how it executes in a standalone mode.

1. **Open Your Terminal or Command Prompt.**
2. **Navigate to Your Script's Directory:**

- Use the cd command to change to the directory where your script is saved. For example:

```
cd path/to/your/script
```

3. Run the Script:

Execute the script by typing:

```
python hello_world.py
```

On systems where Python 3 is not the default, you might need to type:

```
python3 hello_world.py
```

The output should be:

```
Hello, World!
```

### 4. What's Happening Behind the Scenes

When you run the command to execute your script, Python performs the following steps:

- **Interpreter Start-Up:** Python reads your script (hello_world.py) line by line.
- **Execution:** The interpreter processes the print() function call.

- **Output:** The message "Hello, World!" is sent to the standard output (typically your terminal or command prompt).

**5. Tips for Beginners**

- **Comments:**
  Notice the # hello_world.py comment at the beginning of the file. Comments (preceded by #) are used to add notes or explanations in your code. They are ignored by the Python interpreter.

- **Experiment:**
  Try modifying the message inside the print() function. For example, change it to:

```
print("Hello, Python Learner!")
```

- Save the file and run it again to see the new output.

- **Learn by Doing:**
  Writing and running this simple script is a small but significant first step in your Python journey. Experiment with variations and try adding additional print() statements.

In summary, the "Hello, World!" program is more than just a tradition - it's your first foray into coding with Python. By writing and running this simple script, you've learned how to:

- Create a Python file.
- Write a basic line of Python code.
- Run your code using both an interactive shell and the command line.

With this foundation in place, you're now ready to explore more complex concepts and start building your own Python projects. Enjoy your coding journey, and remember: every great program begins with a simple "Hello, World!"!

# Section II: Core Python Fundamentals
# Chapter 3: Python Basics: Syntax and Interactive Shell

## Python Interpreter vs. Scripts

When you begin your journey in Python, it's essential to understand the two primary ways you can run Python code: using the interactive interpreter and executing scripts. Each method has its own advantages and use cases, and knowing when to use one over the other will help streamline your development process.

### 1. The Interactive Interpreter

The interactive interpreter (often referred to simply as the "REPL" - Read-Evaluate-Print Loop) is a tool that lets you type Python code one line at a time and see the results immediately. It is especially useful for experimentation, testing small snippets of code, and learning Python syntax.

### Key Features of the Interactive Interpreter

- **Immediate Feedback:**
  When you type a command, Python evaluates it instantly and displays the result. This allows for quick experimentation.
- **Exploration of Python Features:**
  You can test functions, experiment with data structures, and explore libraries without creating a full script.
- **Learning and Debugging:**
  The interactive shell is an excellent tool for beginners to see how Python behaves with different commands. It's also useful for debugging small sections of code.

### How to Access the Interactive Interpreter

1. **From the Command Line:**
   Open your terminal or command prompt and type:

```
Python
```

or, if Python 3 is not the default:

```
python3
```

You'll see a prompt that looks something like this:

```
>>>
```

2. Example Session in the Interactive Interpreter:

```
>>> # Assigning a value to a variable

>>> x = 5

>>> x

5

>>> # Performing a calculation

>>> print(x * 2)

10

>>> # Exploring a built-in function

>>> len("Hello")

5
```

In this mode, every line is executed as soon as you press Enter. If you make an error, you can immediately correct it and try again.

**2. Python Scripts**

Python scripts are files containing Python code that you execute all at once. They are saved with a .py extension and can be run from the command line. Scripts are ideal for developing programs that require multiple lines of code, managing larger projects, and reusing code across different projects.

### Key Features of Python Scripts

- **Organized Code:**
  Scripts allow you to write, save, and organize code into files and directories, which is crucial for managing larger projects.

- **Reusability:**
  Once a script is written, you can run it multiple times without retyping the code, and you can also import it as a module into other scripts.

- **Automation and Deployment:**
  Scripts can be executed automatically (via scheduling or command-line operations) and are essential for developing applications that are more complex.

### Creating and Running a Python Script

1. Create a Python Script File:
   Open your preferred text editor or IDE and create a new file. Save it as example.py.

2. Write Some Python Code in the Script:

```
# example.py

def greet(name):

    return f"Hello, {name}!"

# Main program execution

if __name__ == "__main__":

    # Calling the greet function and printing the result

    message = greet("World")

    print(message)
```

- **Defining Functions:**
  Functions like greet are defined once and can be reused throughout your script.
- **The if __name__ == "__main__": Block:**
  This special block ensures that the code is executed only when the script is run directly (not when it is imported as a module).

3. Run the Script from the Command Line:

Open your terminal or command prompt, navigate to the directory containing example.py, and run:

```
python example.py
```

or, if needed:

```
python3 example.py
```

The output will be:

```
Hello, World!
```

## 4. Comparing the Two Approaches

| Aspect | Interactive Interpreter | Python Scripts |
|---|---|---|
| Usage Scenario | Quick tests, experiments, learning | Developing larger programs and projects |
| Execution | Executes one line at a time, immediate output | Executes the entire file in one go |
| File Management | No file required; code is temporary | Code is saved in a file ( .py ) for reuse |
| Persistence | Code is lost when you close the session | Code persists on disk for future use |
| Debugging and Prototyping | Ideal for quick debugging and prototyping | Better for structured, multi-line code |

### When to Use Each

- **Interactive Interpreter:**
  Use it for trying out new ideas, testing individual functions, or

learning Python basics. It's perfect for small experiments and quick debugging.

- **Python Scripts:**
  Use scripts when writing programs that are too long for interactive sessions, require organization into functions and modules, or need to be reused and shared with others.

### 4. Transitioning Between the Two

As you develop your Python skills, you'll often start by testing code snippets in the interactive interpreter. Once you're satisfied with how a particular piece of code works, you can transfer it into a script file. This workflow leverages the strengths of both methods:

- **Prototyping in the REPL:**
  Quickly validate ideas and check syntax.
- **Developing in Scripts:**
  Organize and structure your code into a cohesive program.

In summary, understanding the difference between the Python interactive interpreter and Python scripts is fundamental to effective Python programming:

- Interactive Interpreter:
  Provides an immediate, dynamic environment for testing and learning.
- Python Scripts:
  Offer a structured way to write, save, and run comprehensive programs.

By mastering both approaches, you gain the flexibility to experiment with Python concepts in real-time and later build organized, reusable, and scalable code for more complex projects. Happy coding!

## Code Blocks and Indentation

**One of Python's most distinctive features is its use of indentation to define code blocks, rather than using braces ({}) or keywords as in many other programming languages. This design choice not only makes Python code visually appealing but also enforces readability and consistency across codebases.**

### 1. What Are Code Blocks?

In Python, a code block is a group of statements that are executed together. Code blocks appear in many constructs, such as functions, loops, conditionals, and class definitions. The beginning and end of a code block are determined by the level of indentation.

2. The Role of Indentation

Indentation is the whitespace (spaces or tabs) at the beginning of a line of code. In Python:

- Indentation Determines Scope:
  Code that is indented under a statement (like an if, for, or function definition) is considered part of that block.

- Consistency is Key:
  All lines within a block must be indented by the same amount. The recommended style is to use 4 spaces per indentation level.

- Syntax Errors:
  Incorrect indentation leads to a IndentationError or unexpected behavior, as Python will not be able to correctly parse the code structure.

### 3. Examples of Code Blocks with Proper Indentation

#### a. Conditional Statements

Consider an if-else block:

# Using an if-else statement to check a condition

```
x = 10
if x > 5:
    # This block is executed if the condition is True
    print("x is greater than 5")
else:
    # This block is executed if the condition is False
    print("x is 5 or less")
```

- The if and else statements are at the same indentation level.
- The code within each block is indented consistently (by 4 spaces).

**b. Loops**

A for loop also uses indentation to define its code block:

```
# Iterating over a list using a for loop
numbers = [1, 2, 3, 4, 5]
for num in numbers:
    # This block runs once for each element in the list
    print("Number:", num)
    print("Square:", num ** 2)
```

- The two print statements are indented within the for loop, indicating they belong to the loop's block.

**c. Function Definitions**

Defining functions also relies on proper indentation:

```
# Defining a simple function
def greet(name):
```

```
    # The code block of the function starts here
    greeting = f"Hello, {name}!"
    return greeting
# Calling the function and printing the result
print(greet("Alice"))
```

- The function body (the lines inside def greet(name):) is indented to show that they belong to the function.
- The return statement is indented at the same level as the variable assignment.

**d. Nested Blocks**

Python allows nesting blocks within blocks, such as loops inside conditionals or functions within functions:

```
# Nested code blocks example: A function with a conditional statement
def process_number(num):
    if num % 2 == 0:
        # This block executes if num is even
        print(f"{num} is even")
    else:
        # This block executes if num is odd
        print(f"{num} is odd")

# Calling the function for demonstration
process_number(7)
```

```
process_number(8)
```

- The if and else blocks are nested inside the function block, and their statements are further indented.

### 4. Best Practices for Indentation

- **Use 4 Spaces:**
  The PEP 8 style guide recommends 4 spaces per indentation level. Avoid mixing spaces and tabs as this can lead to errors.
- **Maintain Consistency:**
  Consistently indent all lines within the same block. Most modern editors can be configured to insert spaces automatically when you press the Tab key.
- **Readable Code:**
  Clear indentation not only prevents syntax errors but also enhances code readability, making it easier for others (and your future self) to understand the logic.
- **Editor Support:**
  Use an editor or IDE with Python support. Tools like VSCode, PyCharm, or even IDLE highlight indentation levels and help catch mistakes early.

### 5. Why Indentation Matters

The enforced indentation in Python has several benefits:

- **Clarity and Readability:**
  Code is easier to read because its structure is immediately visible.
- **Reduced Boilerplate:**
  There's no need for extra symbols like braces or end statements, which keeps the code clean.

- **Error Prevention:**
  Consistent indentation helps prevent logic errors that can occur when code blocks are not clearly defined.

In summary, understanding code blocks and the role of indentation is fundamental to writing correct and maintainable Python code. With Python, indentation is not just a matter of style - it's a core part of the language's syntax that defines how your code is structured and executed.

By practicing proper indentation and following recommended guidelines (like using 4 spaces per level), you'll develop a solid foundation in Python's syntax and ensure that your code is both readable and error-free. As you move on to more complex topics, these habits will serve as the backbone of all your Python programming endeavors.

## Comments and Docstrings

In Python, writing clear and maintainable code is essential. One of the best practices to achieve this is through the use of **comments** and **docstrings**. They provide context, explanations, and documentation directly within your code.

### 1. Comments

Comments are pieces of text in your code that the Python interpreter ignores. They are used to explain what the code does, provide context, or leave notes for yourself or other developers. Comments can improve the readability and maintainability of your code.

#### 1.1 Single-Line Comments

Single-line comments begin with the hash symbol #. Everything after the # on that line is considered a comment.

**Example:**

```
# This is a single-line comment explaining that the next line prints a message.

print("Hello, World!")  # This comment follows a line of code.
```

### 1.2 Multi-Line Comments

While Python does not have a distinct syntax for multi-line comments like some other languages, you can achieve the same effect in two common ways:

**Using Consecutive Single-Line Comments:**

```
# This is a multi-line comment.

# It spans several lines,

# each prefixed with a hash symbol.

print("Multi-line comments are useful!")
```

**Using Triple-Quoted Strings (Not Assigned to a Variable):**

Although triple-quoted strings are technically string literals, when they are not assigned to any variable, they can serve as multi-line comments.

```
"""

This is another way to write a multi-line comment.

Python will ignore this string literal since it's not used.

It can span multiple lines.

"""

print("Triple-quoted comments are handy for multi-line descriptions!")
```

**Note:** Use triple-quoted strings as comments sparingly, as they are actually string literals that may be stored in memory if not used properly. For actual code comments, the # symbol is generally preferred.

## 2. Docstrings

Docstrings (documentation strings) are a special type of comment used to describe modules, functions, classes, and methods. They provide a convenient way of associating documentation with your code. Unlike regular comments, docstrings are retained as an attribute of the object they document and can be accessed programmatically.

### 2.1 How to Write Docstrings

Docstrings are written using triple quotes ("""Docstring""" or '''Docstring'''). They are placed immediately after the definition of a module, class, or function.

**Example for a Function:**

```
def greet(name):
    """
    Generate a greeting message for the given name.
      Parameters:
    name (str): The name of the person to greet.
      Returns:
    str: A greeting message.
      Example:
    >>> greet("Alice")
    'Hello, Alice!'
```

```
    """
    return f"Hello, {name}!"
```

**Example for a Class:**

```
class Calculator:
    """
    A simple calculator class to perform basic arithmetic operations.
    """
    def add(self, a, b):
        """
        Return the sum of a and b.
        Parameters:
        a (int or float): The first number.
        b (int or float): The second number.
        Returns:
        int or float: The sum of a and b.
        """
        return a + b
    def multiply(self, a, b):
        """
        Return the product of a and b.
        Parameters:
        a (int or float): The first number.
```

```
    b (int or float): The second number.
    Returns:
    int or float: The product of a and b.
    """
    return a * b
```

### 2.2 Accessing Docstrings

Docstrings can be accessed using the .__doc__ attribute on modules, functions, classes, and methods. This is useful for interactive exploration and for generating documentation automatically.

**Example:**

```
print(greet.__doc__)
print(Calculator.__doc__)
```

When you run these commands, Python prints the docstring content for the greet function and the Calculator class, respectively.

## 3. Best Practices for Comments and Docstrings

- **Be Clear and Concise:**
  Write comments and docstrings that are straightforward and to the point. They should help others (and your future self) understand the purpose and functionality of the code.
- **Explain the "Why":**
  Use comments to explain why certain decisions were made, not just what the code does. This context is valuable for maintenance and future modifications.
- **Keep Docstrings Updated:**
  Ensure that your docstrings are accurate and reflect the current

behavior of your code, especially after modifications or refactoring.

- **Follow PEP 257 Guidelines:**
  PEP 257 provides conventions for writing good docstrings in Python. Familiarize yourself with these guidelines to maintain consistency and clarity in your documentation.

**In Summary**

- **Comments** are used for inline explanations and notes that are ignored by the Python interpreter. They are essential for code clarity and are typically written using the # symbol.
- **Docstrings** provide a structured way to document modules, functions, classes, and methods. They are written using triple quotes and are retained with the code for easy access and automatic documentation generation.

By incorporating well-written comments and docstrings into your code, you improve its readability, maintainability, and overall quality. This practice not only helps others understand your work but also serves as a valuable guide for you as your projects grow and evolve.

## Basic I/O (Input/Output)

In any programming language, being able to interact with the user is a fundamental capability. Python makes it simple to perform basic input and output (I/O) operations. In this section, we'll explore how to display output to the user and receive input from the user using built-in functions, along with examples and best practices.

### 1. Output with the print() Function

The primary way to display information to the user in Python is via the print() function. This function converts the provided arguments into a string (if they aren't already) and writes them to the standard output, typically the console.

**Basic Usage:**

```
# Printing a simple message to the console
print("Hello, World!")
```

**Printing Multiple Items:**

You can pass multiple items separated by commas to print(). By default, they will be separated by a space:

```
name = "Alice"
age = 30
print("Name:", name, "- Age:", age)
```

**Customizing the Separator and End Character:**

- **Separator (sep)**: Defines what is printed between the items.
- **End (end)**: Specifies what is printed at the end of the output (by default, a newline).

```
# Using custom separators
print("Python", "is", "fun", sep="-")
# Using a custom end character to continue on the same line
print("Hello", end=" ")
print("World!")
```

**Formatted Output:**

Python offers various methods to format strings:

- **f-Strings (formatted string literals):**
  Introduced in Python 3.6, they allow you to embed expressions inside string literals using curly braces {}.

```
name = "Bob"
```

```
score = 95.5
print(f"Student: {name}, Score: {score}")
```

**str.format() Method:**
A versatile way to format strings, available in earlier Python versions.

```
print("Student: {}, Score: {}".format(name, score))
```

**2. Input with the input() Function**

The input() function allows your program to pause and wait for the user to enter some data. Whatever the user types is returned as a string.

**Basic Usage:**

```
# Asking the user for input
user_name = input("Enter your name: ")
print("Hello,", user_name)
```

**Converting Input to Other Types:**

Since input() always returns a string, you may need to convert the input to another type (such as an integer or float) before processing it further.

```
# Prompting for a number and converting it to an integer
age_input = input("Enter your age: ")
age = int(age_input)  # Convert the input from string to integer
print(f"You are {age} years old.")
```

For floating-point numbers, you can use the float() function:

```
# Prompting for a floating-point number
height_input = input("Enter your height in meters: ")
```

```
height = float(height_input)

print(f"Your height is {height} meters.")
```

### 3. Combining Input and Output

Often, you'll want to capture user input and immediately use it in your program logic. Consider this example of a simple interactive program:

**Example: A Simple Calculator**

```
# A simple program that adds two numbers provided by the user

# Get input from the user for the first number

num1_input = input("Enter the first number: ")

num1 = float(num1_input)

# Get input from the user for the second number

num2_input = input("Enter the second number: ")

num2 = float(num2_input)

# Calculate the sum of the two numbers

result = num1 + num2

# Display the result using an f-string for formatted output

print(f"The sum of {num1} and {num2} is {result}.")
```

In this example:

- The program prompts the user for two numbers.
- The inputs are converted to floating-point numbers.
- The program computes the sum and outputs the result in a clear and formatted message.

## 4. Best Practices for Basic I/O

- **Clear Prompts:**
  Always provide clear and concise prompts so that users know what input is expected.

```
user_input = input("Please enter your email address: ")
```

**Input Validation:**
Consider validating user input to ensure that it meets the expected format or type. For example, when expecting a number, check if the input can be converted to an integer or float.

```
try:
    age = int(input("Enter your age: "))
except ValueError:
    print("Invalid input! Please enter a valid number.")
```

- **Formatted Output:**
  Use formatted strings or the str.format() method to create clear and informative output messages. This makes your output more professional and easier to read.
- **Separation of Concerns:**
  Keep I/O operations separate from the core logic of your program. This separation helps in testing and maintaining your code.

In summary

print() Function:

- Used to display output on the screen.
- Supports printing multiple items and customizing separators and end characters.
- Offers advanced formatting techniques through f-strings and str.format().

input() Function:

- Allows your program to receive input from the user.
- Always returns a string, which can be converted to other data types as needed.
- Enables interactive programs by capturing user responses.

By mastering basic I/O in Python, you can create interactive and user-friendly programs. These fundamental skills form the backbone of more advanced Python programming and will be used extensively as you develop more complex projects.

**<u>Example Exercises</u>: Printing and String Manipulation**

Putting theory into practice is key to learning Python. In this section, we'll work through a series of exercises focused on printing and string manipulation. These exercises will help you understand how to display data using print(), as well as how to work with, transform, and format strings effectively.

**1. Exercise: Basic Printing**

**Objective:**
Practice using the print() function to display various types of data.

**Task 1.1: Print a Simple Message**

Write a Python script that prints the message:

```
Hello, World!
```

Solution:

```
print("Hello, World!")
```

**Task 1.2: Print Multiple Items**

Print your first name, last name, and age on one line separated by commas.

**Solution:**

```
first_name = "John"
last_name = "Doe"
age = 28
print("Name:", first_name, last_name, "- Age:", age)
```

**Task 1.3: Custom Separators and End Characters**

Print the words "Python", "is", and "awesome" separated by a dash (-), and ensure the output does not end with a newline.

**Solution:**

```
print("Python", "is", "awesome", sep="-", end="")
```

**2. Exercise: String Manipulation Basics**

**Objective:**
Learn various string operations including concatenation, repetition, slicing, and case conversion.

**Task 2.1: String Concatenation**

Concatenate two strings "Hello" and "World" with a space in between, and print the result.

**Solution:**

```
greeting = "Hello"
target = "World"
message = greeting + " " + target
print(message)
```

**Task 2.2: String Repetition**

Repeat the string "Ha" 5 times to simulate laughter and print the result.

**Solution:**

```
laughter = "Ha" * 5

print(laughter)
```

**Task 2.3: String Slicing**

Given the string "PythonProgramming", print:

- The first 6 characters.
- The last 6 characters.
- Every second character in the string.

**Solution:**

```
text = "PythonProgramming"

# First 6 characters

print("First 6 characters:", text[:6])

# Last 6 characters

print("Last 6 characters:", text[-6:])

# Every second character

print("Every second character:", text[::2])
```

**Task 2.4: Changing Case**

Convert the string "Hello, World!" to uppercase and then to lowercase.

**Solution:**

```
original_text = "Hello, World!"
```

```
uppercase_text = original_text.upper()

lowercase_text = original_text.lower()

print("Uppercase:", uppercase_text)

print("Lowercase:", lowercase_text)
```

**Task 2.5: Finding and Replacing Substrings**

Given the string "I love Python programming", replace "Python" with "Java" and print the updated string.

**Solution:**

```
sentence = "I love Python programming"

updated_sentence = sentence.replace("Python", "Java")

print(updated_sentence)
```

**3. Exercise: String Formatting**

**Objective:**
Practice formatting strings to produce readable and dynamic output.

**Task 3.1: Using f-Strings (Formatted String Literals)**

Create a script that takes a user's name and age (hard-coded for this exercise) and prints a message in the following format:

```
Alice is 30 years old.
```

Solution:

```
name = "Alice"

age = 30

print(f"{name} is {age} years old.")
```

**Task 3.2: Using the str.format() Method**

Achieve the same output as Task 3.1 using the str.format() method.

**Solution:**

```
name = "Alice"

age = 30

print("{} is {} years old.".format(name, age))
```

**Task 3.3: Formatting Numbers**

Print a floating-point number (e.g., 3.14159265) rounded to 2 decimal places.

**Solution:**

```
pi = 3.14159265

print(f"Pi rounded to 2 decimal places is {pi:.2f}")
```

**4. Putting It All Together: A Mini-Project**

**Objective:**
Combine your skills in printing and string manipulation to build a simple interactive script.

**Task 4.1: Interactive Greeting Script**

Write a script that:

1. Asks the user for their first name and last name.
2. Asks the user for their favorite programming language.
3. Prints a personalized greeting that includes the provided information using string formatting.

**Solution:**

```
# Prompt the user for input

first_name = input("Enter your first name: ")
```

```
last_name = input("Enter your last name: ")

language = input("What is your favorite programming language? ")

# Create a personalized greeting using f-strings

greeting_message = f"Hello, {first_name} {last_name}! It's great to know that you love {language}."

print(greeting_message)
```

In summary

In this section, you learned to:

- **Print Data:** Use the print() function to display messages with various formatting options.
- **Manipulate Strings:** Perform operations such as concatenation, repetition, slicing, and case conversion.
- **Format Strings:** Utilize f-strings and the str.format() method to create dynamic output.
- **Combine I/O with String Operations:** Build interactive scripts that gather input from users and display formatted output.

These exercises reinforce the fundamentals of working with text in Python. By mastering these concepts, you'll be well-equipped to handle more complex tasks and create dynamic, user-friendly programs.

# Chapter 4: Data Types and Variables

## Numeric Types (int, float, complex)

Python provides a rich set of built-in numeric types that allow you to perform arithmetic, scientific computations, and more. The three primary numeric types in Python are **integers** (int), **floating-point numbers** (float), and **complex numbers** (complex). In this section, we'll explore these types in detail, including their properties, usage, and common operations.

### 1. Integers (int)

**Integers** represent whole numbers without a fractional component. They can be positive, negative, or zero.

**Key Characteristics:**

- **Whole Numbers:** No decimal or fractional part.
- **Arbitrary Precision:** Python's integers can grow arbitrarily large as long as there is enough memory.
- **Common Operations:** Addition (+), subtraction (-), multiplication (*), division (/), floor division (//), modulus (%), and exponentiation (**).

**Example Code:**

```
# Integer assignments

a = 10

b = -5

c = 0

# Basic arithmetic operations with integers

sum_result = a + b     # 10 + (-5) = 5
```

```
diff_result = a - b     # 10 - (-5) = 15
prod_result = a * b     # 10 * (-5) = -50
div_result = a / 3      # 10 / 3 ≈ 3.333... (returns float)
floor_div_result = a // 3  # 10 // 3 = 3 (integer division)
mod_result = a % 3      # 10 % 3 = 1 (remainder)
exp_result = a ** 2     # 10 ** 2 = 100
print("Sum:", sum_result)
print("Difference:", diff_result)
print("Product:", prod_result)
print("Division (float):", div_result)
print("Floor Division (int):", floor_div_result)
print("Modulus:", mod_result)
print("Exponentiation:", exp_result)
```

**2. Floating-Point Numbers (float)**

**Floating-point numbers** represent real numbers and are used when precision beyond whole numbers is required. They can include decimals and are represented in Python using the float type.

**Key Characteristics:**

- **Decimal Points:** Can represent fractions and non-whole numbers.
- **Precision Limitations:** Due to their binary representation, floats may introduce small rounding errors.
- **Scientific Notation:** Floats can also be expressed in scientific notation (e.g., 1.23e4 for 12300.0).

**Example Code:**

```
# Floating-point assignments
x = 3.14
y = -0.001
z = 2.0      # Though 2.0 looks like an integer, it is a float.
# Floating-point arithmetic
sum_floats = x + y    # 3.14 + (-0.001) ≈ 3.139
prod_floats = x * z   # 3.14 * 2.0 = 6.28
# Division always returns a float in Python 3.x
div_floats = x / 2    # 3.14 / 2 = 1.57
# Scientific notation
sci_float = 1.23e4    # 1.23e4 is 12300.0
print("Sum of floats:", sum_floats)
print("Product of floats:", prod_floats)
print("Division result:", div_floats)
print("Scientific notation:", sci_float)
```

### 3. Complex Numbers (complex)

**Complex numbers** are used in mathematical computations that require a real part and an imaginary part. In Python, complex numbers are written with a suffix j or J to denote the imaginary component.

**Key Characteristics:**

- **Format:** A complex number is expressed as a + bj where a is the real part and b is the imaginary part.

- **Operations:** You can perform arithmetic operations like addition, subtraction, multiplication, and division on complex numbers.
- **Built-In Functions:** Python provides functions to access the real and imaginary parts.

**Example Code:**

```
# Complex number assignments
z1 = 2 + 3j  # Real part 2, imaginary part 3
z2 = 4 - 1j  # Real part 4, imaginary part -1
# Arithmetic operations on complex numbers
sum_complex = z1 + z2          # (2 + 3j) + (4 - 1j) = 6 + 2j
diff_complex = z1 - z2         # (2 + 3j) - (4 - 1j) = -2 + 4j
prod_complex = z1 * z2         # (2 + 3j) * (4 - 1j)
div_complex = z1 / z2          # Division of complex numbers
# Accessing real and imaginary parts
real_part = z1.real            # 2.0
imag_part = z1.imag            # 3.0
print("Sum of complex numbers:", sum_complex)
print("Difference of complex numbers:", diff_complex)
print("Product of complex numbers:", prod_complex)
print("Division of complex numbers:", div_complex)
print("Real part of z1:", real_part)
print("Imaginary part of z1:", imag_part)
```

### 4. Type Conversion and Functions

Python also allows you to convert between numeric types using built-in functions such as int(), float(), and complex().

**Example Code:**

```
# Converting a float to an integer (note: this truncates the decimal part)

float_num = 3.99

converted_int = int(float_num)   # Result: 3

# Converting an integer to a float

int_num = 5

converted_float = float(int_num) # Result: 5.0

# Converting a number to a complex number

converted_complex = complex(5)   # Result: (5+0j)

converted_complex2 = complex(3, 4)  # Result: (3+4j)

print("Converted int from float:", converted_int)

print("Converted float from int:", converted_float)

print("Converted complex number:", converted_complex)

print("Converted complex number with two arguments:", converted_complex2)
```

In summary

- **Integers (int)** are used for whole numbers, support arithmetic operations, and can be arbitrarily large.

- **Floating-point numbers (float)** represent real numbers with a fractional component, are useful for precision arithmetic, and can be expressed in scientific notation.
- **Complex numbers (complex)** are ideal for computations that involve both a real and an imaginary component, and come with built-in support for arithmetic and accessing individual parts.
- **Type Conversion:**
  You can convert between numeric types using int(), float(), and complex() to ensure that your values are in the correct form for computations.

Understanding these numeric types and how to work with them forms a crucial part of mastering Python's data types and variables. These skills are foundational for further exploring arithmetic operations, algorithm implementations, and more complex programming concepts.

## Strings: Creation, Methods, and Formatting

Strings are one of the most commonly used data types in Python. They represent sequences of characters and are used for storing and manipulating textual data.

### 1. Creating Strings

In Python, strings can be created by enclosing characters in quotes. Python supports single, double, and triple quotes, each serving different purposes.

### 1.1 Single and Double Quotes

Single quotes (' ') and double quotes (" ") are functionally equivalent. They are ideal for short strings that do not span multiple lines.

**Examples:**

```
# Using single quotes

greeting = 'Hello, World!'

# Using double quotes

farewell = "Goodbye, World!"

print(greeting)

print(farewell)
```

### 1.2 Triple Quotes

Triple quotes (''' ''' or """ """) are used for multi-line strings or when you need to include both single and double quotes without escaping them.

**Example:**

```
multi_line_text = """This is a multi-line string.

It spans several lines,

and can contain both 'single' and "double" quotes."""

print(multi_line_text)
```

## 2. String Methods

Python strings come with a variety of built-in methods that make it easy to manipulate and analyze text. Here are some commonly used string methods:

### 2.1 Changing Case

- **upper()**: Converts all characters to uppercase.
- **lower()**: Converts all characters to lowercase.
- **title()**: Converts the first character of each word to uppercase.

- **capitalize()**: Converts the first character of the string to uppercase and the rest to lowercase.

Examples:

```
text = "Hello, Python!"
print(text.upper())     # Output: "HELLO, PYTHON!"
print(text.lower())     # Output: "hello, python!"
print(text.title())     # Output: "Hello, Python!"
print(text.capitalize()) # Output: "Hello, python!"
```

**2.2 Trimming and Splitting**

- **strip()**: Removes leading and trailing whitespace.
- **lstrip()**: Removes leading whitespace.
- **rstrip()**: Removes trailing whitespace.
- **split()**: Splits the string into a list where each word is a list item. By default, it splits by whitespace.

Examples:

```
text_with_spaces = "   Hello, Python!   "
print(text_with_spaces.strip())  # Output: "Hello, Python!"
print(text_with_spaces.lstrip()) # Output: "Hello, Python!   "
print(text_with_spaces.rstrip()) # Output: "   Hello, Python!"
# Splitting a sentence into words
sentence = "Python is fun and powerful"
words = sentence.split()  # Splits on whitespace
print(words)              # Output: ['Python', 'is', 'fun', 'and', 'powerful']
```

## 2.3 Finding and Replacing

- **find()**: Searches the string for a specified value and returns the index of the first occurrence. Returns -1 if not found.
- **replace()**: Replaces a specified phrase with another.

Examples:

```
text = "I love Python programming."

index = text.find("Python")

print("Index of 'Python':", index)  # Output: Index where "Python" starts

new_text = text.replace("Python", "Java")

print(new_text)  # Output: "I love Java programming."
```

## 2.4 Other Useful Methods

- **join()**: Joins the elements of an iterable (e.g., list) into a single string, using a specified separator.
- **splitlines()**: Splits a string at line breaks and returns a list of lines.

Examples:

```
# Using join to combine a list of strings

words = ["Python", "is", "awesome"]

sentence = " ".join(words)

print(sentence)  # Output: "Python is awesome"

# Splitting a multi-line string into a list of lines

multi_line_text = "Line 1\nLine 2\nLine 3"

lines = multi_line_text.splitlines()
```

```
print(lines)  # Output: ['Line 1', 'Line 2', 'Line 3']
```

### 3. String Formatting

String formatting allows you to create dynamic strings by inserting values into a template string. Python provides several methods for string formatting:

#### 3.1 f-Strings (Formatted String Literals)

Introduced in Python 3.6, f-strings provide a concise and readable way to embed expressions within string literals. Enclose the string in quotes prefixed with an f and place expressions in curly braces {}.

Example:

```
name = "Alice"

age = 30

message = f"{name} is {age} years old."

print(message)  # Output: "Alice is 30 years old."
```

#### 3.2 str.format() Method

This method uses placeholders in the form of {} within a string, which are replaced by the arguments passed to the format() method.

Example:

```
name = "Bob"

age = 25

message = "{} is {} years old.".format(name, age)

print(message)  # Output: "Bob is 25 years old."
```

### 3.3 Percent Formatting

An older method for formatting strings using the % operator, similar to printf-style formatting in C. While less common in modern Python, it is still useful in certain contexts.

Example:

```
name = "Charlie"

age = 35

message = "%s is %d years old." % (name, age)

print(message)  # Output: "Charlie is 35 years old."
```

### 3.4 Advanced Formatting Options

Both f-strings and str.format() support advanced formatting options, such as specifying number formats and aligning text.

Example: Formatting Numbers:

```
pi = 3.14159265

# f-string with 2 decimal places

print(f"Pi rounded to 2 decimal places: {pi:.2f}")

# Using str.format() to format a number with 2 decimal places

print("Pi rounded to 2 decimal places: {:.2f}".format(pi))
```

**In summary**

- **String Creation:**
  Strings can be created using single, double, or triple quotes. Triple quotes are ideal for multi-line strings.
- **String Methods:**
  Python provides many built-in methods to manipulate strings, including methods for case conversion (upper(), lower()),

trimming (strip()), splitting (split()), finding (find()), replacing (replace()), and more.

- **String Formatting:**
  Dynamic string generation is achieved using techniques like f-strings, the str.format() method, and percent formatting. These tools allow you to embed variables and expressions within strings, creating clear and adaptable output.

By mastering string creation, methods, and formatting, you enhance your ability to handle textual data efficiently in Python. These fundamental skills are critical as you progress to more advanced topics and develop applications that require robust text processing.

## Boolean and None

In Python, two special types that play a crucial role in decision-making and representing the absence of a value are **Boolean** and **None**.

### 1. Boolean Values

Booleans represent one of two values: **True** or **False**. They are essential in conditional statements, loops, and any scenario where decision-making is required.

### 1.1 Creating Boolean Values

Boolean values are usually the result of comparisons or logical operations. Python has two built-in Boolean constants:

- True
- False

**Examples**

```
# Direct assignment of Boolean values

is_valid = True
```

```
is_empty = False
print("is_valid:", is_valid)  # Output: is_valid: True
print("is_empty:", is_empty)  # Output: is_empty: False
```

### 1.2 Boolean Operations

Python provides several operators to work with Boolean values:

- **Comparison Operators:**
  These include ==, !=, <, >, <=, >=, which compare values and return a Boolean result.

```
a = 10
b = 20
print(a == b)  # Output: False
print(a < b)   # Output: True
```

**Logical Operators:**
and, or, and not are used to combine or invert Boolean values.

```
x = True
y = False
print(x and y)  # Output: False, because both are not True.
print(x or y)   # Output: True, because at least one is True.
print(not x)    # Output: False, because x is True.
```

**Truth Value Testing:**
Python evaluates many non-Boolean values in Boolean contexts. For example, empty sequences (like "", [], {}) and the number 0 are considered **False**, while most other values are **True**.

```
print(bool(0))          # Output: False
```

```
print(bool(42))         # Output: True
print(bool(""))         # Output: False
print(bool("Hello"))   # Output: True
print(bool([]))         # Output: False
print(bool([1, 2, 3])) # Output: True
```

### 1.3 Practical Usage in Conditional Statements

Boolean values are fundamental in control flow. They determine which branch of an if statement is executed.

```
temperature = 25
if temperature > 30:
    print("It's a hot day!")
else:
    print("The day is pleasant.")
```

In this example, the condition temperature > 30 evaluates to a Boolean value (False in this case), so the else block is executed.

## 2. The None Type

None is a special constant in Python that represents the absence of a value or a null value. It is an object of its own datatype, the NoneType.

### 2.1 When to Use None

- **Default Values:**
  None is often used as a default value for function arguments or variables to indicate that no value has been provided.

```
def greet(name=None):
```

```
    if name is None:
        print("Hello, Guest!")
    else:
        print(f"Hello, {name}!")
greet()         # Output: Hello, Guest!
greet("Alice")  # Output: Hello, Alice!
```

**Placeholders:**

Use None as a placeholder when you plan to assign a value later or to signify that a variable currently has no meaningful value.

```
result = None
# Later in the code, result may be assigned a value after some computation
if result is None:
    print("Result is not yet computed.")
```

**2.2 Comparisons Involving None**

It is recommended to use the **is** operator when comparing a variable to None, as None is a singleton in Python (only one instance of None exists).

```
value = None
if value is None:
    print("Value is None")
else:
    print("Value is not None")
```

Using == to compare with None works in many cases but is less explicit and not as reliable when dealing with custom objects that might override the equality operator.

### 2.3 None in Functions

None is frequently used to indicate the absence of a return value from a function.

```
def do_something():
    print("Doing something...")
    # No return statement means the function returns None by
default
result = do_something()  # Output: Doing something...
print(result)            # Output: None
```

In summary

- **Boolean Values (True and False):**
    - Represent the two truth values in Python.
    - Used extensively in conditional statements, logical operations, and comparisons.
    - Can be derived from expressions using comparison and logical operators.
    - Truth value testing determines how non-Boolean values behave in Boolean contexts.
- **None:**
    - Represents the absence of a value.
    - Is an instance of the NoneType.

- Commonly used as a default value, a placeholder, or to indicate no return value from a function.
- Always compared using the is operator for clarity and correctness.

Understanding Booleans and None is vital for writing clear and effective Python code. These types are the backbone of Python's control flow and help manage cases where values may be absent or conditions are tested.

## Variable Assignment and Type Conversion

In Python, variables are used to store information that can be referenced and manipulated throughout your code. Understanding variable assignment and type conversion is essential for writing effective programs.

### 1. Variable Assignment

#### 1.1 Basic Assignment

Variable assignment in Python is straightforward. You simply use the equals sign (=) to assign a value to a variable. Python is a dynamically typed language, which means that you do not need to declare the data type of a variable explicitly; the interpreter infers it at runtime.

**Example:**

```
# Assigning an integer to a variable

age = 25

# Assigning a floating-point number to a variable

pi = 3.14159

# Assigning a string to a variable

name = "Alice"
```

```
# Assigning a Boolean to a variable
is_student = True
print(age)        # Output: 25
print(pi)         # Output: 3.14159
print(name)       # Output: Alice
print(is_student) # Output: True
```

### 1.2 Dynamic Typing

Since Python is dynamically typed, a variable can be reassigned to a value of a different type at any time. This flexibility allows for rapid development but also requires careful management of variable usage to avoid unexpected behavior.

Example:

```
x = 10         # x is an integer
print(x)       # Output: 10
x = "Hello"    # Now x is a string
print(x)       # Output: Hello
x = 3.14       # Now x is a float
print(x)       # Output: 3.14
```

### 1.3 Multiple Assignment

Python allows you to assign values to multiple variables in a single line. This feature can make your code more concise and readable.

Example:

```
# Assigning the same value to multiple variables
a = b = c = 100
```

```
print(a, b, c)  # Output: 100 100 100

# Assigning different values to multiple variables simultaneously

x, y, z = 1, 2, 3

print(x, y, z)  # Output: 1 2 3
```

## 2. Type Conversion

Type conversion (also known as type casting) refers to the process of converting a variable from one data type to another. Python provides several built-in functions for converting between types.

### 2.1 Converting to Integer (int())

The int() function converts a given value to an integer. It can convert floating-point numbers (by truncating the decimal part) and strings that represent integers.

Example:

```
# Converting a float to an integer (truncates the decimal part)

float_num = 3.99

int_num = int(float_num)

print(int_num)  # Output: 3

# Converting a string to an integer

str_num = "42"

int_str = int(str_num)

print(int_str)  # Output: 42
```

### 2.2 Converting to Float (float())

The float() function converts a given value to a floating-point number. It can convert integers and strings that represent numeric values.

Example:

```
# Converting an integer to a float
int_num = 10
float_num = float(int_num)
print(float_num)  # Output: 10.0
# Converting a string to a float
str_num = "3.14"
float_str = float(str_num)
print(float_str)  # Output: 3.14
```

### 2.3 Converting to String (str())

The str() function converts a given value to a string. This is especially useful for concatenating non-string values with strings.

Example:

```
# Converting an integer to a string
int_num = 100
str_int = str(int_num)
print("The number is " + str_int)  # Output: The number is 100
# Converting a float to a string
float_num = 3.14159
```

```
str_float = str(float_num)

print("Pi is approximately " + str_float)  # Output: Pi is approximately 3.14159
```

### 2.4 Converting to Complex (complex())

The complex() function converts numbers to a complex number. If only one argument is provided, it creates a complex number with an imaginary part of zero. If two arguments are provided, the first is the real part and the second is the imaginary part.

Example:

# Converting an integer to a complex number

```
int_num = 5

complex_num = complex(int_num)

print(complex_num)  # Output: (5+0j)

# Creating a complex number with specified real and imaginary parts

complex_num2 = complex(3, 4)

print(complex_num2)  # Output: (3+4j)
```

### 2.5 Converting Between Other Types

Python supports conversion between various data types using similar functions. For example, converting a list to a tuple, a tuple to a list, etc. While these conversions are outside the scope of numeric type conversion, the principle remains the same: using the appropriate function to transform one data type into another.

Example:

```
# Converting a list to a tuple

my_list = [1, 2, 3]
```

```
my_tuple = tuple(my_list)

print(my_tuple)  # Output: (1, 2, 3)

# Converting a tuple to a list

my_tuple = (4, 5, 6)

my_list = list(my_tuple)

print(my_list)  # Output: [4, 5, 6]
```

**3. Best Practices for Variable Assignment and Type Conversion**

- **Descriptive Variable Names:**
  Choose clear, descriptive names for your variables. This practice makes your code more readable and maintainable.
- **Explicit Conversions:**
  While Python performs implicit type conversion in some cases, it's best to be explicit when converting types. This reduces ambiguity and potential errors.
- **Check Input Validity:**
  When converting user input, consider adding error handling (e.g., using try/except) to manage cases where the conversion might fail.

Example with Error Handling:

```
user_input = input("Enter an integer: ")

try:

    user_number = int(user_input)

    print(f"You entered: {user_number}")

except ValueError:

    print("Invalid input! Please enter a valid integer.")
```

- **Consistency:**
  Maintain consistency in how you assign and convert types. Avoid mixing types without proper conversion to prevent bugs.

**In summary**

- **Variable Assignment:**
  - Variables are dynamically typed, meaning their types can change over time.
  - Multiple variables can be assigned in a single line for clarity and efficiency.
- **Type Conversion:**
  - Built-in functions like int(), float(), str(), and complex() are used to convert between types.
  - Explicit conversions help ensure that your data is in the correct format for processing and output.

Mastering variable assignment and type conversion is fundamental to effective Python programming. These concepts allow you to manipulate and transform data seamlessly, laying the groundwork for more advanced programming techniques and applications.

## Example Exercises: Simple Calculators

Putting your knowledge into practice is one of the best ways to solidify your understanding of Python's data types, variables, and basic operations. In this section, you'll work through a series of hands-on exercises designed to reinforce these concepts by building a simple calculator and practicing string formatting.

### 1. Exercise: Building a Simple Calculator

**Objective:**
Create a Python script that prompts the user for two numbers and

performs basic arithmetic operations (addition, subtraction, multiplication, and division).

**Step-by-Step Instructions**

1. **Prompt the User for Input:**
   Use the input() function to capture two numbers.
2. **Convert Inputs to the Appropriate Type:**
   Convert the input strings to floats (or integers) using float() or int().
3. **Perform Arithmetic Operations:**
   Compute the sum, difference, product, and quotient.
4. **Display the Results:**
   Use string formatting to present the results clearly.

Example Code:

```
# Simple Calculator: Performs basic arithmetic operations

# Step 1: Prompt the user for two numbers

num1_input = input("Enter the first number: ")

num2_input = input("Enter the second number: ")

# Step 2: Convert the inputs from strings to floats

try:

    num1 = float(num1_input)

    num2 = float(num2_input)

except ValueError:

    print("Invalid input! Please enter numeric values.")

    exit()  # Exit the program if the conversion fails
```

```
# Step 3: Perform arithmetic operations
sum_result = num1 + num2
difference = num1 - num2
product = num1 * num2
# Check for division by zero
if num2 != 0:
    quotient = num1 / num2
else:
    quotient = "undefined (division by zero)"
# Step 4: Display the results using formatted output
print("\n--- Calculator Results ---")
print(f"{num1} + {num2} = {sum_result}")
print(f"{num1} - {num2} = {difference}")
print(f"{num1} * {num2} = {product}")
print(f"{num1} / {num2} = {quotient}")
```

**Explanation:**

- **Input Conversion:**
  The script converts the user-provided inputs to floats. If the conversion fails (e.g., the user enters non-numeric data), the program prints an error message and exits.
- **Arithmetic Operations:**
  Basic operations are performed, and division includes a check for division by zero to prevent runtime errors.

- **Formatted Output:**
  The results are printed using f-strings, which allow for embedding variables directly into the output string with clear formatting.

## 2. Exercise: String Formatters

**Objective:**
Practice using various string formatting methods to generate dynamic and well-formatted text output.

### Task 2.1: Using f-Strings

Create a script that takes a person's name, age, and city, then prints a greeting using an f-string.

Example Code:

```
# Using f-Strings for formatted output

# Hard-coded example values

name = "Alice"

age = 30

city = "New York"

# Construct a dynamic greeting message using an f-string

greeting = f"Hello, my name is {name}. I am {age} years old and I live in {city}."

print(greeting)
```

### Task 2.2: Using str.format() Method

Achieve the same output as in Task 2.1, but this time using the str.format() method.

Example Code:

```
# Using the str.format() method for formatted output
name = "Alice"
age = 30
city = "New York"
# Construct the greeting message using placeholders
greeting = "Hello, my name is {}. I am {} years old and I live in {}.".format(name, age, city)
print(greeting)
```

**Task 2.3: Percent (%) Formatting**

Finally, create the same greeting message using the older percent formatting method.

Example Code:

```
# Using percent (%) formatting
name = "Alice"
age = 30
city = "New York"
# Construct the greeting message using percent formatting
greeting = "Hello, my name is %s. I am %d years old and I live in %s." % (name, age, city)
print(greeting)
```

**Task 2.4: Advanced Number Formatting**

Format a floating-point number to display only two decimal places.

Example Code:

```
# Advanced number formatting with f-Strings
pi = 3.14159265
formatted_pi = f"Pi rounded to 2 decimal places: {pi:.2f}"
print(formatted_pi)
```

**Explanation:**

- **f-Strings, str.format(), and Percent Formatting:**
  These examples show three different methods for creating dynamic strings. Each method inserts variables into a template string, making it easier to generate user-friendly output.
- **Advanced Number Formatting:**
  The example with the variable pi demonstrates how to round a floating-point number to two decimal places using f-string formatting ({pi:.2f}).

**In summary**

Through these exercises, you've practiced essential techniques in Python:

- **Simple Calculator:**

  - Capturing user input.
  - Converting input types.
  - Performing arithmetic operations.
  - Handling edge cases (such as division by zero).
  - Displaying results using formatted strings.
- **String Formatters:**

  - Using f-strings for concise and readable formatting.

- Employing the str.format() method for versatile formatting.
- Utilizing percent formatting as an alternative method.
- Formatting numbers to a specified number of decimal places.

These exercises not only reinforce your understanding of Python's data types and variable assignments but also help you develop practical skills for creating interactive and well-formatted applications.

# Chapter 5: Operators and Expressions

## Arithmetic Operators

Arithmetic operators are essential tools in Python that allow you to perform mathematical calculations on numeric values. They form the basis of most programs involving numerical computations and are used in various expressions, from simple calculations to complex algorithms.

### 1. Overview of Arithmetic Operators

Python provides several built-in arithmetic operators that can be used to manipulate numbers. Here are the primary arithmetic operators:

- **Addition (+)**
  Adds two numbers together.
- **Subtraction (-)**
  Subtracts one number from another.
- **Multiplication (*)**
  Multiplies two numbers.
- **Division (/)**
  Divides one number by another, always returning a float.
- **Floor Division (//)**
  Divides one number by another and rounds down to the nearest whole number.
- **Modulus (%)**
  Returns the remainder after division.
- **Exponentiation (**)**
  Raises a number to the power of another.

## 2. Detailed Examples and Explanations

### 2.1 Addition and Subtraction

Addition and subtraction are the most straightforward arithmetic operations. They combine or subtract numeric values.

**Example:**

```
a = 10

b = 5

addition = a + b        # 10 + 5 = 15

subtraction = a - b   # 10 - 5 = 5

print("Addition:", addition)       # Output: Addition: 15

print("Subtraction:", subtraction) # Output: Subtraction: 5
```

### 2.2 Multiplication

Multiplication is used to calculate the product of two numbers.

**Example:**

```
a = 7

b = 3

product = a * b  # 7 * 3 = 21

print("Multiplication:", product)  # Output: Multiplication: 21
```

### 2.3 Division

Division returns the quotient of two numbers. In Python 3, division always produces a floating-point result, even if both operands are integers.

**Example:**

```
a = 20

b = 4

division = a / b  # 20 / 4 = 5.0

print("Division:", division)  # Output: Division: 5.0
```

### 2.4 Floor Division

Floor division (//) divides two numbers and returns the largest integer less than or equal to the quotient. This is especially useful when you need an integer result.

**Example:**

```
a = 20

b = 3

floor_division = a // b  # 20 // 3 = 6

print("Floor Division:", floor_division)  # Output: Floor Division: 6
```

### 2.5 Modulus

The modulus operator (%) returns the remainder of the division between two numbers.

**Example:**

```
a = 20

b = 3

remainder = a % b  # 20 % 3 = 2 (since 3*6 = 18 and 20 - 18 = 2)

print("Modulus:", remainder)  # Output: Modulus: 2
```

### 2.6 Exponentiation

Exponentiation (**) raises the first operand to the power of the second operand.

**Example:**

```
base = 2

exponent = 3

power = base ** exponent  # 2 ** 3 = 8

print("Exponentiation:", power)  # Output: Exponentiation: 8
```

## 3. Operator Precedence and Associativity

When combining multiple arithmetic operators in a single expression, Python follows a set of rules known as **operator precedence** to determine the order in which operations are performed. The general precedence from highest to lowest for arithmetic operators is as follows:

1. **Exponentiation (**)**
2. **Unary plus and minus (+, - as in -a or +a)**
3. **Multiplication (*), Division (/), Floor Division (//), Modulus (%)**
4. **Addition (+) and Subtraction (-)**

Operators of the same precedence are evaluated from left to right, except for exponentiation, which is evaluated from right to left.

**Example:**

```
# Expression without parentheses:

result = 2 + 3 * 4 ** 2

# According to precedence:
```

```
# First, exponentiation: 4 ** 2 = 16
# Then, multiplication: 3 * 16 = 48
# Finally, addition: 2 + 48 = 50
print("Result:", result) # Output: Result: 50
# Using parentheses to alter the order:
result_with_parentheses = (2 + 3) * (4 ** 2)
# Parentheses force addition first: 2 + 3 = 5
# Then exponentiation: 4 ** 2 = 16
# Finally, multiplication: 5 * 16 = 80
print("Result with parentheses:", result_with_parentheses) # Output: Result with parentheses: 80
```

In summary

- **Arithmetic operators** in Python allow you to perform mathematical calculations such as addition, subtraction, multiplication, division, floor division, modulus, and exponentiation.
- Python's **operator precedence** rules determine the order in which operations are performed in complex expressions. Parentheses can be used to override these rules and ensure that operations are performed in the desired order.
- Understanding these operators and their behavior is fundamental for working with numerical data in Python and forms the foundation for more advanced mathematical operations and algorithms.

By mastering arithmetic operators, you will be well-equipped to handle numerical computations and build more complex expressions in your Python programs.

## Comparison and Logical Operators

Comparison and logical operators are critical components in Python that enable decision-making by evaluating conditions and combining multiple Boolean expressions. They are widely used in control flow statements (such as if, while, and for) to dictate the path of execution based on dynamic conditions.

### 1. Comparison Operators

Comparison operators compare two values and return a Boolean (True or False) result. They are used to check for equality, inequality, and relational conditions.

#### 1.1 List of Comparison Operators

- **Equality (==)**
  Checks if two values are equal.
- **Inequality (!=)**
  Checks if two values are not equal.
- **Greater Than (>)**
  Checks if the left value is greater than the right value.
- **Less Than (<)**
  Checks if the left value is less than the right value.
- **Greater Than or Equal To (>=)**
  Checks if the left value is greater than or equal to the right value.
- **Less Than or Equal To (<=)**
  Checks if the left value is less than or equal to the right value.

#### 1.2 Examples of Comparison Operators

```
# Define two numbers for comparison
a = 10
b = 20
# Equality and Inequality
print("a == b:", a == b)  # Output: False
print("a != b:", a != b)  # Output: True
# Relational comparisons
print("a < b:", a < b)    # Output: True
print("a > b:", a > b)    # Output: False
print("a <= b:", a <= b)  # Output: True
print("a >= b:", a >= b)  # Output: False
# Comparing strings
str1 = "apple"
str2 = "banana"
print("str1 == str2:", str1 == str2)  # Output: False
print("str1 < str2:", str1 < str2)    # Lexicographical comparison: Output depends on alphabetic order
```

## 2. Logical Operators

Logical operators allow you to combine multiple Boolean expressions into a single condition. They evaluate to either True or False based on the logic of the combination.

### 2.1 List of Logical Operators

- **Logical AND (and)**
  Returns True if **both** operands are True; otherwise, returns False.

- **Logical OR (or)**
  Returns True if **at least one** of the operands is True; otherwise, returns False.
- **Logical NOT (not)**
  Returns True if the operand is False; returns False if the operand is True.

### 2.2 Examples of Logical Operators

```
# Define some Boolean variables
x = True
y = False
# Logical AND
print("x and y:", x and y)  # Output: False (because y is False)
# Logical OR
print("x or y:", x or y)    # Output: True (because x is True)
# Logical NOT
print("not x:", not x)      # Output: False (because x is True)
print("not y:", not y)      # Output: True (because y is False)
```

### 2.3 Combining Comparison and Logical Operators

You can combine comparison operators with logical operators to form complex conditional expressions.

**Example:**

```
age = 25
income = 50000
```

```
# Check if a person is eligible for a loan

# Condition: age must be at least 21 AND income must be greater than 40000

eligible = (age >= 21) and (income > 40000)

print("Eligible for loan:", eligible)  # Output: True

# Alternatively, check if a person qualifies for a discount:

# Condition: age is less than 18 OR greater than 65

age = 70

qualifies_discount = (age < 18) or (age > 65)

print("Qualifies for discount:", qualifies_discount)  # Output: True
```

**3. Operator Precedence**

When combining multiple operators in a single expression, Python follows a specific order of operations (operator precedence):

1. **Comparison Operators:**
   Evaluate before logical operators. For example, in the expression (a > b) and (a != c), both comparisons are evaluated first.
2. **Logical NOT (not):**
   Has higher precedence than and and or.
3. **Logical AND (and):**
   Evaluated before logical OR.
4. **Logical OR (or):**
   Evaluated last.

**Example:**

```
a, b, c = 10, 20, 10

# Expression without parentheses
```

```
result = a == c or a > b and b != c

# Operator precedence:

# 1. Evaluate comparisons: a == c -> True; a > b -> False; b != c -> True

# 2. Evaluate "and": False and True -> False

# 3. Evaluate "or": True or False -> True

print("Result:", result)  # Output: True

# Using parentheses to change evaluation order

result_with_parentheses = (a == c or a > b) and b != c

# 1. Evaluate inside parentheses: (a == c or a > b) -> (True or False) -> True

# 2. Then, evaluate: True and (b != c) -> True and True -> True

print("Result with parentheses:", result_with_parentheses)  # Output: True
```

**4. Truth Value Testing in Python**

Python's logical operators also work on non-Boolean values. Each object in Python has an inherent truth value. The following values are considered **False** in Boolean contexts:

- False
- None
- Numeric zero values: 0, 0.0, 0j
- Empty sequences or collections: "", (), [], {}, set()

All other values are considered **True**.

**Example:**

```
print(bool(0))        # Output: False
print(bool(1))        # Output: True
print(bool(""))       # Output: False
print(bool("Python")) # Output: True
print(bool([]))       # Output: False
print(bool([1, 2, 3])) # Output: True
```

In summary

- **Comparison Operators:**
  - Allow you to compare values (e.g., ==, !=, <, >, <=, >=).
  - Return Boolean results based on the relationship between operands.
- **Logical Operators:**
  - Enable you to combine multiple Boolean expressions (and, or, not).
  - Follow a specific precedence where comparisons are evaluated first, then not, followed by and, and finally or.
- **Combining Both:**
  - Complex expressions can be created by mixing comparison and logical operators.
  - Parentheses can be used to control the order of evaluation explicitly.

Understanding these operators is crucial for making decisions in your code. Mastery of comparison and logical operators not only simplifies the creation of conditional statements but also forms the foundation for more advanced programming techniques.

## Assignment Operators and Expressions

Assignment operators are essential in Python, allowing you to store, update, and manipulate data throughout your programs. They not only assign values to variables but also provide shortcuts for performing arithmetic or other operations before assignment. Additionally, Python supports assignment expressions (popularly known as the "walrus operator") which allow you to assign values as part of larger expressions.

### 1. Basic Assignment

The simplest assignment operator in Python is the equals sign (=), which assigns the value on the right-hand side (RHS) to the variable on the left-hand side (LHS). Python is dynamically typed, so you don't need to declare a variable's type before assignment.

**Example:**

```
# Basic assignment of values to variables
x = 10          # x is assigned the integer 10
name = "Alice"  # name is assigned the string "Alice"
pi = 3.14159    # pi is assigned a floating-point number
print(x)    # Output: 10
print(name) # Output: Alice
print(pi)   # Output: 3.14159
```

### 2. Compound Assignment Operators

Compound assignment operators combine an arithmetic or bitwise operation with assignment. They provide a shorthand way to update the value of a variable.

**Common Compound Assignment Operators:**

- **Addition Assignment (+=):**
  Adds the right-hand operand to the left-hand operand and assigns the result to the left-hand operand.
- **Subtraction Assignment (-=):**
  Subtracts the right-hand operand from the left-hand operand and assigns the result to the left-hand operand.
- **Multiplication Assignment (*=):**
  Multiplies the left-hand operand by the right-hand operand and assigns the result.
- **Division Assignment (/=):**
  Divides the left-hand operand by the right-hand operand and assigns the result as a float.
- **Floor Division Assignment (//=):**
  Divides the left-hand operand by the right-hand operand, floors the result, and assigns it.
- **Modulus Assignment (%=):**
  Applies the modulus operation on the left-hand operand with the right-hand operand and assigns the result.
- **Exponentiation Assignment (**=):**
  Raises the left-hand operand to the power of the right-hand operand and assigns the result.

**Examples:**

```
# Compound assignment examples

# Addition assignment
```

```
x = 5
x += 3  # Equivalent to: x = x + 3
print("After += :", x)  # Output: 8
# Subtraction assignment
y = 10
y -= 2  # Equivalent to: y = y - 2
print("After -= :", y)  # Output: 8
# Multiplication assignment
z = 4
z *= 2  # Equivalent to: z = z * 2
print("After *= :", z)  # Output: 8
# Division assignment
a = 16
a /= 4  # Equivalent to: a = a / 4 (result is a float)
print("After /= :", a)  # Output: 4.0
# Floor division assignment
b = 17
b //= 4  # Equivalent to: b = b // 4
print("After //= :", b)  # Output: 4
# Modulus assignment
c = 17
c %= 4  # Equivalent to: c = c % 4
```

```
print("After %= :", c)  # Output: 1

# Exponentiation assignment

d = 3

d **= 2  # Equivalent to: d = d ** 2

print("After **= :", d)  # Output: 9
```

### 3. Assignment Expressions (The Walrus Operator)

Introduced in Python 3.8, assignment expressions (denoted by the := operator, colloquially known as the "walrus operator") allow you to assign a value to a variable as part of a larger expression. This can simplify code by reducing redundancy and improving readability.

**Use Cases for the Walrus Operator:**

- **In Loops:**
  You can assign and test a condition in a single line.
- **In Conditional Statements:**
  It enables you to compute and use a value without needing a separate assignment statement.

**Example 1: Using the Walrus Operator in a Loop**

```
# Read lines from a file (or any iterable) until an empty line is encountered.

# Here, we simulate this with a list of strings.

lines = ["First line", "Second line", "", "Fourth line"]

# Using a while loop with the walrus operator

i = 0

while (line := lines[i]) != "":

    print(f"Line {i+1}: {line}")
```

```
    i += 1
# Output:
# Line 1: First line
# Line 2: Second line
```

**Example 2**: Using the Walrus Operator in an If Statement

```
# Check if a user input (a number as a string) can be converted to an integer
user_input = "1234"
if (num := int(user_input)) > 1000:
    print(f"The number {num} is greater than 1000.")
else:
    print(f"The number {num} is not greater than 1000.")
# Output: The number 1234 is greater than 1000.
```

**4. Best Practices for Assignment and Type Conversion**

- **Clarity Over Brevity:**
  While compound assignments and the walrus operator can make your code more concise, ensure that your code remains readable. Overusing compact expressions can lead to code that is difficult to understand.
- **Consistent Use:**
  Be consistent in how you use assignment operators throughout your code to maintain clarity.
- **Type Awareness:**
  Python's dynamic typing makes implicit type conversion common, but be explicit when necessary, especially when

converting user inputs or performing arithmetic operations that require specific types.

**In summary**

- **Basic Assignment (=):**
  The foundation for storing values in variables. Python's dynamic typing means you do not declare a variable's type explicitly.
- **Compound Assignment Operators:**
  Provide a shorthand for performing an operation and assignment in one step (e.g., +=, -=, *=, /=, //=, %= and **=).
- **Assignment Expressions (Walrus Operator :=):**
  Allow you to assign values within an expression, reducing redundancy and often improving code readability when used appropriately.

Mastering assignment operators and expressions is essential for efficient Python programming. These tools not only simplify code by reducing repetition but also allow you to write more dynamic and expressive programs.

## Operator Precedence and Associativity

When writing complex expressions in Python, understanding **operator precedence** and **associativity** is essential. These rules determine the order in which parts of an expression are evaluated. This ensures that operations are performed in a predictable manner, without requiring excessive use of parentheses.

### 1. Operator Precedence

Operator precedence defines the order in which different operators in an expression are evaluated. Operators with higher precedence are evaluated before operators with lower precedence. Below is a simplified list of Python operator precedence, from highest to lowest, relevant to common arithmetic and logical expressions:

1. **Parentheses (())**
   Expressions within parentheses are always evaluated first.

2. **Exponentiation (**)**
   Evaluated next and is right-associative (see below).

3. **Unary Operators (+, -, ~)**
   These operators (unary plus, unary minus, bitwise NOT) operate on a single operand.

4. **Multiplication (*), Division (/), Floor Division (//), and Modulus (%)**
   These are evaluated after unary operators.

5. **Addition (+) and Subtraction (-)**
   Evaluated after the multiplication group.

6. **Comparison Operators (<, <=, >, >=, ==, !=)**
   Evaluated after arithmetic operators.

7. **Logical NOT (not)**
   Higher precedence than and and or.

8. **Logical AND (and)**
   Evaluated before logical OR.

9. **Logical OR (or)**
   Evaluated last among these groups.

**2. Associativity**

**Associativity** determines the order in which operators of the same precedence level are evaluated. Operators can be **left-associative** or **right-associative**:

**Left-Associative:**
Most binary operators (such as addition, subtraction, multiplication, division, floor division, modulus) are left-associative. This means that

when operators of the same precedence appear in an expression, evaluation occurs from left to right.

**Example:**

```
# Left-associative example

result = 10 - 3 - 2

# Evaluated as: (10 - 3) - 2 = 7 - 2 = 5

print("Result:", result)  # Output: 5
```

**Right-Associative:**
The exponentiation operator (**) is right-associative, meaning it is evaluated from right to left.

**Example:**

```
# Right-associative example for exponentiation

result = 2 ** 3 ** 2

# Evaluated as: 2 ** (3 ** 2) = 2 ** 9 = 512

print("Result:", result)  # Output: 512
```

In contrast, if exponentiation were left-associative, the expression would be evaluated as (2 ** 3) ** 2 = 8 ** 2 = 64, which is not the case in Python.

### 3. Using Parentheses to Control Evaluation

Parentheses can be used to override the default precedence and associativity rules. This is useful for clarifying the intended order of operations and ensuring that your expression is evaluated in the correct order.

**Example Without Parentheses:**

```
# Consider the following expression:
```

```
result = 2 + 3 * 4

# According to operator precedence, multiplication is performed before addition.

# So, result is evaluated as: 2 + (3 * 4) = 2 + 12 = 14

print("Result without parentheses:", result)  # Output: 14
```

Example With Parentheses:

```
# If you want the addition to occur first, use parentheses:

result = (2 + 3) * 4

# Now, addition is performed first: (2 + 3) = 5, then multiplication: 5 * 4 = 20

print("Result with parentheses:", result)  # Output: 20
```

Parentheses not only enforce the order of operations but also enhance code readability by clearly indicating the intended grouping of operations.

**4. Complex Expression Example**

Let's look at a more complex example that combines several operators, demonstrating both precedence and associativity:

```
# Complex expression example:

result = 2 + 3 * 4 ** 2 / (5 - 3) % 2

# Evaluation step-by-step:

# 1. Parentheses: (5 - 3) = 2

# 2. Exponentiation: 4 ** 2 = 16

# 3. Multiplication: 3 * 16 = 48
```

```
# 4. Division: 48 / 2 = 24.0 (division always yields a float in Python 3)

# 5. Modulus: 24.0 % 2 = 0.0 (remainder of division by 2)

# 6. Addition: 2 + 0.0 = 2.0

print("Complex expression result:", result)  # Output: 2.0
```

Here, each operator is evaluated according to its precedence:

- Parentheses are evaluated first.
- Exponentiation comes next.
- Multiplication and division follow.
- Modulus is then computed.
- Finally, addition is performed.

**In summary**

- **Operator Precedence:**
  Determines the order in which different types of operators are evaluated in an expression. Operators with higher precedence are executed before those with lower precedence.
- **Associativity:**
  Defines the order of evaluation for operators of the same precedence. Most arithmetic operators are left-associative (evaluated left to right), while the exponentiation operator is right-associative (evaluated right to left).
- **Parentheses:**
  Can be used to override the default rules, forcing a specific evaluation order. This not only ensures the correct outcome but also improves code readability.

Understanding operator precedence and associativity is fundamental to writing correct and efficient Python expressions. It allows you to construct complex expressions confidently, knowing that Python will evaluate them as intended.

## Example Exercises:

### *Evaluating Expressions and Building Small Formulas*

Practicing with exercises that evaluate expressions and build small formulas is an excellent way to reinforce your understanding of Python's operators and expressions. In these exercises, you'll combine arithmetic, comparison, and logical operators to solve problems and create formulas that perform useful calculations.

Below are several example exercises along with detailed explanations and code samples.

### 1. Evaluating Expressions

Evaluating expressions involves combining operators to calculate a result. These exercises help you understand how Python applies operator precedence and associativity.

### Exercise 1.1: Compute a Mathematical Expression

**Objective:**
Evaluate the expression:
result=2+3×42(5−3)mod 2
where exponentiation is represented by ** and modulus by %.

**Steps:**

1. Evaluate the parentheses.
2. Apply exponentiation.
3. Perform multiplication.
4. Execute division.

5. Compute the modulus.
6. Finally, perform addition.

**Code Example:**

```
# Step-by-step evaluation:

# Parentheses: (5 - 3) = 2

# Exponentiation: 4 ** 2 = 16

# Multiplication: 3 * 16 = 48

# Division: (2 + 48) / 2 -> First, addition: 2 + 48 = 50, then
division: 50 / 2 = 25.0

# Modulus: 25.0 % 2 = 1.0

result = (2 + 3 * 4 ** 2) / (5 - 3) % 2

print("Result of the expression:", result)  # Expected output: 1.0
```

**Exercise 1.2: Logical Expression Evaluation**

**Objective:**
Evaluate a logical expression that combines comparison and logical operators. For instance:
result=((10>5) and (3≤3)) or (5==2+3

**Code Example:**

```
# Breaking down the expression:

# (10 > 5) evaluates to True.

# (3 <= 3) evaluates to True.

# Therefore, (10 > 5) and (3 <= 3) is True.

# (5 == 2 + 3) evaluates to True since 2 + 3 equals 5.

# Combining with OR: True or True is True.
```

```
result = ((10 > 5) and (3 <= 3)) or (5 == 2 + 3)

print("Result of the logical expression:", result)  # Expected output: True
```

**2. Building Small Formulas**

In addition to evaluating static expressions, you can build small formulas to perform calculations dynamically based on variable values.

**Exercise 2.1: Calculate the Area of a Circle**

**Objective:**
Write a formula to calculate the area of a circle given its radius. The formula for the area is:
Area=π×radius2

**Code Example:**

```
import math  # Importing math module for pi

# Define the radius

radius = 5

# Calculate the area using the formula: area = pi * radius^2

area = math.pi * radius ** 2

print(f"The area of a circle with radius {radius} is {area:.2f}")

# Expected output: The area of a circle with radius 5 is 78.54 (approximately)
```

**Exercise 2.2: Compute the Average of Three Numbers**

**Objective:**
Create a formula to compute the average of three numbers. The

average is calculated as:
Average=(a+b+c)/3

**Code Example:**

```
# Define three numbers

a = 10

b = 15

c = 20

# Calculate the average

average = (a + b + c) / 3

print("The average of", a, b, c, "is", average)

# Expected output: The average of 10 15 20 is 15.0
```

**Exercise 2.3: Convert Temperature from Celsius to Fahrenheit**

**Objective:**
Use the formula to convert a temperature from Celsius to Fahrenheit. The formula is:
Fahrenheit=(Celsius×(9/5))+32

**Code Example:**

```
# Define a temperature in Celsius

celsius = 25

# Convert to Fahrenheit using the formula

fahrenheit = (celsius * 9/5) + 32

print(f"{celsius}°C is equivalent to {fahrenheit}°F")

# Expected output: 25°C is equivalent to 77.0°F
```

**3. Combining Expressions in a Single Script**

You can combine various expressions and formulas in one script to build more comprehensive applications.

**Exercise 3.1: A Mini Finance Calculator**

**Objective:**
Write a small script that calculates the final amount after applying compound interest. The formula for compound interest is:
A=P×(1+r/n)n×t where:

- *P* is the principal amount,
- *r* is the annual interest rate (in decimal),
- *n* is the number of times interest is compounded per year,
- t is the number of years,
- *A* is the amount after ttt years.

**Code Example:**

```
# Compound interest calculator

# Input variables

principal = 1000  # Principal amount

annual_rate = 0.05  # 5% annual interest rate

compounds_per_year = 4  # Quarterly compounding

years = 5  # Investment period in years

# Calculate the final amount using the compound interest formula

amount = principal * (1 + annual_rate / compounds_per_year) **
(compounds_per_year * years)
```

```
print(f"After {years} years, an initial investment of ${principal} grows to ${amount:.2f}")

# Expected output: After 5 years, an initial investment of $1000 grows to a calculated amount based on the formula.
```

**In summary**

- **Evaluating Expressions:**
  - Practice breaking down complex expressions into simpler components.
  - Understand and apply operator precedence and associativity to obtain the correct result.
  - Use examples that combine arithmetic, comparison, and logical operators.
- **Building Small Formulas:**
  - Use mathematical formulas to perform dynamic calculations.
  - Implement real-world applications such as calculating the area of a circle, the average of numbers, and temperature conversion.
  - Combine multiple expressions in a single script to create mini-applications (e.g., a finance calculator).

By working through these exercises, you'll strengthen your grasp of Python's operators and expressions, improve your problem-solving skills, and prepare yourself for more complex programming challenges.

## Section III: Flow Control and Structured Programming
## Chapter 6: Control Structures – Conditionals

Conditionals are the cornerstone of flow control in Python. They allow your program to execute different blocks of code based on whether certain conditions are met.

### Basic Conditional Statements

#### *if, elif, else Statements*

Conditional statements are essential tools in Python that enable your program to make decisions based on dynamic conditions. By using if, elif, and else statements, you can control the flow of your program, executing different blocks of code depending on whether certain conditions are met.

#### 1. The if Statement

The if statement is the simplest form of a conditional. It evaluates a condition and, if the condition is True, executes a block of code.

**Syntax**

```
if condition:
    # Code block executed when condition is True
```

Example

```
temperature = 25
if temperature > 20:
    print("It is warm outside!")
```

**Explanation:**
In the example above, the condition temperature > 20 is checked. Since 25 is greater than 20, the code within the if block is executed, and the message "It is warm outside!" is printed.

### 2. The if-else Statement

An if-else statement extends the basic if statement by adding an alternative block of code that is executed when the condition is False.

**Syntax**

```
if condition:
    # Code block executed when condition is True
else:
    # Code block executed when condition is False
```

Example

```
temperature = 15
if temperature > 20:
    print("It is warm outside!")
else:
    print("It is cool outside!")
```

**Explanation:**
Here, the condition temperature > 20 is False because 15 is not greater than 20. Therefore, the code in the else block runs, and "It is cool outside!" is printed.

### 3. The if-elif-else Statement

When you need to test multiple conditions sequentially, the if-elif-else construct is used. It allows your program to check several conditions one after another until one is found to be True.

**Syntax**

```
if condition1:
```

```
    # Code block executed when condition1 is True
elif condition2:
    # Code block executed when condition2 is True
...
else:
    # Code block executed if none of the above conditions are True
```

Example

```
score = 85
if score >= 90:
    grade = "A"
elif score >= 80:
    grade = "B"
elif score >= 70:
    grade = "C"
elif score >= 60:
    grade = "D"
else:
    grade = "F"
print(f"Score: {score} -> Grade: {grade}")
```

**Explanation:**

In this grading example:

- The condition score >= 90 is checked first. Since 85 is not greater than or equal to 90, Python moves on to the next condition.
- The condition score >= 80 evaluates to True because 85 is at least 80, so grade is set to "B".
- No further conditions are evaluated once a True condition is found.
- The final output is "Score: 85 -> Grade: B".

**4. Nested Conditionals**

Nested conditionals involve placing one or more conditional statements inside another. This allows for more detailed decision-making.

**Example**

```
age = 25

citizen = True

if age >= 18:

    if citizen:

        print("You are eligible to vote.")

    else:

        print("You must be a citizen to vote.")

else:

    print("You are not eligible to vote.")
```

**Explanation:**

- The outer if checks whether the person is at least 18 years old.

- If True, the program then checks if the person is a citizen using a nested if statement.
- Depending on the nested condition, the appropriate message is printed.
- This structure enables multi-layered decision making in a clear and organized manner.

### 5. Combining Conditions with Logical Operators

You can combine multiple conditions within a single if statement using logical operators such as and, or, and not.

**Example**

```
temperature = 22

humidity = 60

if temperature > 20 and humidity < 70:

    print("The weather is pleasant!")

else:

    print("The weather is not ideal.")
```

**Explanation:**

- Both conditions must be met for the if block to execute. Here, temperature > 20 is True and humidity < 70 is also True.
- Since both conditions are satisfied, the program prints "The weather is pleasant!".

### 6. The Ternary Conditional Operator

For simple conditional assignments, Python offers a concise one-line expression known as the ternary conditional operator.

**Syntax**

```
value_if_true if condition else value_if_false
```

Example

```
age = 16

status = "adult" if age >= 18 else "minor"

print(f"Status: {status}")  # Output: "Status: minor"
```

**Explanation:**
This one-liner checks if age is greater than or equal to 18. If it is, status is assigned "adult"; otherwise, it is assigned "minor". Since 16 is less than 18, status becomes "minor".

**7. Best Practices for Conditionals**

- **Clarity and Readability:**
  Use clear and straightforward conditions. Adding comments and appropriate spacing can help maintain readability.

- **Avoid Deep Nesting:**
  Deeply nested conditions can make your code hard to read and maintain. Consider refactoring or using logical operators to simplify conditions.

- **Test All Branches:**
  Ensure that every branch (if, elif, and else) is correctly executed by testing with different input values.

- **Consistent Style:**
  Follow Python's style guidelines (PEP 8) for indentation (typically 4 spaces per level) to maintain consistency.

**In Summary**

- **if Statement:**
  Executes a block of code if a condition is True.

- **if-else Statement:**
  Provides an alternative code block when the condition is False.
- **if-elif-else Statement:**
  Evaluates multiple conditions sequentially, executing the first block with a True condition.
- **Nested Conditionals:**
  Allow for complex decision-making by embedding one conditional inside another.
- **Logical Operators:**
  Enable combining multiple conditions into one.
- **Ternary Conditional Operator:**
  Offers a compact way to assign a value based on a condition in a single line.

By mastering these control structures, you gain the ability to direct the flow of your Python programs based on dynamic conditions, enabling you to build interactive, responsive, and robust applications.

## Nested Conditionals and Best Practices

Nested conditionals allow you to handle complex decision-making scenarios by embedding one conditional statement inside another. They are particularly useful when multiple layers of criteria must be met before executing a specific block of code.

### 1. Understanding Nested Conditionals

Nested conditionals occur when an if, elif, or else block contains another conditional statement. This allows for more granular control over program flow. However, overusing nesting can lead to code that is difficult to read and maintain. Therefore, it is important to balance complexity with clarity.

## Example of a Nested Conditional

Consider a scenario where you determine voting eligibility based on age and citizenship:

```
age = 25

is_citizen = True

if age >= 18:

    # First level of decision: Check if the person is an adult.

    if is_citizen:

        # Second level: Check citizenship if the person is old enough.

        print("You are eligible to vote.")

    else:

        print("You must be a citizen to vote.")

else:

    print("You are not eligible to vote.")
```

**Explanation:**

- The outer if checks if the person is at least 18 years old.
- If true, the program then evaluates whether the person is a citizen using an inner if statement.
- Depending on the result of the inner condition, the appropriate message is printed.
- If the outer condition fails (i.e., the person is younger than 18), the program directly prints that the person is not eligible to vote.

## 2. Best Practices for Nested Conditionals

While nested conditionals are powerful, following best practices can help keep your code organized and maintainable:

### 2.1 Limit Nesting Depth

**Avoid Deep Nesting:**
Deeply nested code can become difficult to follow. If you find yourself nesting more than three or four levels deep, consider refactoring your logic into functions or using other control structures.

**Example:** Instead of:

```
if condition1:
    if condition2:
        if condition3:
            # Deeply nested logic here
```

Refactor into separate functions:

```
def check_conditions():
    if condition1 and condition2 and condition3:
        # Process logic here
check_conditions()
```

### 2.2 Use Descriptive Variable and Function Names

**Clear Naming:**
Use names that clearly describe the purpose of the variables and functions. This helps anyone reading your code (including future you) understand what each part does.

**Example:**

```
def is_eligible_to_vote(age, is_citizen):
```

```
    if age >= 18:
        if is_citizen:
            return True
        else:
            return False
    else:
        return False
# Now call the function with clear arguments
eligibility = is_eligible_to_vote(age=25, is_citizen=True)
if eligibility:
    print("You are eligible to vote.")
else:
    print("You are not eligible to vote.")
```

### 2.3 Comment and Document Your Code

**Inline Comments:**
Add comments to explain the purpose of each nested level, especially if the conditions are not immediately obvious.

**Example:**

```
if age >= 18:
    # The person is an adult; now check citizenship
    if is_citizen:
        print("You are eligible to vote.")
    else:
```

```
        # The person is an adult but not a citizen
        print("You must be a citizen to vote.")
else:
    # The person is not an adult
    print("You are not eligible to vote.")
```

## 2.4 Use Logical Operators to Simplify Conditions

**Combine Conditions When Appropriate:**
If two conditions are closely related, consider using logical operators (and, or) to combine them, reducing the need for nesting.

**Example:** Instead of:

```
if age >= 18:
    if is_citizen:
        print("Eligible to vote")
    else:
        print("Not eligible due to citizenship")
else:
    print("Not eligible due to age")
```

You can simplify it:

```
if age >= 18 and is_citizen:
    print("Eligible to vote")
elif age >= 18 and not is_citizen:
    print("Not eligible due to citizenship")
else:
```

```
    print("Not eligible due to age")
```

### 2.5 Consider Alternative Structures

**Early Exits:**
Sometimes, it is clearer to handle exceptional or negative conditions first and then proceed with the main logic. This can reduce the nesting depth.

**Example:**

```
if age < 18:
    print("Not eligible to vote.")
elif not is_citizen:
    print("Not eligible due to citizenship.")
else:
    print("Eligible to vote.")
```

## 3. Comprehensive Example: Student Grade Evaluation

Let’s put nested conditionals into practice with a more comprehensive example: determining a student's performance based on their score and attendance.

**Scenario:**

- If the student's score is 90 or above, they receive an "A".
- If the score is between 80 and 89:
    - If attendance is above 90%, they receive a "B".
    - Otherwise, they receive a "C".
- If the score is below 80, they receive a "D".

**Code Example:**

```
score = 85
attendance = 92  # Percentage
if score >= 90:
    grade = "A"
else:
    if 80 <= score < 90:
        if attendance > 90:
            grade = "B"
        else:
            grade = "C"
    else:
        grade = "D"
print(f"Score: {score}, Attendance: {attendance}% -> Grade: {grade}")
```

**Explanation:**

- The outer if checks if the score is 90 or above.
- If not, the nested condition checks if the score is between 80 and 89.
    - Within that, another nested condition checks the attendance to decide between a "B" and a "C".
- If the score is below 80, the else block assigns a "D".
- This structured approach ensures each condition is evaluated in a logical order while remaining readable.

**In Summary**

- **Nested Conditionals:**
  Allow you to make complex decisions by embedding conditions within one another. They are essential for handling multi-layered decision logic.

- **Best Practices:**

  - **Limit Nesting Depth:** Simplify logic by breaking it into functions or combining conditions.
  - **Descriptive Naming:** Use clear variable and function names.
  - **Commenting:** Add inline comments to explain each logical step.
  - **Logical Operators:** Combine conditions to reduce unnecessary nesting.
  - **Early Exits:** Handle negative conditions early to simplify the main logic.

By following these guidelines, you can effectively manage nested conditionals in your Python programs, ensuring that your code remains both powerful and maintainable. Mastery of these techniques is crucial for building robust, clear, and scalable applications.

## Example Control Structures

### *Simple Decision Programs*

Simple decision programs leverage conditional statements to make choices based on user input or computed values. These exercises are designed to help you practice using if, elif, and else statements, enabling your program to execute different code paths depending on dynamic conditions. Below are several example exercises with detailed explanations and code samples.

### 1. Exercise: Even or Odd Number Checker

**Objective:**
Write a program that determines whether a given number is even or odd.

**Steps:**

1. Prompt the user for an integer.
2. Use the modulus operator (%) to check if the number is divisible by 2.
3. Use an if-else statement to print whether the number is even or odd.

**Code Example:**

```
# Even or Odd Number Checker

# Prompt the user for input and convert it to an integer

number_input = input("Enter an integer: ")

try:

    number = int(number_input)

except ValueError:

    print("Invalid input! Please enter a valid integer.")

    exit()  # Exit if conversion fails

# Check if the number is even or odd using the modulus operator

if number % 2 == 0:

    print(f"{number} is even.")
```

```
else:
    print(f"{number} is odd.")
```

**Explanation:**

- The program reads input from the user.
- It attempts to convert the input to an integer; if the conversion fails, an error message is printed.
- The condition number % 2 == 0 checks for even numbers.
- Based on the result, the program prints whether the number is even or odd.

**2. Exercise: Temperature-Based Clothing Suggestion**

**Objective:**
Create a program that suggests clothing based on the current temperature.

**Steps:**

1. Prompt the user for the current temperature (in Celsius).
2. Use if-elif-else statements to evaluate the temperature range.
3. Print an appropriate suggestion based on the temperature.

**Code Example:**

```
# Temperature-Based Clothing Suggestion

# Prompt the user for the current temperature

temperature_input = input("Enter the current temperature (in Celsius): ")
```

```
try:
    temperature = float(temperature_input)
except ValueError:
    print("Invalid input! Please enter a numeric value for the temperature.")
    exit()
# Use conditionals to provide clothing suggestions
if temperature < 0:
    print("It's freezing! Wear a heavy coat, scarf, and gloves.")
elif 0 <= temperature < 15:
    print("It's chilly. Wear a jacket and perhaps a sweater.")
elif 15 <= temperature < 25:
    print("The weather is mild. A light jacket or long sleeves should suffice.")
else:
    print("It's warm outside. Wear something light like a t-shirt and shorts.")
```

**Explanation:**

- The program converts the user input to a float.
- An if-elif-else structure checks multiple temperature ranges.
- Based on the evaluated condition, the program suggests appropriate clothing.

**3. Exercise: Simple Grading System**

**Objective:**

Write a program that assigns a grade based on a student's score.

**Steps:**

1. Prompt the user for the student's score.
2. Use an if-elif-else chain to determine the grade.
3. Print the corresponding grade.

**Code Example:**

```
# Simple Grading System
# Prompt the user for the student's score
score_input = input("Enter the student's score (0-100): ")
try:
    score = float(score_input)
except ValueError:
    print("Invalid input! Please enter a numeric value for the score.")
    exit()
# Determine the grade using conditional statements
if score >= 90:
    grade = "A"
elif score >= 80:
    grade = "B"
elif score >= 70:
    grade = "C"
elif score >= 60:
```

```
    grade = "D"
else:
    grade = "F"
print(f"Score: {score} -> Grade: {grade}")
```

**Explanation:**

- The program reads a score from the user and converts it to a float.
- An if-elif-else chain determines the corresponding grade.
- The grade is then printed in a formatted string.

**4. Exercise: Discount Eligibility Checker**

**Objective:**
Create a program that checks whether a customer is eligible for a discount based on their membership status and total purchase amount.

**Steps:**

1. Prompt the user for membership status and total purchase amount.
2. Use conditionals to check if the customer is a member and if their purchase exceeds a threshold.
3. Print a message indicating discount eligibility.

**Code Example:**

```
# Discount Eligibility Checker
# Prompt the user for membership status and total purchase amount
membership = input("Are you a member? (yes/no): ").strip().lower()
```

```
purchase_input = input("Enter your total purchase amount: ")
try:
    purchase_amount = float(purchase_input)
except ValueError:
    print("Invalid input! Please enter a numeric value for the purchase amount.")
    exit()
# Check discount eligibility using conditionals
if membership == "yes" and purchase_amount >= 100:
    print("Congratulations! You are eligible for a discount.")
else:
    print("Sorry, you are not eligible for a discount at this time.")
# Note: This simple program assumes that the purchase amount threshold for discount eligibility is $100.
```

**Explanation:**

- The program collects the user's membership status and purchase amount.
- It then evaluates whether the user is a member and if the purchase meets the minimum amount for a discount.
- Based on the evaluation, it outputs an appropriate message.

**In Summary**

These example exercises demonstrate how to use conditional statements in Python to create simple decision programs. By practicing these examples, you learn how to:

- Use if, elif, and else statements to control program flow.
- Evaluate conditions using arithmetic, logical, and comparison operators.
- Combine user input with conditional logic to build interactive applications.
- Structure your code to handle various scenarios in a clear and readable manner.

Mastering these control structures is key to developing robust and dynamic Python applications.

# Chapter 7: Control Structures

## For Loops and Ranges

Loops are a core part of programming that allow you to execute a block of code repeatedly. In Python, the for loop is particularly powerful because it enables you to iterate over any sequence - including lists, strings, and even ranges of numbers - with simple, readable syntax. The built-in range() function is commonly used with for loops to generate sequences of numbers, making it easy to repeat operations a specific number of times.

### 1. Understanding the for Loop

A for loop in Python allows you to iterate over a sequence (e.g., list, string, tuple) and execute a block of code for each element in that sequence.

**Syntax**

```
for variable in sequence:
    # Code block executed for each element in the sequence
```

Example: Iterating Over a List

```
fruits = ["apple", "banana", "cherry"]
for fruit in fruits:
    print(f"I like {fruit}")
```

**Explanation:**

- The loop assigns each element of the fruits list to the variable fruit one by one.
- The code inside the loop prints a message for each fruit.

## 2. The range() Function

The range() function is used to generate a sequence of numbers, which is especially useful when you need to perform an action a specific number of times. The function supports several forms:

### Forms of range()

1. **range(stop)**
   Generates numbers from 0 up to (but not including) stop.

```
for i in range(5):
    print(i)  # Outputs: 0, 1, 2, 3, 4
```

2. **range(start, stop)**
   Generates numbers from start up to (but not including) stop.

```
for i in range(3, 8):
    print(i)  # Outputs: 3, 4, 5, 6, 7
```

3. **range(start, stop, step)**
   Generates numbers from start up to (but not including) stop, incrementing by step. The step can be positive or negative.

```
# Positive step
for i in range(2, 11, 2):
    print(i)  # Outputs: 2, 4, 6, 8, 10
# Negative step: counting backwards
for i in range(10, 0, -2):
    print(i)  # Outputs: 10, 8, 6, 4, 2
```

## 3. Practical Examples with for Loops and range()

### 3.1 Summing Numbers

Calculate the sum of numbers from 1 to 10.

```
total = 0
for number in range(1, 11):  # Numbers 1 through 10
    total += number
print("The sum of numbers from 1 to 10 is:", total)
```

**Explanation:**

- The loop iterates over the sequence generated by range(1, 11).
- Each number is added to the total.
- The final sum is printed after the loop completes.

**3.2 Creating a Multiplication Table**

Generate a multiplication table for a specific number.

```
number = 5
print(f"Multiplication Table for {number}:")
for i in range(1, 11):  # Multiplying by numbers 1 through 10
    result = number * i
    print(f"{number} x {i} = {result}")
```

**Explanation:**

- The loop goes through the numbers 1 to 10.
- For each iteration, the product of number and the loop variable i is calculated and printed.

**3.3 Iterating Over a String**

Loop through each character in a string.

```
message = "Hello, Python!"
```

```
for char in message:
    print(char)
```

**Explanation:**

- A string in Python is a sequence of characters.
- The for loop iterates over each character and prints it on a new line.

### 3.4 List Comprehensions as a Concise Alternative

List comprehensions offer a compact syntax for creating lists based on existing iterables.

```
# Create a list of squares for numbers 1 through 10
squares = [x**2 for x in range(1, 11)]
print("Squares from 1 to 10:", squares)
```

**Explanation:**

- The list comprehension iterates over range(1, 11) and computes x**2 for each x.
- The resulting list of squares is printed.

## 4. Best Practices for Using for Loops and range()

- **Choose Descriptive Variable Names:**
  Use names like item, number, or index instead of generic names (e.g., i) when possible, especially in more complex loops.
- **Avoid Off-By-One Errors:**
  Remember that the stop value in range(start, stop) is exclusive. Ensure that your range boundaries are correctly set.

- **Keep Loop Bodies Simple:**
  If the loop body becomes too complex, consider breaking it into functions. This enhances readability and maintainability.
- **Utilize List Comprehensions:**
  For operations that generate a new list, list comprehensions provide a concise and often more readable alternative.
- **Be Mindful of Performance:**
  Although for loops in Python are efficient for many tasks, processing very large datasets may require more advanced techniques or using libraries such as NumPy for vectorized operations.

**In Summary**

- **For Loops:**
  - Allow iteration over sequences like lists, strings, and ranges.
  - Enable the execution of a block of code repeatedly for each element in a sequence.
- **Range Function:**
  - Generates a sequence of numbers and can be customized with start, stop, and step values.
  - Is widely used with for loops to control the number of iterations.
- **Practical Applications:**
  - Summing numbers, generating multiplication tables, iterating over strings, and creating lists via comprehensions.
  - Combined, these structures facilitate the development of dynamic, efficient, and readable Python programs.

Mastering for loops and the range() function is essential for handling repetitive tasks and processing data in Python. With these tools, you can write clean, efficient code that automates a wide range of programming tasks.

## While Loops

While loops are a fundamental control structure in Python that allow you to repeatedly execute a block of code as long as a specified condition remains true. They are particularly useful when the number of iterations is not known beforehand and depends on dynamic conditions during runtime.

### 1. Understanding the while Loop

The while loop repeatedly executes a block of code as long as its controlling condition evaluates to True. It is ideal for situations where the number of iterations cannot be predetermined.

#### Syntax

```
while condition:
    # Code block to be executed repeatedly
```

#### How It Works

- The loop first checks the condition.
- If the condition is True, the code block inside the loop is executed.
- After executing the block, the condition is checked again.
- This process repeats until the condition becomes False.

### 2. Basic Examples

#### Example 1: Simple Counter

This example demonstrates a simple counter that increments a variable until a condition is met.

```
# Initialize a counter variable
```

```
counter = 1

# Loop until counter exceeds 5

while counter <= 5:

    print("Counter:", counter)

    counter += 1  # Increment counter by 1

# Output:

# Counter: 1

# Counter: 2

# Counter: 3

# Counter: 4

# Counter: 5
```

**Explanation:**

- The loop condition counter <= 5 is evaluated before each iteration.
- The variable counter starts at 1 and is incremented by 1 in each iteration.
- Once counter becomes 6, the condition evaluates to False, and the loop terminates.

**Example 2: User Input Validation**

A while loop can be used to repeatedly prompt the user for input until valid data is provided.

```
# Prompt the user until a positive number is entered

number = -1  # Initialize with a negative number to enter the loop
```

```
while number <= 0:
    user_input = input("Please enter a positive number: ")
    try:
        number = float(user_input)
        if number <= 0:
            print("The number must be positive. Try again.")
    except ValueError:
        print("Invalid input! Please enter a numeric value.")

print(f"Thank you! You entered: {number}")
```

**Explanation:**

- The loop continues as long as number is less than or equal to 0.
- The program prompts the user for input, converting it to a float.
- If the input is not valid or the number is not positive, an error message is displayed.
- The loop only terminates when a valid, positive number is entered.

### 3. Handling Infinite Loops

An infinite loop occurs when the loop's condition never becomes False. While sometimes intentional (e.g., for server loops or event listeners), infinite loops are often the result of a programming error.

**Example: Avoiding Infinite Loops**

```
# Example of an infinite loop (uncomment to test with caution)

# while True:
```

```
#     print("This loop will run forever unless you break out of it.")


# Preventing an infinite loop with a break statement:
counter = 0
while True:
    print("Loop iteration:", counter)
    counter += 1
    if counter >= 5:
        break  # Exit the loop when counter reaches 5
print("Loop terminated.")
```

**Explanation:**

- The first commented-out loop demonstrates an infinite loop.
- The second loop uses while True but includes a break statement that terminates the loop when counter reaches 5.

**4. Using continue in While Loops**

The continue statement skips the current iteration and proceeds to the next one. It is useful when you want to skip over certain iterations based on a condition.

**Example: Skipping Iterations**

```
# Print numbers from 1 to 10, skipping even numbers
counter = 0
while counter < 10:
    counter += 1  # Increment the counter first
```

```
    if counter % 2 == 0:
        continue  # Skip printing if the number is even
    print("Odd number:", counter)
# Output:
# Odd number: 1
# Odd number: 3
# Odd number: 5
# Odd number: 7
# Odd number: 9
```

**Explanation:**

- The loop increments counter from 1 to 10.
- The if condition checks whether the number is even.
- If the number is even, continue is executed, skipping the print statement.
- Only odd numbers are printed.

**5. Best Practices for Using While Loops**

- **Ensure Termination:**
  Always verify that the loop's condition will eventually become False to avoid unintended infinite loops.
- **Use Meaningful Conditions:**
  Write clear and understandable loop conditions to enhance readability and maintenance.
- **Minimize Complexity in the Loop Body:**
  Keep the code within the loop simple. If the loop body becomes too complex, consider refactoring it into functions.

- **Leverage Break and Continue:**
  Use break to exit the loop early when necessary, and continue to skip certain iterations. This helps in managing loop control effectively.

- **Test Edge Cases:**
  Validate that the loop behaves correctly for boundary conditions to ensure robust program behavior.

**In Summary**

- **While Loops:**
    - Execute a block of code repeatedly as long as a given condition is true.
    - Are ideal when the number of iterations is not predetermined.
- **Key Concepts:**
    - **Basic Syntax:** while condition:
    - **Incrementing Counters:** Ensure conditions change over time to avoid infinite loops.
    - **Break and Continue:** Use these statements to manage loop control effectively.
- **Practical Examples:**
    - Simple counters, user input validation, avoiding infinite loops, and skipping iterations.

Mastering while loops equips you with the ability to handle dynamic and condition-dependent repetition in your programs. With careful construction and adherence to best practices, while loops become a powerful tool for writing efficient, clear, and robust Python code.

## Loop Control Statements

Loop control statements - namely break and continue - are powerful tools that allow you to alter the normal flow of a loop. They help you manage the execution of loops by providing mechanisms to either exit the loop early or skip certain iterations.

### 1. The break Statement

The break statement immediately terminates the loop in which it appears. When a break is encountered, the loop stops executing, and control is transferred to the first statement following the loop.

**When to Use break:**

- **Exiting Early:** When a certain condition is met and there is no need to continue iterating.
- **Search Operations:** For instance, when looking for a specific element in a list; once found, you can stop further iterations.

**Example: Searching for a Value in a List**

```
# Searching for a specific fruit in a list
fruits = ["apple", "banana", "cherry", "date", "elderberry"]
target = "cherry"
for fruit in fruits:
    if fruit == target:
        print(f"Found {target}!")
        break  # Exit the loop once the target is found
    print(f"Checked {fruit}")
else:
```

```
    # This block executes if the loop completes without encountering a break
    print(f"{target} not found in the list.")
```

**Explanation:**

- The loop iterates over each fruit in the list.
- When fruit matches target, the program prints a message and executes break, exiting the loop immediately.
- The else clause attached to the loop will only execute if the loop is not terminated by a break (i.e., if the target is not found).

**2. The continue Statement**

The continue statement skips the rest of the code inside the loop for the current iteration and proceeds with the next iteration of the loop.

**When to Use continue:**

**Skipping Iterations:** When you want to skip certain iterations based on a condition, but still continue looping through the rest of the elements.

**Example: Skipping Even Numbers**

```
# Print only odd numbers from 1 to 10
for number in range(1, 11):
    if number % 2 == 0:
        continue  # Skip the current iteration for even numbers
    print(f"Odd number: {number}")
```

**Explanation:**

- The loop iterates over numbers 1 through 10.

- For each number, it checks if the number is even (number % 2 == 0).
- If the condition is true, continue is executed, and the print statement is skipped for that iteration.
- Only odd numbers are printed.

### 3. Combining break and continue in Loops

In some scenarios, both break and continue may be used within the same loop to handle different conditions.

**Example: Processing a List with Multiple Conditions**

```
# Process a list of numbers, skipping negatives and stopping when a number greater than 50 is encountered

numbers = [5, 12, -3, 8, 25, 47, -10, 60, 15]

for num in numbers:

    if num < 0:

        # Skip negative numbers

        continue

    if num > 50:

        print(f"Number {num} exceeds the limit. Exiting loop.")

        break

    print(f"Processing number: {num}")

print("Loop terminated.")
```

**Explanation:**

- The loop iterates over a list of numbers.

- The first condition checks if the number is negative. If it is, continue skips the rest of the loop body for that iteration.
- The second condition checks if the number is greater than 50. If so, it prints a message and uses break to exit the loop immediately.
- Otherwise, the number is processed (in this example, simply printed).

**4. Best Practices for Using break and continue**

- **Clarity and Readability:**
  Use break and continue judiciously to avoid making the loop logic confusing. Clearly comment on why a loop is exited or an iteration skipped.
- **Avoid Overuse:**
  Excessive use of these statements can lead to spaghetti code. If your loop requires multiple break or continue conditions, consider refactoring your logic into functions or simplifying the conditions.
- **Loop else Clause:**
  Take advantage of the loop else clause when appropriate. It executes only if the loop is not terminated by a break, providing a clear way to handle cases where no break occurs.
- **Consistent Formatting:**
  Keep your code formatted and indented properly to ensure that the flow of control is easy to follow.

**In Summary**

- **break:**

  - Immediately terminates the loop when executed.

    - Useful for exiting early from loops when a specific condition is met.

- **continue:**
    - Skips the current iteration and proceeds to the next one.
    - Ideal for bypassing certain iterations without stopping the loop entirely.

- **Combined Use:**
  Both statements can be used together in loops to handle complex conditions, such as skipping unwanted elements and terminating loops when necessary.

Mastering loop control statements like break and continue empowers you to write efficient and clear loops that can handle a wide range of tasks, from simple filtering to more complex data processing. By following best practices and using these tools thoughtfully, you can greatly improve the clarity and performance of your Python code.

## Example Exercises

Working with loops is central to controlling the flow of a Python program. To solidify your understanding of loops, it's very helpful to practice with real-world exercises.

### 1. FizzBuzz

**Objective:**

Write a program that prints the numbers from 1 to 100. For multiples of 3, print "Fizz" instead of the number; for multiples of 5, print "Buzz" instead; and for numbers which are multiples of both 3 and 5, print "FizzBuzz."

**Concepts Covered:**

- Loop iteration using for loops and range()

- Conditional statements (if, elif, else)
- Combining conditions with logical operators

**Code Example:**

```
# FizzBuzz: Print numbers from 1 to 100 with special rules for multiples of 3 and 5.

for num in range(1, 101):
    if num % 3 == 0 and num % 5 == 0:
        print("FizzBuzz")
    elif num % 3 == 0:
        print("Fizz")
    elif num % 5 == 0:
        print("Buzz")
    else:
        print(num)
```

**Explanation:**

- The loop iterates from 1 to 100.
- The program first checks if the number is divisible by both 3 and 5 using the condition num % 3 == 0 and num % 5 == 0 (this must come first).
- Then it checks for divisibility by 3 and by 5 separately.
- If none of the conditions apply, it prints the number itself.

**2. Summations**

**Objective:**

Calculate summations using loops. For example, compute the sum of all numbers from 1 to 50, and separately, calculate the sum of even numbers within a given range.

**Concepts Covered:**

- Iterating over a range of numbers with for loops
- Accumulating a result using a variable
- Conditional filtering within a loop

**Code Example 1: Sum of Numbers from 1 to 50**

```
# Calculate the sum of all numbers from 1 to 50
total_sum = 0
for i in range(1, 51):
    total_sum += i
print("Sum of numbers from 1 to 50 is:", total_sum)
```

Code Example 2: Sum of Even Numbers from 1 to 50

```
# Calculate the sum of even numbers from 1 to 50
even_sum = 0
for i in range(1, 51):
    if i % 2 == 0:
        even_sum += i
print("Sum of even numbers from 1 to 50 is:", even_sum)
```

**Explanation:**

- In the first example, the loop accumulates all integers from 1 to 50 into total_sum.

- In the second example, a condition if i % 2 == 0 ensures that only even numbers are added to even_sum.

### 3. Pattern Printing

**Objective:**

Print various patterns using loops. For example, print a simple pyramid of asterisks (*), where the number of asterisks increases with each row.

**Concepts Covered:**

- Nested loops
- Controlling output with loops
- String multiplication and formatting

**Code Example 1: Right-Angled Triangle Pattern**

```
# Print a right-angled triangle pattern with asterisks
rows = 5
for i in range(1, rows + 1):
    # Print i asterisks on the ith row
    print("*" * i)
```

Output:

```
*
**
***
****
*****
```

Code Example 2: Pyramid Pattern

```
# Print a centered pyramid pattern with asterisks
rows = 5
for i in range(1, rows + 1):
    # Calculate the number of spaces
    spaces = " " * (rows - i)
    # Calculate the number of asterisks (2*i - 1 ensures an odd number)
    stars = "*" * (2 * i - 1)
    # Print the combined string
    print(spaces + stars + spaces)
```

Output:

```
    *
   ***
  *****
 *******
*********
```

Code Example 3: Inverted Pyramid Pattern

```
# Print an inverted pyramid pattern with asterisks
rows = 5
for i in range(rows, 0, -1):
    spaces = " " * (rows - i)
    stars = "*" * (2 * i - 1)
```

```
    print(spaces + stars + spaces)
```

Output:

```
*********
 *******
  *****
   ***
    *
```

**Explanation:**

- **Right-Angled Triangle:** A single loop increases the number of asterisks printed per line.
- **Pyramid Pattern:** A nested approach where the outer loop controls the row, and the inner logic computes the required number of spaces and stars.
- **Inverted Pyramid:** Similar to the pyramid pattern, but the loop runs in reverse to decrease the number of stars per row.

**In Summary**

These exercises provide practical experience with loops in Python:

- **FizzBuzz:** Uses a for loop and conditional statements to print a sequence with specific replacements.
- **Summations:** Demonstrates how to accumulate values using a loop and conditionally filter elements (e.g., summing even numbers).
- **Pattern Printing:** Illustrates the power of loops for generating visual patterns, utilizing string multiplication, nested loops, and formatting.

By working through these examples, you'll gain a deeper understanding of how to use loops effectively in your programs, enabling you to automate repetitive tasks and solve complex problems with clarity and precision.

# Section IV: Data Structures and Collections
# Chapter 8: Lists, Tuples, and Sets

## Creating and Modifying Lists

Lists are one of Python's most versatile and widely used data structures. They are ordered, mutable collections that can store items of different types.

### 1. Creating Lists

### 1.1 Literal List Creation

Lists can be created by placing comma-separated values inside square brackets ([]).

**Example:**

```
# Creating a list of integers
numbers = [1, 2, 3, 4, 5]
print("Numbers:", numbers)
# Creating a list of strings
fruits = ["apple", "banana", "cherry"]
print("Fruits:", fruits)
# Creating a list with mixed data types
mixed_list = [1, "two", 3.0, True]
print("Mixed List:", mixed_list)
```

### 1.2 Using the list() Constructor

You can also create a list by passing an iterable (e.g., a string, tuple, or range) to the list() constructor.

**Example:**

```
# Converting a tuple to a list
tuple_data = (10, 20, 30)
list_from_tuple = list(tuple_data)
print("List from tuple:", list_from_tuple)
# Creating a list from a range
list_from_range = list(range(1, 6))
print("List from range:", list_from_range)
```

**2. Accessing List Elements**

Lists are indexed, with the first element at index 0. You can access elements using square brackets ([]).

**2.1 Indexing and Slicing**

**Example:**

```
fruits = ["apple", "banana", "cherry", "date", "elderberry"]
# Accessing the first element
print("First fruit:", fruits[0])
# Accessing the last element using negative indexing
print("Last fruit:", fruits[-1])
# Slicing: Extracting a sub-list
print("Middle fruits:", fruits[1:4])  # Elements at index 1, 2, and 3
```

**3. Modifying Lists**

Since lists are mutable, you can change their content after creation. There are several ways to modify lists, including changing individual elements, appending new items, extending with other lists, and more.

### 3.1 Changing Elements by Index

**Example:**

```
numbers = [1, 2, 3, 4, 5]

# Update the third element (index 2)

numbers[2] = 99

print("Updated numbers:", numbers)  # Output: [1, 2, 99, 4, 5]
```

### 3.2 Appending Elements

Use the append() method to add an element to the end of the list.

**Example:**

```
fruits = ["apple", "banana", "cherry"]

fruits.append("date")

print("After append:", fruits)  # Output: ["apple", "banana", "cherry", "date"]
```

### 3.3 Inserting Elements

Use the insert() method to add an element at a specific index.

**Example:**

```
fruits = ["apple", "banana", "cherry"]

# Insert "orange" at index 1

fruits.insert(1, "orange")

print("After insert:", fruits)  # Output: ["apple", "orange", "banana", "cherry"]
```

### 3.4 Removing Elements

There are several methods to remove elements from a list:

- **pop()**: Removes and returns the element at a given index (default is the last element).
- **remove()**: Removes the first occurrence of a specified value.
- **del Statement**: Deletes an element or a slice of the list without returning it.

**Examples:**

```
# Using pop()
numbers = [1, 2, 3, 4, 5]
last_number = numbers.pop()  # Removes the last element
print("After pop:", numbers, " | Popped value:", last_number)
# Using remove()
fruits = ["apple", "banana", "cherry", "banana"]
fruits.remove("banana")  # Removes the first "banana"
print("After remove:", fruits)
# Using del
del fruits[1]  # Deletes the element at index 1
print("After del:", fruits)
```

### 3.5 Extending Lists

To add multiple elements from another iterable, use the extend() method or the += operator.

**Examples:**

```
# Using extend()
numbers = [1, 2, 3]
numbers.extend([4, 5, 6])
print("After extend:", numbers)  # Output: [1, 2, 3, 4, 5, 6]
# Using += operator
letters = ["a", "b", "c"]
letters += ["d", "e"]
print("After +=:", letters)  # Output: ["a", "b", "c", "d", "e"]
```

### 3.6 Sorting and Reversing

Lists provide methods to sort and reverse their elements.

**Examples:**

```
numbers = [4, 2, 5, 1, 3]
numbers.sort()  # Sorts the list in ascending order
print("Sorted numbers:", numbers)
numbers.reverse()  # Reverses the order of the list
print("Reversed numbers:", numbers)
```

## 4. List Comprehensions

List comprehensions provide a concise way to create lists based on existing iterables.

**Example:**

```
# Creating a list of squares from 1 to 10
squares = [x**2 for x in range(1, 11)]
print("Squares:", squares)
```

**Explanation:**

- The list comprehension iterates over the range from 1 to 10.
- For each element, it calculates the square and builds a new list containing these values.

**5. Best Practices for Creating and Modifying Lists**

- **Clarity and Readability:**
  Choose descriptive variable names and keep list operations simple. When multiple modifications are required, consider breaking them into separate, well-documented steps.
- **Avoid Unnecessary Copies:**
  Be mindful of how you modify lists, as creating unnecessary copies of large lists can affect performance.
- **Use List Comprehensions When Appropriate:**
  For simple transformations and filtering, list comprehensions offer a more concise and often more readable alternative to traditional loops.
- **Error Handling:**
  When modifying lists (e.g., removing elements), ensure that the element exists or handle potential exceptions to avoid runtime errors.

**In Summary**

Lists are dynamic, mutable data structures that allow you to store and manipulate collections of items. In this section, we covered:

- **Creating Lists:** Using literal syntax and the list() constructor.
- **Accessing Elements:** Through indexing and slicing.
- **Modifying Lists:** Updating elements, appending, inserting, removing, extending, sorting, and reversing.

- **List Comprehensions:** A concise method for creating and transforming lists.

By mastering these techniques, you can effectively manage and manipulate collections in your Python programs.

## Tuples: Immutable Sequences

Tuples are one of Python's core sequence data types and share many similarities with lists. However, a key difference is that tuples are **immutable**, meaning that once a tuple is created, its elements cannot be modified. This immutability makes tuples useful for representing fixed collections of items and for ensuring that data does not get accidentally altered.

### 1. Creating Tuples

Tuples can be created in several ways. The most common method is by placing comma-separated values within parentheses. However, parentheses are optional in some contexts.

**Example: Basic Tuple Creation**

```
# Creating a tuple with multiple items

coordinates = (10, 20, 30)

print("Coordinates:", coordinates)

# Creating a tuple without parentheses

colors = "red", "green", "blue"

print("Colors:", colors)

# Creating a tuple with a single element

single_element_tuple = (42,)  # Note the trailing comma

print("Single element tuple:", single_element_tuple)
```

**Explanation:**

- **Multiple Items:** The tuple coordinates contains three integers.
- **Implicit Tuple:** The tuple colors is created without explicit parentheses.
- **Singleton Tuple:** A single element tuple must include a trailing comma; otherwise, Python will interpret it as a different data type (e.g., an integer).

2. Accessing Tuple Elements

Tuples, like lists, are ordered sequences, meaning each element can be accessed by its index. Indexing starts at 0.

Example: Indexing and Slicing

```
fruits = ("apple", "banana", "cherry", "date")

# Accessing elements by index

print("First fruit:", fruits[0])

print("Last fruit:", fruits[-1])

# Slicing: Getting a sub-tuple

print("Middle fruits:", fruits[1:3])
```

**Explanation:**

- **Indexing:** fruits[0] accesses the first element ("apple"), and fruits[-1] accesses the last element ("date").
- **Slicing:** fruits[1:3] returns a new tuple with elements from index 1 up to, but not including, index 3.

**3. Immutability of Tuples**

Once a tuple is created, its contents cannot be changed. This means you cannot add, remove, or modify its elements. Immutability provides benefits such as data integrity and can improve performance in certain contexts (e.g., as keys in dictionaries).

**Example: Attempting to Modify a Tuple**

```
numbers = (1, 2, 3, 4, 5)

try:

    # Trying to modify the first element (this will raise a TypeError)

    numbers[0] = 10

except TypeError as e:

    print("Error:", e)
```

**Explanation:**

- The code attempts to change the first element of the tuple numbers.
- Python raises a TypeError because tuples are immutable.

**4. Benefits of Using Tuples**

Tuples have several advantages that make them a good choice in certain situations:

- **Immutability:**
  Ensures that the data remains constant, preventing accidental modifications.
- **Hashability:**
  Because they are immutable, tuples can be used as keys in dictionaries or elements of sets.
- **Performance:**
  Tuples are typically faster than lists for certain operations due to their immutable nature.

- **Semantic Clarity:**
  Tuples can be used to represent fixed collections of related values, such as coordinates, RGB values, or a record from a database.

**Example: Using Tuples as Dictionary Keys**

```
# Tuples as keys in a dictionary

location = {

    (40.7128, -74.0060): "New York",

    (34.0522, -118.2437): "Los Angeles",

    (41.8781, -87.6298): "Chicago"

}

print("City at coordinates (40.7128, -74.0060):", location[(40.7128, -
74.0060)])
```

**Explanation:**

- Tuples representing coordinates are used as keys in the dictionary location.
- Their immutability guarantees that the keys remain consistent.

**5. Converting Between Tuples and Lists**

Even though tuples are immutable, you can convert them to lists to perform modifications and then convert them back to tuples if needed.

**Example: Converting and Modifying a Tuple**

```
# Original tuple

fruits = ("apple", "banana", "cherry")

# Convert tuple to list
```

```
fruits_list = list(fruits)
print("List:", fruits_list)
# Modify the list
fruits_list.append("date")
print("Modified List:", fruits_list)
# Convert the list back to a tuple
new_fruits = tuple(fruits_list)
print("New Tuple:", new_fruits)
```

**Explanation:**

- The tuple fruits is converted to a list to allow modifications.
- After appending a new element, the list is converted back to a tuple, resulting in a new immutable sequence.

**6. Best Practices for Using Tuples**

- **Use Tuples for Fixed Data:**
  When you have a collection of items that should not change throughout the program, tuples provide a clear indication that the data is constant.
- **Prefer Tuples for Heterogeneous Data:**
  Tuples are ideal for storing a record with different types of data, such as (name, age, occupation).
- **Utilize Tuples as Dictionary Keys:**
  When you need to use compound keys in a dictionary, tuples are the appropriate choice due to their immutability.
- **Convert Only When Necessary:**
  Avoid unnecessary conversions between tuples and lists to maintain performance and code clarity.

### In Summary

Tuples are immutable sequences in Python that offer a lightweight and efficient way to store fixed collections of items. They support indexing and slicing like lists, but once created, their content cannot be modified. This immutability makes tuples useful in scenarios where data integrity is crucial, such as using them as dictionary keys or representing fixed sets of values.

Key points covered include:

- **Creating Tuples:** Using parentheses or comma-separated values.
- **Accessing Elements:** Through indexing and slicing.
- **Immutability:** Understanding that tuples cannot be modified after creation.
- **Conversion:** How to convert between tuples and lists for modifications.
- **Benefits and Best Practices:** Utilizing tuples for fixed data, improved performance, and safe usage in hashable contexts.

Mastering the use of tuples enhances your ability to work with immutable data in Python, ensuring that your code is robust, efficient, and semantically clear.

## Set Operations: Union and Intersection

Sets in Python are unordered collections of unique elements. They are particularly useful for performing mathematical set operations such as union, intersection, difference, and symmetric difference.

### 1. Understanding Sets in Python

Before diving into operations, it's important to understand a few key characteristics of sets:

- **Unordered:**
  The elements in a set are not stored in any particular order.
- **Unique Elements:**
  Sets automatically remove duplicate elements.
- **Mutable:**
  You can add or remove elements from a set after its creation.

**Creating a Set**

```
# Creating a set of integers

numbers = {1, 2, 3, 4, 5}

print("Numbers:", numbers)

# Creating a set from a list (duplicates are removed)

fruits_list = ["apple", "banana", "apple", "cherry"]

fruits_set = set(fruits_list)

print("Fruits Set:", fruits_set)
```

**2. Union of Sets**

The **union** of two sets is a set containing all unique elements from both sets. In Python, you can perform a union in two main ways:

**Using the union() method:**

```
set1.union(set2)
```

Using the | operator:

```
set1 | set2
```

Example: Union Operation

```
# Define two sets

set_a = {1, 2, 3, 4}
```

```
set_b = {3, 4, 5, 6}

# Using the union() method

union_result = set_a.union(set_b)

print("Union using method:", union_result)  # Output: {1, 2, 3, 4, 5, 6}

# Using the | operator

union_result_operator = set_a | set_b

print("Union using operator:", union_result_operator)  # Output: {1, 2, 3, 4, 5, 6}
```

**Explanation:**

- Both approaches produce a set containing all elements that are in either set_a or set_b (or both).
- Duplicates are automatically removed.

**3. Intersection of Sets**

The **intersection** of two sets is a set containing only the elements that are common to both sets. Similar to union, intersection can be performed using:

**The intersection() method:**

```
set1.intersection(set2)
```

The & operator:

```
set1 & set2
```

Example: Intersection Operation

```
# Define two sets

set_a = {1, 2, 3, 4}
```

```
set_b = {3, 4, 5, 6}

# Using the intersection() method

intersection_result = set_a.intersection(set_b)

print("Intersection using method:", intersection_result)  # Output: {3, 4}

# Using the & operator

intersection_result_operator = set_a & set_b

print("Intersection using operator:", intersection_result_operator)  # Output: {3, 4}
```

**Explanation:**

- Both methods yield a set containing only the elements that appear in both set_a and set_b.
- In this case, the common elements are 3 and 4.

**4. Practical Applications of Set Operations**

Set operations are very useful in scenarios where you need to compare collections of data. Here are a couple of practical examples:

**Example: Finding Unique Elements Across Data Sources**

Suppose you have two lists representing participants from two different events, and you want to find all unique participants.

```
event1 = ["Alice", "Bob", "Charlie", "David"]

event2 = ["Charlie", "Eve", "Frank", "Alice"]

# Convert lists to sets

participants_event1 = set(event1)

participants_event2 = set(event2)
```

```
# Get the union of both sets
all_participants = participants_event1 | participants_event2
print("All unique participants:", all_participants)
```

**Example: Identifying Common Elements**

Suppose you want to find participants who attended both events

```
# Get the intersection of both sets
common_participants = participants_event1 & participants_event2
print("Participants in both events:", common_participants)
```

**Explanation:**

- The union operation provides a complete list of unique participants from both events.
- The intersection operation reveals the participants common to both events.

**In Summary**

- **Sets** are collections of unique, unordered elements.
- **Union Operation:**
  - Combines two sets, yielding a set with all elements from both sets.
  - Can be performed using the union() method or the | operator.
- **Intersection Operation:**
  - Produces a set with elements common to both sets.
  - Can be performed using the intersection() method or the & operator.
- **Practical Uses:**

- Useful in scenarios like data deduplication, comparing collections, and identifying common or unique elements across datasets.

Understanding set operations is a crucial part of Python's data structures. They provide efficient and expressive ways to handle and compare collections of data, making your code more robust and easier to maintain.

## List and Set Comprehensions

Python's comprehensions are a concise and powerful way to generate new collections by iterating over existing iterables. They combine looping and conditional logic in a single, readable expression.

### 1. List Comprehensions

List comprehensions allow you to create lists in a concise manner. They replace the need for verbose loops by embedding the loop and any necessary conditions directly inside square brackets.

#### 1.1 Basic Syntax

The general syntax for a list comprehension is:

```
[expression for item in iterable]
```

Example: Creating a List of Squares

```
# Generate a list of squares for numbers 1 through 10

squares = [x**2 for x in range(1, 11)]

print("Squares:", squares)
```

**Explanation:**

- **Expression:** x**2 calculates the square of each number.
- **Loop:** for x in range(1, 11) iterates over numbers from 1 to 10.
- **Result:** A new list squares is created containing the squared values.

### 1.2 Filtering with Conditions

You can add an if clause to include only items that meet a certain condition.

Example: Generating Even Squares Only

```
# Generate a list of squares for even numbers between 1 and 10

even_squares = [x**2 for x in range(1, 11) if x % 2 == 0]

print("Even Squares:", even_squares)
```

**Explanation:**

The if x % 2 == 0 clause ensures that only even numbers are squared and included in the resulting list.

### 1.3 Multiple For Clauses

List comprehensions can contain multiple for clauses to handle nested iterations.

**Example: Creating Pairs from Two Lists**

```
colors = ["red", "green", "blue"]

objects = ["ball", "car"]

# Generate all possible color-object pairs as tuples

pairs = [(color, obj) for color in colors for obj in objects]

print("Color-Object Pairs:", pairs)
```

**Explanation:**

- The comprehension iterates over every color and, for each color, iterates over every object.
- The resulting list pairs contains tuples representing every combination.

## 2. Set Comprehensions

Set comprehensions are similar to list comprehensions but are used to create sets, which automatically eliminate duplicate elements. The syntax is nearly identical, but curly braces {} are used instead of square brackets.

### 2.1 Basic Syntax

The general syntax for a set comprehension is:

```
{expression for item in iterable}
```

Example: Creating a Set of Unique Squares

```
# Generate a set of squares for numbers 1 through 10

squares_set = {x**2 for x in range(1, 11)}

print("Squares Set:", squares_set)
```

**Explanation:**

- Even though the operation is similar to a list comprehension, the resulting collection is a set, which holds only unique values.
- If the expression produced duplicate values, the set would automatically ensure each element appears only once.

### 2.2 Filtering with Conditions

Just like list comprehensions, set comprehensions can include conditions to filter the elements.

**Example: Generating a Set of Even Squares**

```
# Generate a set of squares for even numbers between 1 and 10

even_squares_set = {x**2 for x in range(1, 11) if x % 2 == 0}

print("Even Squares Set:", even_squares_set)
```

**Explanation:**

- The comprehension filters for even numbers using the condition if x % 2 == 0 and then squares them.
- The resulting set even_squares_set contains only the squared values of even numbers.

### 3. Benefits of Using Comprehensions

- **Conciseness:**
  Comprehensions allow you to write compact code that is often more expressive than equivalent multi-line loops.
- **Readability:**
  When used appropriately, comprehensions make it clear what transformation or filtering is being performed on the data.
- **Performance:**
  Python comprehensions are optimized for performance and are typically faster than their loop-based counterparts.

### 4. Best Practices

- **Keep it Simple:**
  If a comprehension becomes overly complex (e.g., multiple nested loops and conditions), consider refactoring the code into a conventional loop or splitting the logic into helper functions for clarity.
- **Use Descriptive Variables:**
  Choose variable names that make the purpose of the comprehension clear. Avoid overly terse names that might obscure meaning.
- **Balance Readability and Conciseness:**
  While comprehensions are powerful, readability should not be sacrificed for brevity. If a comprehension is hard to understand at a glance, a regular loop might be a better choice.

## In Summary

List and set comprehensions are essential tools in Python for creating and transforming collections in a concise and readable manner:

- **List Comprehensions:**
  - Syntax: [expression for item in iterable [if condition]]
  - Use cases include generating lists, filtering data, and performing operations on each element.
- **Set Comprehensions:**
  - Syntax: {expression for item in iterable [if condition]}
  - Ideal for creating sets, ensuring uniqueness of elements while applying transformations or filters.

By mastering comprehensions, you can write more efficient, elegant, and Pythonic code.

## Example Exercises

Working with collections is an essential part of Python programming. Lists, tuples, and sets provide powerful ways to store and manage data.

### 1. Filtering Collections

Filtering involves selecting a subset of elements from a collection based on a condition. Python offers several ways to filter collections, including list comprehensions, the built-in filter() function, and using loops.

### 1.1 Filtering with List Comprehensions

#### Example: Filtering a List of Numbers

Suppose you have a list of numbers and you want to filter out only the even numbers.

```
numbers = [1, 2, 3, 4, 5, 6, 7, 8, 9, 10]

# Using a list comprehension to filter even numbers

even_numbers = [num for num in numbers if num % 2 == 0]

print("Even Numbers:", even_numbers)
```

**Explanation:**

- The list comprehension iterates over numbers.
- The condition if num % 2 == 0 ensures only even numbers are included in the new list even_numbers.

### 1.2 Filtering with the filter() Function

You can achieve the same result using the built-in filter() function combined with a lambda function.

```
# Using filter() to select even numbers

even_numbers_filter = list(filter(lambda x: x % 2 == 0, numbers))

print("Even Numbers (filter):", even_numbers_filter)
```

**Explanation:**

- The filter() function applies the lambda function to each element.
- Elements for which the lambda returns True are included in the resulting iterator, which is then converted to a list.

### 1.3 Filtering Elements in Tuples and Sets

Filtering works similarly with tuples and sets, though you may often want to convert the result back to the original data type.

**Example: Filtering a Tuple of Strings**

```
names = ("Alice", "Bob", "Charlie", "David", "Eve")
```

```
# Filter names that start with 'A' or 'E'
filtered_names = tuple(name for name in names if name[0] in ("A",
"E"))
print("Filtered Names (Tuple):", filtered_names)
```

Example: Filtering a Set of Numbers

```
number_set = {10, 15, 20, 25, 30, 35}
# Filter numbers greater than 20
filtered_set = {num for num in number_set if num > 20}
print("Filtered Set:", filtered_set)
```

**2. Sorting Collections**

Sorting arranges the elements of a collection in a specific order (ascending or descending). Python provides built-in functions to sort lists, and you can use similar techniques to sort other types of collections (often by converting them to lists).

**2.1 Sorting a List**

**Example: Sorting Numbers**

```
unsorted_numbers = [4, 2, 9, 1, 5, 6]
sorted_numbers = sorted(unsorted_numbers)  # Returns a new
sorted list
print("Sorted Numbers (Ascending):", sorted_numbers)
# Sorting in descending order
sorted_numbers_desc = sorted(unsorted_numbers, reverse=True)
print("Sorted Numbers (Descending):", sorted_numbers_desc)
```

**Explanation:**

- The sorted() function returns a new sorted list from the iterable.
- The reverse=True argument sorts the list in descending order.

### 2.2 Sorting with List Methods

Lists also provide an in-place sort() method.

```
fruits = ["banana", "apple", "cherry", "date"]
fruits.sort()  # Sorts the list in place in ascending order
print("Sorted Fruits:", fruits)
```

**Explanation:**

The sort() method rearranges the elements of fruits without creating a new list.

### 2.3 Sorting Complex Data

When working with collections of complex data, such as dictionaries or lists of tuples, you can use the key parameter in sorted() to specify a custom sort order.

**Example: Sorting a List of Tuples by the Second Element**

```
students = [("Alice", 88), ("Bob", 95), ("Charlie", 70), ("David", 85)]
# Sort by score (the second element of each tuple)
sorted_students = sorted(students, key=lambda student: student[1])
print("Students Sorted by Score:", sorted_students)
```

**Explanation:**

The lambda function lambda student: student[1] tells sorted() to use the second element (score) of each tuple as the sort key.

## 3. Simple Data Analysis

Data analysis often involves filtering, sorting, and then computing summary statistics on collections.

### 3.1 Calculating the Average

**Example: Average of a List of Numbers**

```
data = [10, 20, 30, 40, 50]

# Calculate the average

average = sum(data) / len(data)

print("Average:", average)
```

**Explanation:**

- The sum() function adds all numbers in the list.
- The len() function provides the number of elements, and dividing the total by this number yields the average.

### 3.2 Finding the Maximum and Minimum

**Example: Using Built-In Functions**

```
max_value = max(data)

min_value = min(data)

print("Maximum:", max_value)

print("Minimum:", min_value)
```

**Explanation:**

- The max() function returns the highest value in the collection.
- The min() function returns the lowest value.

### 3.3 Counting Occurrences

**Example: Frequency Count Using a Dictionary**

```
words = ["apple", "banana", "apple", "cherry", "banana", "apple"]
frequency = {}
for word in words:
    frequency[word] = frequency.get(word, 0) + 1
print("Word Frequency:", frequency)
```

**Explanation:**

- The loop iterates over the list of words.
- The get() method with a default value of 0 counts the occurrences of each word.
- The result is a dictionary mapping each word to its frequency.

**In Summary**

In these exercises, we've explored how to:

- **Filter** data from lists, tuples, and sets using comprehensions and the filter() function.
- **Sort** collections using both the built-in sorted() function and in-place list methods like sort(), including custom sorting for complex data.
- **Perform simple data analysis** by calculating averages, finding maximum and minimum values, and counting occurrences.

These operations are fundamental for many applications in data processing, cleaning, and analysis. Mastering these techniques will enable you to work more effectively with data structures in Python, making your code both efficient and expressive.

# Chapter 10: Working with Strings in Depth

## String Methods

Strings are one of Python's most frequently used data types and come equipped with a rich set of built-in methods for manipulation and analysis. These methods allow you to transform, search, and modify text in a variety of ways.

### 1. Splitting Strings

The split() method divides a string into a list of substrings based on a specified delimiter. By default, it splits on any whitespace.

**Basic Usage**

```
text = "Python is fun and powerful"

words = text.split()

print("Words:", words)
```

**Explanation:**

The string text is split at every whitespace, resulting in a list of words.

**Specifying a Delimiter**

```
csv_data = "Alice,Bob,Charlie,David"

names = csv_data.split(",")

print("Names:", names)
```

**Explanation:**

Here, the delimiter is a comma. The method splits the string at each comma, producing a list of names.

**Limiting the Number of Splits**

```
sentence = "one two three four five"
limited_split = sentence.split(" ", 2)
print("Limited Split:", limited_split)
```

**Explanation:**

The second argument (2) limits the number of splits to 2, resulting in a list with three elements: the first two words and the remainder of the string.

**2. Trimming Strings**

Trimming methods remove unwanted whitespace or characters from the beginning and/or end of a string.

**strip() Method**

Removes both leading and trailing whitespace.

```
messy_string = "   Hello, World!   "
clean_string = messy_string.strip()
print("Stripped String:", clean_string)
```

**Explanation:**

strip() removes spaces from both the start and the end of the string.

**lstrip() and rstrip() Methods**

- lstrip() removes leading whitespace.
- rstrip() removes trailing whitespace.

```
messy_string = "   Hello, World!   "
left_clean = messy_string.lstrip()
right_clean = messy_string.rstrip()
```

```
print("Left Stripped:", left_clean)
print("Right Stripped:", right_clean)
```

**Explanation:**

- lstrip() only removes spaces at the beginning.
- rstrip() only removes spaces at the end.

### 3. Replacing Substrings

The replace() method substitutes occurrences of a specified substring with another substring.

#### Basic Replacement

```
text = "I love Python. Python is awesome."
new_text = text.replace("Python", "JavaScript")
print("Replaced Text:", new_text)
```

**Explanation:**

- Every occurrence of "Python" is replaced with "JavaScript".
- This operation returns a new string, leaving the original string unchanged (since strings are immutable in Python).

#### Replacing with a Limit

```
text = "spam spam spam spam"
limited_replace = text.replace("spam", "eggs", 2)
print("Limited Replace:", limited_replace)
```

**Explanation:**

The third argument limits the number of replacements to 2, so only the first two occurrences of "spam" are replaced with "eggs".

### 4. Joining Strings

While not a trimming or splitting method, join() is essential for working with strings, particularly when you need to combine a list of strings into a single string.

**Basic Usage**

```
words = ["Python", "is", "awesome"]

sentence = " ".join(words)

print("Joined Sentence:", sentence)
```

**Explanation:**

- The string " " (a space) is used as a separator between the words.
- The join() method concatenates all elements in the list words into one string.

**Custom Separator**

```
names = ["Alice", "Bob", "Charlie"]

csv_line = ", ".join(names)

print("CSV Line:", csv_line)
```

**Explanation:**

The elements of the list are joined using a comma followed by a space, producing a CSV-like string.

### 5. Additional Useful String Methods

Beyond splitting, stripping, and replacing, there are several other string methods that can help in data processing:

**Case Conversion**

- **upper()**: Converts all characters to uppercase.

- **lower()**: Converts all characters to lowercase.
- **title()**: Capitalizes the first letter of each word.
- **capitalize()**: Capitalizes the first letter of the string and lowercases the rest.

```
text = "hello, python!"

print("Uppercase:", text.upper())

print("Lowercase:", text.lower())

print("Title Case:", text.title())

print("Capitalized:", text.capitalize())
```

**Finding Substrings**

- **find()**: Returns the lowest index of the substring if found, otherwise returns -1.
- **index()**: Similar to find(), but raises a ValueError if the substring is not found.

```
phrase = "The quick brown fox jumps over the lazy dog"

position = phrase.find("fox")

print("Position of 'fox':", position)
```

**Splitting Lines**

**splitlines()**: Splits the string at line breaks and returns a list of lines.

```
multiline_text = "Line one\nLine two\nLine three"

lines = multiline_text.splitlines()

print("Lines:", lines)
```

**6. Best Practices for String Methods**

- **Immutable Nature:**
  Remember that strings in Python are immutable. Methods like replace() and strip() do not modify the original string but return a new one.

- **Chaining Methods:**
  You can chain string methods for more concise operations. However, ensure that the chain is clear and does not compromise readability.

```
messy_text = "   hello, python!   "
clean_text = messy_text.strip().capitalize()
print("Clean Text:", clean_text)
```

- **Error Handling:**
  When searching for substrings using methods like index(), consider using exception handling to manage cases where the substring may not be present.

```
try:
    position = phrase.index("cat")
except ValueError:
    position = -1
print("Position of 'cat':", position)
```

**In Summary**

String methods are a powerful part of Python's standard library that enable efficient and effective text manipulation. Key methods include:

- **split()**: Divides a string into a list of substrings based on a delimiter.

- **strip(), lstrip(), rstrip()**: Remove unwanted whitespace from the beginning and/or end of a string.
- **replace()**: Substitutes occurrences of a substring with another substring.
- **join()**: Combines a list of strings into a single string with a specified separator.
- **Additional Methods**: Case conversion (upper(), lower(), title(), capitalize()), substring searching (find(), index()), and splitting lines (splitlines()).

By mastering these string methods, you can manipulate text data more effectively, making your code both more concise and more readable.

## Advanced Formatting

Advanced string formatting in Python allows you to generate dynamic, well-formatted output with minimal code. Two of the most powerful techniques for advanced formatting are **f-strings** (formatted string literals) and the **format()** method. These tools enable you to embed expressions, control number precision, align text, and more.

### 1. f-Strings (Formatted String Literals)

Introduced in Python 3.6, f-strings offer a concise and readable way to format strings. By prefixing a string with the letter f or F, you can embed Python expressions inside curly braces {} directly within the string.

#### 1.1 Basic Usage

**Example: Embedding Variables**

```
name = "Alice"

age = 30
```

```
message = f"My name is {name} and I am {age} years old."

print(message)
```

**Explanation:**

The f-string automatically replaces {name} and {age} with the values of the corresponding variables.

### 1.2 Expression Evaluation

f-Strings support the evaluation of arbitrary Python expressions.

**Example: Inline Calculations**

```
a = 5

b = 3

result = f"The product of {a} and {b} is {a * b}."

print(result)
```

**Explanation:**

- The expression {a * b} is evaluated in place, and its result is formatted into the string.

### 1.3 Advanced Formatting Options

f-Strings allow you to specify detailed formatting options using a colon : followed by format specifiers.

**Example: Formatting Numbers**

```
pi = 3.14159265

# Rounding to 2 decimal places

formatted_pi = f"Pi rounded to 2 decimal places: {pi:.2f}"

print(formatted_pi)
```

```
# Displaying in scientific notation
formatted_scientific = f"Pi in scientific notation: {pi:.3e}"
print(formatted_scientific)
```

**Explanation:**

- {pi:.2f} rounds the value of pi to two decimal places.
- {pi:.3e} formats pi in scientific notation with three digits after the decimal.

**Example: Width and Alignment**

```
text = "Hello"
# Align text within a field of width 10
left_aligned = f"|{text:<10}|"
center_aligned = f"|{text:^10}|"
right_aligned = f"|{text:>10}|"
print("Left Aligned:  ", left_aligned)
print("Center Aligned:", center_aligned)
print("Right Aligned: ", right_aligned)
```

**Explanation:**

<, ^, and > specify left, center, and right alignment within a field of a given width (10 in this case).

**2. The format() Method**

Before f-strings, the format() method was the primary way to format strings in Python. It offers similar capabilities and remains widely used, especially in codebases that need to support earlier versions of Python.

## 2.1 Basic Usage

**Example: Inserting Values**

```
name = "Bob"

age = 25

message = "My name is {} and I am {} years old.".format(name, age)

print(message)
```

**Explanation:**

The curly braces {} act as placeholders that are replaced by the arguments passed to format() in order.

## 2.2 Positional and Keyword Arguments

The format() method supports both positional and keyword arguments for greater control over the output.

**Example: Positional Arguments**

```
message = "The {0} is {1} years old.".format("cat", 3)

print(message)
```

Example: Keyword Arguments

```
message = "My favorite fruit is {fruit} and I have {quantity} of them.".format(fruit="apple", quantity=5)

print(message)
```

## 2.3 Advanced Formatting with format()

You can use format specifiers within the curly braces to control the output, similar to f-strings.

**Example: Formatting Numbers and Alignment**

```
pi = 3.14159265
```

```
formatted_pi = "Pi rounded to 2 decimal places: {:.2f}".format(pi)

print(formatted_pi)

# Alignment

text = "World"

aligned_text = "|{:<10}|{:^10}|{:>10}|".format("Left", "Center", "Right")

print("Aligned Text:", aligned_text)
```

**Explanation:**

- {:.2f} rounds the floating-point number to 2 decimal places.
- The alignment specifiers <, ^, and > work similarly to those in f-strings, specifying left, center, and right alignment, respectively.

**3. Choosing Between f-Strings and format()**

Both f-strings and the format() method are powerful and flexible, but there are some considerations for choosing one over the other:

- **f-Strings:**
  - **Pros:**
    - Concise and more readable when embedding expressions.
    - Often more efficient and clearer for simple substitutions.
  - **Cons:**
    - Only available in Python 3.6 and later.
- **format() Method:**
  - **Pros:**
    - More versatile in scenarios where older versions of Python must be supported.

    - Can be useful in complex formatting cases where positional and keyword arguments are beneficial.

- **Cons:**
    - Can be more verbose and less intuitive than f-strings for straightforward cases.

**In Summary**

Advanced string formatting in Python is a critical tool for creating clear and dynamic output. Key points include:

- **f-Strings:**
  - Introduced in Python 3.6.
  - Allow inline expression evaluation and support advanced formatting (precision, alignment, etc.) with a clear and concise syntax.
- **format() Method:**
  - A versatile method that works in earlier Python versions.
  - Supports both positional and keyword arguments, along with detailed formatting specifiers.

By mastering these advanced formatting techniques, you can significantly enhance the readability and functionality of your Python programs, making them both more professional and user-friendly.

## Regular Expressions with the re Module

Regular expressions (regex) provide a powerful way to search, match, and manipulate text. In Python, the re module offers robust support for working with regular expressions, enabling complex string processing tasks with concise syntax.

## 1. Getting Started with the re Module

Before using regular expressions, you must import the module:

```
import re
```

## 2. Basic Functions and Their Usage

### 2.1 re.search()

The re.search() function scans through a string and returns a match object if a match is found anywhere in the string; otherwise, it returns None.

**Example:**

```
import re

text = "The quick brown fox jumps over the lazy dog."

pattern = "fox"

match = re.search(pattern, text)

if match:

    print("Match found:", match.group())

else:

    print("No match found.")
```

**Explanation:**

- re.search(pattern, text) searches for the substring "fox" in text.
- If a match is found, match.group() returns the matched substring.

### 2.2 re.match()

The re.match() function checks for a match only at the beginning of the string.

**Example:**

```
import re
text = "Hello, world!"
pattern = "Hello"
match = re.match(pattern, text)
if match:
    print("Match found at the beginning:", match.group())
else:
    print("No match at the beginning.")
```

**Explanation:**

- re.match(pattern, text) attempts to match "Hello" at the start of text.
- Since text starts with "Hello", a match is found.

**2.3 re.findall()**

The re.findall() function returns all non-overlapping matches of a pattern in a string as a list.

**Example:**

```
import re
text = "The rain in Spain falls mainly in the plain."
pattern = "ain"
matches = re.findall(pattern, text)
print("Matches found:", matches)
```

**Explanation:**

- re.findall(pattern, text) finds all occurrences of the substring "ain" in text.
- The result is a list of all matching substrings.

### 2.4 re.split()

The re.split() function splits a string by the occurrences of a pattern, similar to the built-in str.split() but with regex support.

**Example:**

```
import re

text = "apple, banana; cherry: date"

# Split on commas, semicolons, or colons

parts = re.split(r'[,:;]\s*', text)

print("Splitted parts:", parts)
```

**Explanation:**

- The pattern [,:;]\s* matches a comma, colon, or semicolon followed by any whitespace.
- re.split() uses this pattern to divide the string into a list of substrings.

### 2.5 re.sub()

The re.sub() function replaces occurrences of a pattern in a string with a replacement string.

**Example:**

```
import re

text = "The quick brown fox jumps over the lazy dog."
```

```
pattern = "fox"
replacement = "cat"
new_text = re.sub(pattern, replacement, text)
print("Replaced Text:", new_text)
```

**Explanation:**

- re.sub(pattern, replacement, text) replaces "fox" with "cat" in text.
- The function returns a new string with the substitutions made.

**3. Compiling Regular Expressions**

For patterns that are used repeatedly, you can compile them into a regex object using re.compile(). This can improve performance and code clarity.

**Example:**

```
import re
pattern = re.compile(r'\d+')
text = "There are 123 apples and 45 oranges."
# Use the compiled pattern to find all sequences of digits
numbers = pattern.findall(text)
print("Numbers found:", numbers)
```

**Explanation:**

- re.compile(r'\d+') compiles a pattern that matches one or more digits.
- The findall() method of the compiled pattern is then used to extract all matching substrings.

## 4. Best Practices for Using Regular Expressions

- **Keep Patterns Simple:**
  Write clear and concise regex patterns. Overly complex expressions can be difficult to read and maintain.
- **Use Raw Strings:**
  Prefix your regex patterns with r (e.g., r'\d+') to avoid issues with escape sequences in Python strings.
- **Comment Your Patterns:**
  When using complex patterns, consider adding comments or breaking the regex into smaller parts with the re.VERBOSE flag.

**Example:**

```
pattern = re.compile(r"""
    \d{3}     # Area code
    -         # Separator
    \d{3}     # First three digits
    -         # Separator
    \d{4}     # Last four digits
    """, re.VERBOSE)
```

- **Test Thoroughly:**
  Regular expressions can be error-prone. Test your regex patterns with various inputs to ensure they work as expected.
- **Prefer Specificity:**
  Avoid overly broad patterns that might match unintended parts of your text.

## In Summary

Regular expressions provide a powerful toolkit for working with strings in Python. With the re module, you can:

- **Search and Match:**
  - Use re.search() and re.match() to locate patterns in text.
- **Find All Matches:**
  - Use re.findall() to retrieve all occurrences of a pattern.
- **Split and Replace:**
  - Use re.split() to divide a string based on a regex pattern.
  - Use re.sub() to replace parts of a string that match a pattern.
- **Compile Patterns:**
  - Use re.compile() to create reusable regex objects for improved performance and clarity.

By mastering regular expressions, you'll be able to perform sophisticated text manipulation and data extraction tasks efficiently.

## Example Exercises

Parsing and cleaning text data are common tasks in data processing and analysis. In Python, you can leverage a variety of string methods, regular expressions (via the re module), and other tools to extract useful information and prepare text for further processing.

### 1. Exercise: Extracting Email Addresses from a Block of Text

**Objective:**
Given a block of text, extract all email addresses present within it. This exercise demonstrates the use of regular expressions for pattern matching and the re.findall() method for extracting multiple occurrences.

**Code Example:**

```
import re

# Sample text containing email addresses

text = """

Hello, you can contact us at support@example.com for assistance.

Alternatively, reach out to sales-info@company.org or
feedback@service.net.

Please do not reply to noreply@domain.com.

"""

# Define a regex pattern for matching email addresses

email_pattern = r"[a-zA-Z0-9_.+-]+@[a-zA-Z0-9-]+\.[a-zA-Z0-9-
.]+"

# Use re.findall() to extract all email addresses

emails = re.findall(email_pattern, text)

print("Extracted Email Addresses:")

for email in emails:

    print(email)
```

**Explanation:**

- The regex pattern [a-zA-Z0-9_.+-]+@[a-zA-Z0-9-]+\.[a-zA-Z0-9-.]+ is designed to match common email formats.
- The re.findall() function searches the text and returns a list of all matches.
- The output lists each email found in the sample text.

2. Exercise: Cleaning and Normalizing a Raw Text Document

Objective:

Clean a raw text document by removing extra whitespace, punctuation, and converting the text to lowercase. This exercise uses string methods such as strip(), replace(), and regular expressions for further cleaning.

Code Example:

```
import re

# Raw text with unwanted characters, extra whitespace, and inconsistent casing

raw_text = """

   Hello!!! This is an example document.

It contains extra spaces, punctuation... and CAPITAL letters!

Visit https://example.com for more info.

"""

# Step 1: Strip leading and trailing whitespace and convert to lowercase

clean_text = raw_text.strip().lower()

print("After strip and lower:")

print(clean_text)

# Step 2: Remove punctuation (except for basic sentence structure, e.g., periods)

# Here we remove any character that is not alphanumeric, whitespace, or a period.

clean_text = re.sub(r"[^a-z0-9\s.]", "", clean_text)

print("\nAfter removing punctuation:")
```

```
print(clean_text)
# Step 3: Replace multiple whitespace characters with a single space
clean_text = re.sub(r"\s+", " ", clean_text)
print("\nAfter normalizing whitespace:")
print(clean_text)
```

**Explanation:**

- The strip() method removes leading and trailing whitespace, and lower() converts the text to lowercase.
- A regular expression re.sub(r"[^a-z0-9\s.]", "", clean_text) removes any character that is not a lowercase letter, a digit, whitespace, or a period.
- Another regex re.sub(r"\s+", " ", clean_text) replaces multiple spaces or newline characters with a single space.
- The result is a cleaned and normalized version of the raw text.

3. Exercise: Splitting a Paragraph into Sentences

Objective:

Parse a paragraph of text into individual sentences. This can be useful for tasks like text summarization or further natural language processing.

Code Example:

```
import re
# A paragraph of text
paragraph = """
Natural language processing (NLP) is a field of artificial intelligence.
```

```
It focuses on the interaction between computers and humans.

Understanding language is a complex challenge.

"""

# Use re.split() to split the paragraph into sentences

# The pattern splits at a period, question mark, or exclamation point, followed by one or more spaces or a newline.

sentences = re.split(r'[.?!]+\s*', paragraph.strip())

# Remove any empty strings that might result from trailing punctuation

sentences = [sentence for sentence in sentences if sentence]

print("Sentences:")

for idx, sentence in enumerate(sentences, start=1):

    print(f"{idx}. {sentence}")
```

**Explanation:**

- The regex pattern [.?!]+\s* is used to split the paragraph at punctuation marks that typically denote the end of a sentence.
- The strip() method is used to remove any leading or trailing whitespace from the paragraph.
- A list comprehension filters out any empty strings that may be produced if the paragraph ends with a punctuation mark.
- The output is a numbered list of sentences extracted from the paragraph.

**4. Exercise: Tokenizing and Counting Word Frequencies**

**Objective:**

Break a text document into individual words (tokens) and compute the frequency of each word. This exercise is a common task in text analysis and preprocessing.

**Code Example:**

```
import re

from collections import Counter

# Sample text

text = """

Data science is an interdisciplinary field.

It uses scientific methods, processes, algorithms, and systems to
extract knowledge and insights from noisy, structured, and
unstructured data.

Data science is related to data mining, machine learning and big data.

"""

# Step 1: Convert text to lowercase

text = text.lower()

# Step 2: Remove punctuation using regex

text = re.sub(r"[^a-z\s]", "", text)

# Step 3: Split the text into words

words = text.split()

# Step 4: Count word frequencies using Counter

word_frequencies = Counter(words)

print("Word Frequencies:")

for word, count in word_frequencies.items():
```

```
print(f"{word}: {count}")
```

**Explanation:**

- The text is first converted to lowercase to ensure that word counts are case-insensitive.
- A regex removes punctuation, leaving only letters and whitespace.
- The cleaned text is split into words using split().
- The Counter from the collections module tallies the occurrences of each word.
- The output displays each word alongside its frequency count.

**In Summary**

These exercises demonstrate how to parse and clean text data using Python's string methods and regular expressions:

- **Extracting Data:**
  Use regular expressions with functions like re.findall() to extract patterns such as email addresses.
- **Cleaning Data:**
  Employ string methods (strip(), lower(), split()) and regex substitutions to remove unwanted characters, normalize whitespace, and standardize text.
- **Parsing Text:**
  Split paragraphs into sentences using regex and tokenize text for analysis.
- **Data Analysis:**
  Count word frequencies using tokenization and Python's Counter class.

Mastering these techniques is essential for effective text processing and lays a strong foundation for more advanced natural language processing tasks.

# Section V: Functions, Modules, and Packages
# Chapter 11: Functions – Building Blocks of Reusability

## Defining and Calling Functions

Functions are fundamental building blocks in Python that encapsulate a block of code into a single, reusable unit. They enable you to write modular code by grouping related operations, making your programs easier to read, maintain, and test.

### 1. Defining Functions

In Python, functions are defined using the def keyword, followed by the function name and a pair of parentheses. Any parameters the function accepts are placed within these parentheses. The function body is indented and contains the code that runs each time the function is called.

### 1.1 Basic Function Definition

**Example: A Simple Greeting Function**

```
def greet():
    """Print a simple greeting message."""
    print("Hello, World!")
# Calling the function
greet()
```

**Explanation:**

- The function greet() is defined with no parameters.
- A docstring is included to describe what the function does.
- When greet() is called, it prints "Hello, World!" to the console.

### 1.2 Functions with Parameters

Parameters allow functions to accept input values that can be used within the function body, making the function more versatile.

**Example: A Personalized Greeting Function**

```
def greet_person(name):
    """
    Print a personalized greeting message.
    Parameters:
    name (str): The name of the person to greet.
    """
    print(f"Hello, {name}! Welcome to Python programming.")
# Calling the function with an argument
greet_person("Alice")
```

**Explanation:**

- The function greet_person(name) takes one parameter name.
- The function uses an f-string to embed the name parameter in the greeting message.
- Calling greet_person("Alice") prints a personalized greeting for Alice.

### 1.3 Functions with Return Values

Often, functions perform computations and return a result instead of just printing output. Use the return statement to send a value back to the caller.

**Example: A Function to Add Two Numbers**

```
def add_numbers(a, b):
    """
    Return the sum of two numbers.
     Parameters:
    a (int or float): The first number.
    b (int or float): The second number.
      Returns:
    int or float: The sum of a and b.
    """
    return a + b
# Calling the function and storing the result
result = add_numbers(5, 7)
print("The sum is:", result)
```

**Explanation:**

- The function add_numbers(a, b) takes two parameters and returns their sum.
- The returned value is stored in the variable result and then printed.

**2. Calling Functions**

Calling a function means executing the code defined within it. You can call functions multiple times, which is one of the key benefits of reusability.

### 2.1 Basic Function Call

Once a function is defined, call it by using its name followed by parentheses. If the function requires parameters, pass the appropriate arguments inside the parentheses.

**Example:**

```
def say_hello():
    print("Hello!")
# Calling the function
say_hello()
say_hello()  # The function can be called as many times as needed
```

### 2.2 Passing Arguments to Functions

When functions accept parameters, you must pass arguments when calling them. Arguments can be passed positionally or by keyword.

**Example: Positional Arguments**

```
def multiply(a, b):
    return a * b
product = multiply(3, 4)  # 3 is assigned to 'a' and 4 to 'b'
print("Product:", product)
```

Example: Keyword Arguments

```
def subtract(a, b):
    return a - b
# Calling the function with keyword arguments
difference = subtract(b=5, a=10)
```

```
print("Difference:", difference)
```

**Explanation:**

- In the first example, arguments are passed by their position in the function definition.
- In the second example, keyword arguments explicitly specify which parameter each value should be assigned to, making the call clearer and order-independent.

**3. Best Practices for Defining and Calling Functions**

- **Write Clear Function Names:**
  Choose descriptive names that convey the purpose of the function. For instance, use calculate_sum() instead of calc().
- **Include Docstrings:**
  Provide a docstring immediately after the function definition to explain what the function does, its parameters, and its return value. This is useful for both documentation and tools that generate API docs.
- **Keep Functions Focused:**
  Each function should perform a single, well-defined task. If a function becomes too complex, consider breaking it into smaller helper functions.
- **Avoid Side Effects:**
  Functions should ideally return values and not modify global variables unless explicitly intended. This makes them easier to test and reuse.
- **Use Default Parameters When Appropriate:**
  Default parameters allow functions to be called with fewer arguments while still providing flexibility.

**Example:**

```
def greet_person(name, greeting="Hello"):
    print(f"{greeting}, {name}!")
greet_person("Alice")  # Uses default greeting "Hello"
greet_person("Bob", greeting="Hi")  # Uses custom greeting "Hi"
```

**In Summary**

- **Defining Functions:**
  - Use the def keyword to create a function.
  - Include parameters in parentheses to accept inputs.
  - Write a docstring to describe the function's purpose.
  - Use the return statement to send results back to the caller.
- **Calling Functions:**
  - Invoke functions by using their name followed by parentheses.
  - Pass arguments either positionally or by keyword.
  - Functions can be called multiple times, promoting code reuse.

By mastering the art of defining and calling functions, you create modular, reusable code that enhances both the readability and maintainability of your programs. Functions are the backbone of structured programming in Python, enabling you to build complex systems out of simple, well-defined components.

## Function Arguments and Return Values

Functions are one of the most powerful constructs in Python, allowing you to encapsulate logic into reusable blocks of code. Two fundamental aspects of functions are **arguments** (the inputs that a function accepts) and **return values** (the output produced by a function). Understanding how to use and design function parameters and return values is critical for writing modular, reusable, and maintainable code.

### 1. Function Arguments

Arguments allow you to pass data into functions so they can operate on that data. Python supports several types of function arguments:

#### 1.1 Positional Arguments

Positional arguments are the simplest form of function parameters. When you call the function, the values are assigned to the parameters based on their position in the function definition.

**Example:**

```
def add(a, b):
    """Return the sum of two numbers."""
    return a + b
# Calling the function with positional arguments
result = add(3, 5)  # 3 is assigned to 'a' and 5 to 'b'
print("Sum:", result)  # Output: Sum: 8
```

**Explanation:**
Here, a is explicitly set to 10 and b to 4, regardless of their order in the function call.

#### 1.3 Default Arguments

Default arguments allow you to assign a default value to a parameter. If the caller does not provide a value for that parameter, the default is used.

**Example:**

```
def greet(name, greeting="Hello"):
    """Print a greeting message to the given name."""
    print(f"{greeting}, {name}!")
# Calling the function with and without providing the greeting
greet("Alice")                # Uses the default greeting "Hello"
greet("Bob", greeting="Hi")   # Uses the custom greeting "Hi"
```

**Explanation:**
The greeting parameter has a default value of "Hello". If no greeting is provided, the default is used.

### 1.4 Variable-Length Arguments

Sometimes you might need to write functions that accept an arbitrary number of arguments. Python supports two ways to achieve this:

#### 1.4.1 *args for Non-Keyword Arguments

*args allows a function to accept any number of positional arguments. Inside the function, args is a tuple of all additional positional arguments.

**Example:**

```
def multiply(*args):
    """Return the product of all given numbers."""
    product = 1
    for num in args:
        product *= num
    return product
```

```
# Calling the function with a variable number of arguments
result = multiply(2, 3, 4)
print("Product:", result)  # Output: Product: 24
```

**Explanation:**
All additional positional arguments passed to multiply are captured in the tuple args.

### 1.4.2 **kwargs for Keyword Arguments

**kwargs allows a function to accept an arbitrary number of keyword arguments. Inside the function, kwargs is a dictionary of all additional keyword arguments.

**Example:**

```
def display_info(**kwargs):
    """Print out key-value pairs of provided information."""
    for key, value in kwargs.items():
        print(f"{key}: {value}")
# Calling the function with multiple keyword arguments
display_info(name="Charlie", age=28, occupation="Engineer")
```

**Explanation:**
All additional keyword arguments are captured in the dictionary kwargs, which the function iterates over to display the information.

## 2. Return Values

Functions in Python often compute and return a value using the return statement. The value can be of any data type, and you can also return multiple values using tuples.

### 2.1 Returning a Single Value

**Example:**

```
def square(x):
    """Return the square of a number."""
    return x ** 2
result = square(5)
print("Square:", result)  # Output: Square: 25
```

**Explanation:**
The square function computes x ** 2 and returns the result, which is then stored in result.

### 2.2 Returning Multiple Values

When you return multiple values separated by commas, Python implicitly packs them into a tuple.

**Example:**

```
def min_max(numbers):
    """Return the minimum and maximum values from a list of numbers."""
    return min(numbers), max(numbers)
# Call the function and unpack the returned tuple
minimum, maximum = min_max([3, 1, 4, 1, 5, 9])
print("Minimum:", minimum)  # Output: Minimum: 1
print("Maximum:", maximum)  # Output: Maximum: 9
```

**Explanation:**
The function min_max returns two values: the minimum and

maximum of the list. These values are automatically packed into a tuple, which can then be unpacked into separate variables.

### 3. Best Practices for Function Arguments and Return Values

- **Write Clear and Descriptive Parameter Names:**
  Choose names that clearly describe the data expected by the function.
- **Include Docstrings:**
  Always add a docstring to describe the function's purpose, its parameters, and its return value. This helps in documentation and maintenance.
- **Avoid Side Effects:**
  Functions should ideally compute and return values without modifying global state unless explicitly intended.
- **Keep Functions Focused:**
  Each function should perform a single, well-defined task. If a function is doing too much, consider breaking it into smaller functions.
- **Use Default Parameters Wisely:**
  Default parameters can simplify function calls, but be cautious of mutable default arguments (e.g., lists or dictionaries).
- **Return Early:**
  Consider returning early from a function if certain conditions are met, to avoid deep nesting and improve clarity.

### In Summary

Understanding function arguments and return values is crucial for writing modular, reusable, and maintainable code in Python. Key points include:

- **Positional and Keyword Arguments:**

- o Positional arguments are assigned based on order.
- o Keyword arguments allow explicit assignment by parameter name.
- **Default Arguments:**
  Provide default values for parameters to simplify function calls.
- **Variable-Length Arguments:**
- o Use *args to accept any number of positional arguments.
- o Use **kwargs to accept any number of keyword arguments.
- **Return Values:**
- o Functions use the return statement to output results.
- o Multiple return values are automatically packed into a tuple.

By mastering these techniques, you can design functions that are both flexible and robust, enabling code reuse and simplifying complex programming tasks.

## Variable Scope: Local vs. Global

Understanding variable scope is crucial for writing modular and maintainable code in Python. Variable scope determines where a variable is accessible within a program. In Python, variables can either be **local** (defined within a function) or **global** (defined at the module level).

### 1. Local Scope

Local variables are those defined within a function. They are accessible only within the function in which they are declared. Once the function finishes execution, the local variables are typically discarded.

**Example: Local Variables**

```
def greet():
    # 'message' is a local variable
    message = "Hello, World!"
    print(message)
greet()  # Output: Hello, World!
# Trying to access 'message' outside the function will result in a NameError
try:
    print(message)
except NameError as e:
    print("Error:", e)  # Output: Error: name 'message' is not defined
```

**Explanation:**

- The variable message is defined inside the function greet(), so its scope is limited to that function.
- Attempting to access message outside greet() raises an error because it is not visible in the global scope.

**2. Global Scope**

Global variables are defined outside of any function and are accessible from any part of the module. They persist throughout the lifetime of the program and can be read by functions, though modifications require special handling.

**Example: Global Variables**

```
# Global variable
```

```
greeting = "Hello, World!"
def print_greeting():
    # Accessing the global variable 'greeting'
    print(greeting)
print_greeting()  # Output: Hello, World!
print(greeting)   # Output: Hello, World!
```

**Explanation:**

The variable greeting is defined at the top level and can be accessed both inside the function print_greeting() and outside of it.

**3. Modifying Global Variables Inside Functions**

If you need to modify a global variable inside a function, you must declare it as global within the function. Without this declaration, Python treats any assignment to a variable inside a function as creating a new local variable.

**Example: Using the global Keyword**

```
x = 10  # Global variable
def modify_global():
    global x  # Declare that we are referring to the global variable x
    x = 20
    print("Inside function, x =", x)
modify_global()  # Output: Inside function, x = 20
print("Outside function, x =", x)  # Output: Outside function, x = 20
```

**Explanation:**

- The global keyword tells Python to use the variable x defined in the global scope.
- The function modifies x to 20, and this change is reflected outside the function.

### 4. Local Variables Shadowing Global Variables

If a local variable has the same name as a global variable, the local variable **shadows** the global one within the function. Outside the function, the global variable remains unchanged.

**Example: Variable Shadowing**

```
x = 10  # Global variable

def shadow_variable():

    x = 5  # Local variable shadows the global x within this function

    print("Inside function, x =", x)

shadow_variable()  # Output: Inside function, x = 5

print("Outside function, x =", x)  # Output: Outside function, x = 10
```

**Explanation:**

- The assignment x = 5 inside shadow_variable() creates a local variable x that is independent of the global variable x.
- Outside the function, x remains 10.

### 5. The LEGB Rule

Python resolves variable names using the **LEGB** rule, which stands for:

- **L: Local** — Variables defined within the current function.

- **E: Enclosing** — Variables in the local scope of any enclosing functions (applicable for nested functions).
- **G: Global** — Variables defined at the top level of a module.
- **B: Built-in** — Names preassigned in Python's built-in namespace (e.g., len, str).

**Example: Nested Function and LEGB Rule**

```
x = "global"

def outer():

    x = "enclosing"

        def inner():

        x = "local"

        print("Inside inner:", x)  # Outputs "local" (Local scope takes precedence)

      inner()

    print("Inside outer:", x)  # Outputs "enclosing" (Local to outer, but enclosing for inner)

outer()

print("In global scope:", x)   # Outputs "global"
```

**Explanation:**

- In the inner() function, x is defined locally, so it takes precedence.
- The outer() function has its own x, which is used when inner() isn't accessing its own x.
- Outside all functions, the global x is used.

**6. Best Practices for Managing Variable Scope**

- **Minimize the Use of Global Variables:**
  Rely on function parameters and return values to pass data between functions. This promotes modularity and reduces side effects.

- **Explicitly Declare Globals When Necessary:**
  If a function must modify a global variable, clearly declare it with the global keyword to avoid accidental creation of local variables.

- **Prefer Local Variables:**
  Use local variables within functions whenever possible. This confines changes to a limited scope, making your code easier to debug and maintain.

- **Avoid Naming Conflicts:**
  Choose distinct names for variables in different scopes to avoid confusion and unintentional shadowing.

**In Summary**

- **Local Variables:**
  - Defined within a function.
  - Accessible only within that function.
- **Global Variables:**
  - Defined outside of any function.
  - Accessible from anywhere in the module.
- **Modifying Globals:**
  - Use the global keyword inside functions to modify global variables.
- **Shadowing and the LEGB Rule:**
  - Local variables can shadow global variables.

- Python follows the LEGB rule (Local, Enclosing, Global, Built-in) to resolve variable names.

By understanding and managing variable scope effectively, you create functions that are both reusable and less prone to bugs. Proper scope management leads to cleaner, more modular code, which is easier to test and maintain.

## Lambda Functions and Higher-Order Functions

Python's functional programming features enable concise and expressive code by treating functions as first-class objects. Two key concepts in this paradigm are **lambda functions** (anonymous functions) and **higher-order functions**. Lambda functions allow you to create small, one-off functions without formally defining them using def, while higher-order functions can accept functions as arguments or return functions as results. Together, they form powerful tools for writing modular, reusable code.

### 1. Lambda Functions

Lambda functions, or anonymous functions, are defined using the lambda keyword. They are best suited for simple operations that can be expressed in a single expression.

#### 1.1 Syntax

The general syntax of a lambda function is:

```
lambda arguments: expression
```

- **Arguments:** One or more parameters separated by commas.
- **Expression:** A single expression that is evaluated and returned.

#### 1.2 Examples

**Basic Lambda Function:**

```
# A lambda function to add two numbers
```

```
add = lambda a, b: a + b
print("Sum:", add(3, 5))  # Output: Sum: 8
```

Lambda Function for String Manipulation:

```
# A lambda function to convert a string to uppercase
to_upper = lambda s: s.upper()
print("Uppercase:", to_upper("hello"))  # Output: Uppercase:
HELLO
```

No-Parameter Lambda:

```
# A lambda function with no parameters
greet = lambda: "Hello, World!"
print(greet())  # Output: Hello, World!
```

### 1.3 When to Use Lambda Functions

- **Short, Simple Functions:** Lambda functions are ideal for operations that can be expressed in one line.
- **Inline Usage:** They are often used as arguments to higher-order functions (e.g., map(), filter(), sorted()).
- **Avoiding Verbosity:** For small, throwaway functions, lambda functions help keep the code concise and readable.

## 2. Higher-Order Functions

Higher-order functions are functions that can take other functions as arguments, return functions as results, or both. This feature allows you to create flexible and reusable components that can operate on behavior rather than just data.

### 2.1 Key Higher-Order Functions

- **map(function, iterable)**: Applies a function to each element of an iterable and returns an iterator with the results.
- **filter(function, iterable)**: Filters elements of an iterable for which the function returns True.
- **sorted(iterable, key=function)**: Sorts elements of an iterable based on a function applied to each element.
- **reduce(function, iterable)** (from the functools module): Applies a function cumulatively to the items of an iterable to reduce it to a single value.

### 2.2 Examples Using Lambda Functions with Higher-Order Functions

**Example: Using map() to Transform Data**

```
# Use map to square each number in a list

numbers = [1, 2, 3, 4, 5]

squares = list(map(lambda x: x ** 2, numbers))

print("Squares:", squares)  # Output: Squares: [1, 4, 9, 16, 25]
```

**Explanation:**

- The lambda function lambda x: x ** 2 is applied to each element of the list.
- The map() function returns an iterator, which is converted to a list.

**Example: Using filter() to Select Data**

```
# Use filter to select even numbers from a list

numbers = [1, 2, 3, 4, 5, 6, 7, 8, 9, 10]
```

```
even_numbers = list(filter(lambda x: x % 2 == 0, numbers))

print("Even Numbers:", even_numbers)  # Output: Even Numbers: [2, 4, 6, 8, 10]
```

**Explanation:**

- The lambda function lambda x: x % 2 == 0 returns True for even numbers.
- The filter() function returns an iterator of the elements that satisfy the condition.

**Example: Using sorted() with a Key Function**

```
# Use sorted with a lambda function to sort a list of tuples by the second element

students = [("Alice", 88), ("Bob", 95), ("Charlie", 70), ("David", 85)]

sorted_students = sorted(students, key=lambda student: student[1])

print("Students Sorted by Score:", sorted_students)
```

**Explanation:**

- The lambda function lambda student: student[1] extracts the score (second element) from each tuple.
- The sorted() function uses this key to sort the list of tuples in ascending order.

**Example: Using reduce() for Cumulative Computation**

```
from functools import reduce

# Use reduce to compute the product of a list of numbers

numbers = [1, 2, 3, 4, 5]

product = reduce(lambda a, b: a * b, numbers)
```

```
print("Product:", product)  # Output: Product: 120
```

**Explanation:**

- The lambda function lambda a, b: a * b multiplies two numbers.
- The reduce() function applies this multiplication cumulatively across the list, resulting in the product of all numbers.

**3. Best Practices and Considerations**

- **Keep Lambda Functions Simple:**
  Lambda functions should be used for small, simple operations. For complex logic, define a regular function with def.
- **Readability Matters:**
  While lambda functions can make code more concise, overusing them or creating overly complex lambdas can reduce readability. When in doubt, use a named function.
- **Use Higher-Order Functions Judiciously:**
  Higher-order functions like map(), filter(), and reduce() can make code concise and expressive. However, ensure that the use of these functions does not obscure the overall logic.
- **Explicit Over Implicit:**
  Although lambda functions and higher-order functions promote brevity, make sure your code remains clear to other developers (or your future self).

**In Summary**

- **Lambda Functions:**

  - Allow you to define anonymous functions in a single expression.
  - Are ideal for simple, throwaway operations.

- **Higher-Order Functions:**

- Accept functions as arguments or return them as results.
- Enable concise data transformations and computations using functions like map(), filter(), sorted(), and reduce().

By mastering lambda functions and higher-order functions, you can write more modular, reusable, and expressive code in Python. These techniques not only reduce boilerplate code but also empower you to process data in a functional programming style.

## Example Exercises

One of the most significant benefits of functions is their ability to encapsulate reusable logic. In many applications, you may need to perform common mathematical or utility operations, and writing these as functions helps you keep your code modular, organized, and easy to maintain.

### 1. Factorial Function

The factorial of a non-negative integer *n*, denoted by *n!*, is the product of all positive integers less than or equal to *n*. Factorials are widely used in mathematics, particularly in combinatorics and probability.

**Example: Implementing a Factorial Function**

```
def factorial(n):
    """
    Compute the factorial of a non-negative integer n.
    Parameters:
    n (int): A non-negative integer whose factorial is to be computed.
    Returns:
    int: The factorial of n.
```

```
    Raises:
    ValueError: If n is negative.
    """
    if n < 0:
        raise ValueError("Factorial is not defined for negative numbers.")
    # Base case: factorial of 0 is 1
    if n == 0:
        return 1
    result = 1
    for i in range(1, n + 1):
        result *= i
    return result
# Testing the factorial function
print("Factorial of 5:", factorial(5))  # Expected output: 120
print("Factorial of 0:", factorial(0))  # Expected output: 1
```

**Explanation:**

- The function factorial(n) first checks if the input is negative and raises a ValueError if so.
- For *n* equal to 0, it returns 1 (by definition).
- For positive *n*, it iterates from 1 to *n*, multiplying the results cumulatively.
- This function demonstrates using a loop, handling edge cases, and raising exceptions for invalid input.

## 2. Fibonacci Sequence Generator

The Fibonacci sequence is a series where each number is the sum of the two preceding ones, starting from 0 and 1. Generating Fibonacci numbers is a classic exercise to demonstrate iterative or recursive function design.

**Example: Implementing an Iterative Fibonacci Function**

```
def fibonacci(n):
    """
    Generate the first n Fibonacci numbers.
    Parameters:
    n (int): The number of Fibonacci numbers to generate.
    Returns:
    list: A list containing the first n Fibonacci numbers.
    """
    if n <= 0:
        return []  # Return an empty list for non-positive input
    elif n == 1:
        return [0]
    # Start with the first two Fibonacci numbers
    fib_sequence = [0, 1]
    while len(fib_sequence) < n:
        # Next number is the sum of the last two numbers in the
sequence
        next_number = fib_sequence[-1] + fib_sequence[-2]
```

```
        fib_sequence.append(next_number)
    return fib_sequence
# Testing the Fibonacci function
print("First 10 Fibonacci numbers:", fibonacci(10))
```

**Explanation:**

- The function fibonacci(n) returns an empty list if *n* is non-positive and returns [0] if *n* is 1.
- It initializes the sequence with the first two Fibonacci numbers.
- A while loop continues generating new numbers until the sequence contains *n* numbers.
- The result is a list of the first *n* Fibonacci numbers.

**3. Prime Number Checker**

Determining whether a number is prime (i.e., only divisible by 1 and itself) is a common utility function in mathematics and computer science.

**Example: Implementing a Prime Checker Function**

```
def is_prime(n):
    """
    Determine whether an integer n is a prime number.
    Parameters:
    n (int): The number to check for primality.
    Returns:
    bool: True if n is prime, False otherwise.
    """
```

```
    if n <= 1:
        return False  # 0 and 1 are not prime numbers
    if n <= 3:
        return True  # 2 and 3 are prime numbers
    # If n is divisible by 2 or 3, it is not prime
    if n % 2 == 0 or n % 3 == 0:
        return False
    # Check for factors up to the square root of n
    i = 5
    while i * i <= n:
        if n % i == 0 or n % (i + 2) == 0:
            return False
        i += 6  # Check next potential factors (skipping multiples of 2 and 3)
    return True
# Testing the prime checker function
print("Is 29 prime?", is_prime(29))  # Expected output: True
print("Is 30 prime?", is_prime(30))  # Expected output: False
```

**Explanation:**

- The function first handles small numbers and simple cases.
- It then checks divisibility by 2 and 3.
- For larger numbers, it tests potential factors up to the square root of *n*, incrementing by 6 to skip unnecessary checks.

- This efficient approach minimizes the number of iterations.

### 4. Greatest Common Divisor (GCD) Function

The greatest common divisor of two numbers is the largest integer that divides both numbers without leaving a remainder. Euclid's algorithm is a classic method for computing the GCD.

**Example: Implementing GCD using Euclid's Algorithm**

```
def gcd(a, b):
    """
    Compute the greatest common divisor (GCD) of two integers a and b using Euclid's algorithm.
    Parameters:
    a (int): The first integer.
    b (int): The second integer.
    Returns:
    int: The GCD of a and b.
    """
    while b:
        a, b = b, a % b  # Replace a with b and b with the remainder
    return a
# Testing the GCD function
print("GCD of 48 and 18:", gcd(48, 18))  # Expected output: 6
print("GCD of 100 and 85:", gcd(100, 85))  # Expected output: 5
```

**Explanation:**

- The function repeatedly replaces the pair (a, b) with (b, a % b) until b becomes zero.
- When b is zero, a holds the GCD.
- This efficient algorithm quickly computes the GCD even for large numbers.

**5. Best Practices for Implementing Utility Functions**

- **Single Responsibility:**
  Each function should have a clear, single purpose. For example, a factorial function should only compute factorials.
- **Docstrings and Comments:**
  Include a clear docstring that explains what the function does, its parameters, return values, and any exceptions it might raise.
- **Input Validation:**
  Validate input values and handle exceptional cases (e.g., negative numbers for factorials).
- **Reusability:**
  Design functions to be reusable in various contexts. Utility functions, by nature, should be generic and adaptable.
- **Testing:**
  Write test cases for your functions to ensure they work as expected across a range of inputs.

**In Summary**

Utility functions are essential for building reusable, modular code in Python. In this section, we implemented several math/utility functions, including:

- **Factorial Function:**
  Computes the factorial of a non-negative integer.

- **Fibonacci Generator:**
  Generates the first *n* Fibonacci numbers iteratively.

- **Prime Checker:**
  Determines whether a number is prime using an efficient algorithm.

- **GCD Function:**
  Uses Euclid's algorithm to compute the greatest common divisor of two numbers.

By encapsulating these common operations into functions, you can simplify your code, reduce repetition, and make your programs easier to maintain and extend.

# Chapter 12: Modules and Packages

## Creating and Importing Modules

Modules are an essential part of Python's ecosystem that allow you to organize your code into separate, reusable files. A module is simply a Python file (with a .py extension) that contains definitions of functions, classes, and variables. By creating and importing modules, you can break up large programs into manageable pieces, promote code reuse, and improve maintainability.

### 1. Creating a Module

Creating a module is straightforward: you write your Python code in a file with a .py extension. This file can contain functions, classes, and variables that you want to reuse in other parts of your application.

### Example: Creating a Simple Module

Let's create a module named math_utils.py that contains several utility functions for mathematical operations.

**Content of math_utils.py:**

```
# math_utils.py

"""

A simple module for basic mathematical operations.

"""

def add(a, b):

    """Return the sum of a and b."""

    return a + b

def subtract(a, b):

    """Return the difference of a and b."""
```

```
    return a - b
def multiply(a, b):
    """Return the product of a and b."""
    return a * b
def divide(a, b):
    """
    Return the division of a by b.
    Raises:
        ValueError: If b is zero.
    """
    if b == 0:
        raise ValueError("Cannot divide by zero.")
    return a / b
# A simple test block (optional)
if __name__ == "__main__":
    print("Testing math_utils module:")
    print("3 + 4 =", add(3, 4))
    print("10 - 2 =", subtract(10, 2))
    print("6 * 7 =", multiply(6, 7))
    print("8 / 2 =", divide(8, 2))
```

**Explanation:**

- The module math_utils.py defines four functions: add(), subtract(), multiply(), and divide().

- A docstring at the top describes the purpose of the module.
- The if __name__ == "__main__": block provides a simple test when the module is run directly, but it does not execute when the module is imported elsewhere.

## 2. Importing Modules

Once you have created a module, you can import it into other Python scripts to reuse its functions.

### 2.1 Basic Import

Use the import statement to load the entire module. When you do this, you need to use the module name as a prefix to access its functions.

**Example: Using import**

```
# main.py

import math_utils

result_add = math_utils.add(5, 3)

result_divide = math_utils.divide(10, 2)

print("5 + 3 =", result_add)          # Output: 5 + 3 = 8

print("10 / 2 =", result_divide)         # Output: 10 / 2 = 5.0
```

**Explanation:**

- The entire module is imported using import math_utils.
- Functions are accessed using the dot notation (e.g., math_utils.add()).

### 2.2 Importing Specific Functions

You can import individual functions (or classes/variables) from a module using the from ... import ... syntax. This method allows you to use the imported names directly without the module prefix.

**Example: Using from ... import ...**

```
# main.py

from math_utils import add, subtract

print("7 + 2 =", add(7, 2))         # Output: 7 + 2 = 9

print("10 - 3 =", subtract(10, 3))   # Output: 10 - 3 = 7
```

**Explanation:**

- Only the add and subtract functions are imported from math_utils.
- These functions can be called directly without the math_utils. prefix.

**2.3 Using Aliases**

Sometimes, you may want to shorten the module name or avoid name conflicts by using an alias. This is done using the as keyword.

**Example: Importing with an Alias**

```
# main.py

import math_utils as mu

print("8 * 3 =", mu.multiply(8, 3))   # Output: 8 * 3 = 24
```

**Explanation:**

- The module math_utils is imported with the alias mu.
- All functions are accessed using the alias (e.g., mu.multiply()).

### 3. Module Search Path

When you import a module, Python searches for the module in a series of directories defined in the module search path (stored in sys.path). By default, this includes:

- The directory containing the input script (or the current directory).
- The list of directories specified by the environment variable PYTHONPATH.
- The installation-dependent default directories.

**Example: Displaying the Module Search Path**

```
import sys

print("Module Search Path:")

for path in sys.path:

    print(path)
```

**Explanation:**

- The code prints all directories where Python looks for modules.
- Understanding sys.path can help diagnose import issues.

### 4. Best Practices for Creating and Importing Modules

- **Organize Code Logically:**
  Group related functions, classes, and variables into separate modules. For example, you might have modules for math utilities, string operations, or file handling.
- **Use Meaningful Names:**
  Choose module names that clearly indicate their purpose.

- **Document Your Modules:**
  Include docstrings at the beginning of each module to explain what it does and how to use it.
- **Avoid Circular Imports:**
  Structure your modules to prevent circular dependencies, where two modules depend on each other.
- **Test Modules Separately:**
  Use the if __name__ == "__main__": block to include tests that run only when the module is executed directly, not when imported.

## In Summary

Creating and importing modules is a fundamental practice in Python that enhances code reuse and maintainability. Key points include:

- **Creating a Module:**
  - Write your code in a .py file.
  - Define functions, classes, and variables that encapsulate specific functionality.
  - Include a module-level docstring for documentation.
- **Importing Modules:**
  - Use import module_name to import the entire module.
  - Use from module_name import item to import specific items.
  - Use the as keyword to create aliases for modules.
- **Module Search Path:**
  - Python searches for modules in directories listed in sys.path.

By effectively creating and importing modules, you can write modular, maintainable code that is easier to understand and reuse.

## Working with Built-in Modules

Python's standard library comes with a rich collection of built-in modules that extend the core language capabilities. These modules provide ready-made functions and classes for common tasks such as mathematical computations, generating random numbers, manipulating dates and times, and more. In this section, we will explore several key built-in modules - **math**, **random**, and **datetime** - and demonstrate how to import and use them in your Python programs.

### 1. The math Module

The math module provides access to a wide range of mathematical functions and constants. It is particularly useful for complex mathematical operations that go beyond basic arithmetic.

#### 1.1 Importing the math Module

```
import math
```

#### 1.2 Key Functions and Constants

- **Mathematical Functions:**
    - math.sqrt(x): Returns the square root of x.
    - math.sin(x), math.cos(x), math.tan(x): Trigonometric functions.
    - math.log(x[, base]): Returns the logarithm of x to the given base (default is e).
    - math.factorial(x): Returns the factorial of x.
- **Mathematical Constants:**
    - math.pi: The value of π (pi).
    - math.e: The base of natural logarithms.

#### 1.3 Example: Using the math Module

```
import math
# Square root and factorial
number = 16
sqrt_number = math.sqrt(number)
fact_number = math.factorial(5)
# Using trigonometric functions and constants
angle = math.pi / 4  # 45 degrees in radians
sin_angle = math.sin(angle)
cos_angle = math.cos(angle)
print("Square root of", number, "is", sqrt_number)
print("Factorial of 5 is", fact_number)
print("Sine of 45 degrees is", sin_angle)
print("Cosine of 45 degrees is", cos_angle)
```

**Explanation:**

- The script imports the math module.
- It calculates the square root of 16 and the factorial of 5.
- It computes the sine and cosine of 45 degrees (π/4 radians) using the module's trigonometric functions.
- The constants math.pi and functions like math.sqrt() and math.sin() simplify complex mathematical calculations.

**2. The random Module**

The random module offers functions for generating random numbers and performing random operations on sequences. This module is useful in simulations, games, testing, and any application that requires random behavior.

### 2.1 Importing the random Module

```
import random
```

### 2.2 Key Functions

- **Random Number Generation:**
  - random.random(): Returns a random float in the range [0.0, 1.0).
  - random.randint(a, b): Returns a random integer between a and b (inclusive).
- **Random Choices:**
  - random.choice(seq): Returns a random element from a non-empty sequence.
  - random.shuffle(seq): Shuffles the sequence in place.
  - random.sample(population, k): Returns a list of k unique random elements from the population.

### 2.3 Example: Using the random Module

```
import random

# Generate a random float between 0 and 1

rand_float = random.random()

# Generate a random integer between 10 and 20

rand_int = random.randint(10, 20)

# Choose a random element from a list

colors = ["red", "green", "blue", "yellow"]

rand_color = random.choice(colors)
```

```
# Shuffle a list
numbers = [1, 2, 3, 4, 5]
random.shuffle(numbers)
# Get a sample of 3 unique elements from a list
sample_numbers = random.sample(numbers, 3)
print("Random float:", rand_float)
print("Random integer between 10 and 20:", rand_int)
print("Random color:", rand_color)
print("Shuffled numbers:", numbers)
print("Sample of 3 numbers:", sample_numbers)
```

**Explanation:**

- The module is imported and various random functions are demonstrated.
- random.random() produces a random float.
- random.randint() generates an integer within a specified range.
- random.choice() selects an element from a list.
- random.shuffle() randomly rearranges the list in place.
- random.sample() extracts a specified number of unique elements from the list.

### 3. The datetime Module

The datetime module supplies classes for manipulating dates and times. It is widely used for tasks involving scheduling, time tracking, or formatting date and time information.

#### 3.1 Importing the datetime Module

```
import datetime
```

### 3.2 Key Classes and Functions

- **datetime.date:**
  Represents a date (year, month, day).
- **datetime.time:**
  Represents a time (hour, minute, second, microsecond).
- **datetime.datetime:**
  Combines date and time.
- **datetime.timedelta:**
  Represents the difference between two dates or times.

### 3.3 Example: Working with Dates and Times

```
import datetime

# Current date and time

now = datetime.datetime.now()

print("Current Date and Time:", now)

# Create a specific date

birthday = datetime.date(1990, 5, 21)

print("Birthday:", birthday)

# Create a specific time

meeting_time = datetime.time(14, 30, 0)

print("Meeting Time:", meeting_time)

# Calculate the difference between two dates

today = datetime.date.today()

delta = today - birthday
```

```
print("Days since birthday:", delta.days)
# Using timedelta to add days to the current date
future_date = today + datetime.timedelta(days=30)
print("Date after 30 days:", future_date)
```

**Explanation:**

- The code demonstrates how to obtain the current date and time using datetime.datetime.now().
- It creates specific date and time objects.
- It computes the difference between two dates using subtraction, resulting in a timedelta object.
- The timedelta is used to calculate a future date by adding 30 days.

**4. Best Practices for Using Built-in Modules**

- **Read Documentation:**
  Familiarize yourself with the official Python documentation for each module to understand all available functions and classes.
- **Use Aliases When Appropriate:**
  For commonly used modules, consider using aliases (e.g., import numpy as np, although not a built-in module) to shorten code and improve readability.
- **Handle Exceptions:**
  When working with modules such as datetime or math, ensure you handle potential exceptions (e.g., division by zero in math or invalid date inputs in datetime).
- **Modular Code Organization:**
  Use modules to organize related functionality. This makes your code easier to maintain and test.

**In Summary**

Python's built-in modules like **math**, **random**, and **datetime** offer a wide array of functionalities that simplify many common programming tasks:

- **math Module:**
  Provides mathematical functions and constants for complex calculations.
- **random Module:**
  Enables random number generation, shuffling, and selection from collections.
- **datetime Module:**
  Facilitates working with dates and times, including formatting, manipulation, and arithmetic.

By effectively using these built-in modules, you can write more efficient, readable, and powerful code, leveraging Python's extensive standard library.

## Structuring Large Projects into Packages

As your Python projects grow in complexity, it becomes essential to organize your code in a logical and maintainable way. Packages provide a mechanism for structuring large projects by grouping related modules together. This not only improves code readability and reusability but also makes it easier to manage, distribute, and collaborate on your projects.

### 1. What Is a Package?

A **package** in Python is a directory that contains a collection of related modules and sub-packages. The presence of an __init__.py file in a directory indicates to Python that the directory should be treated as a package. This file can be empty or contain initialization code for the package.

**Key Points:**

- **Modularity:** Packages allow you to separate different parts of your project into logical groups.
- **Namespace Management:** Packages help prevent naming conflicts by encapsulating modules in their own namespace.
- **Reusability:** Code organized into packages can be easily reused across different projects.

## 2. Creating a Package Structure

Let's consider a sample project for a simple application that performs mathematical operations and string utilities. Below is an example of how you might structure such a project:

```
my_project/
│
├── README.md
├── setup.py
└── my_package/
    ├── __init__.py
    ├── math_utils.py
    ├── string_utils.py
    └── subpackage/
        ├── __init__.py
        └── advanced_math.py
```

**Explanation:**

- **my_project/**: The root directory of your project.

- **README.md**: A file containing documentation or information about your project.
- **setup.py**: A script for packaging and distribution.
- **my_package/**: The main package containing modules related to your project.
  - **__init__.py**: This file indicates that my_package is a package. It can be used to initialize package-level variables or import submodules.
  - **math_utils.py**: A module with basic mathematical utility functions.
  - **string_utils.py**: A module with string manipulation utility functions.
- **my_package/subpackage/**: A sub-package for more specialized functionality.
  - **__init__.py**: Indicates that subpackage is a package.
  - **advanced_math.py**: A module containing advanced mathematical operations.

**3. Creating and Using Modules in a Package**

**3.1 Example Module: math_utils.py**

```
# my_package/math_utils.py
def add(a, b):
    """Return the sum of a and b."""
    return a + b
def subtract(a, b):
    """Return the difference of a and b."""
```

```
    return a – b
```

3.2 Example Module: string_utils.py

```
# my_package/string_utils.py
def capitalize_words(text):
    """Capitalize the first letter of each word in the text."""
    return text.title()
def reverse_string(text):
    """Return the reversed version of the input string."""
    return text[::-1]
```

3.3 Example Module in Sub-Package: advanced_math.py

```
# my_package/subpackage/advanced_math.py
def factorial(n):
    """Return the factorial of n (n!)."""
    if n < 0:
        raise ValueError("Factorial is not defined for negative
numbers.")
    result = 1
    for i in range(1, n + 1):
        result *= i
    return result
```

**3.4 Initializing a Package with __init__.py**

The __init__.py file can be used to expose certain functions or classes at the package level. For instance, you might want to import key functions from your modules so that they can be accessed directly from the package.

```
# my_package/__init__.py

from .math_utils import add, subtract

from .string_utils import capitalize_words, reverse_string

# Optionally, you can also import sub-packages

from .subpackage import advanced_math
```

**Explanation:**

- The dot (.) in from .math_utils indicates a relative import from the current package.
- This setup allows users of your package to access add(), subtract(), etc., directly from my_package without needing to reference the specific module.

**4. Importing and Using Your Package in Other Scripts**

Once your package is structured, you can import it in your scripts. Suppose you have a script main.py in the root directory my_project/ that uses your package.

**Example: main.py**

```
# main.py

import my_package

# Using functions imported in the package's __init__.py

sum_result = my_package.add(10, 5)

print("Sum:", sum_result)

capitalized_text = my_package.capitalize_words("hello world")
```

```
print("Capitalized:", capitalized_text)

# Accessing a function from the sub-package

fact = my_package.advanced_math.factorial(6)

print("Factorial of 6:", fact)
```

**Explanation:**

- The script imports the entire package using import my_package.
- Functions such as add and capitalize_words are accessed directly via the package.
- Functions in the sub-package, like factorial, are accessed through the package's submodule.

**5. Best Practices for Structuring Large Projects**

- **Logical Organization:**
  Group related modules into packages and sub-packages. This improves readability and maintainability.
- **Modularization:**
  Ensure that each module has a clear purpose. Keep functions and classes focused on a single task.
- **Documentation:**
  Include docstrings and comments in your modules and packages. A well-documented project is easier to understand and collaborate on.
- **Consistent Naming Conventions:**
  Follow Python's naming conventions (PEP 8) for module and package names to ensure consistency across your project.
- **Testing:**
  Write tests for each module and package. Organize tests in a

separate directory (e.g., tests/) to ensure that your code works as expected.

- **Version Control:**
  Use version control systems (like Git) to manage your project and track changes.

**In Summary**

Structuring large projects into packages is a key aspect of writing scalable and maintainable Python code. By organizing your code into logical groups (modules and packages), you can:

- Promote reusability and modularity.
- Simplify code management and collaboration.
- Enhance readability and maintainability through clear organization and documentation.

Key points:

- **Create Modules:** Write Python code in .py files to define functions, classes, and variables.
- **Organize into Packages:** Use directories with an __init__.py file to group related modules.
- **Importing:** Use absolute or relative imports to access functionality from your packages.
- **Best Practices:** Follow logical organization, naming conventions, documentation, and testing strategies.

With this structured approach, your large projects will be easier to navigate, maintain, and extend, ultimately leading to more robust and scalable applications.

## Example Exercises

Creating reusable modules is a cornerstone of Python programming. It allows you to encapsulate frequently used functions, classes, and variables in separate files so that they can be imported and used across multiple projects. This approach promotes modularity, improves code organization, and makes maintenance easier.

### 1. Creating a Simple Utility Module

In this exercise, we'll create a module named utilities.py that contains several math utility functions. This module can be reused in different projects whenever you need to perform basic mathematical operations.

### Step 1: Create the Module File

Create a file named utilities.py and add the following code:

```
# utilities.py

"""

A reusable module for basic mathematical operations.

This module provides functions for addition, subtraction,
multiplication,

and division, along with error handling for division by zero.

"""

def add(a, b):

    """

    Return the sum of a and b.

    Parameters:

    a (int or float): The first number.
```

```
    b (int or float): The second number.
    Returns:
    int or float: The sum of a and b.
    """
    return a + b
def subtract(a, b):
    """
    Return the difference of a and b.
    Parameters:
    a (int or float): The first number.
    b (int or float): The second number.
    Returns:
    int or float: The difference of a and b.
    """
    return a - b
def multiply(a, b):
    """
    Return the product of a and b.
    Parameters:
    a (int or float): The first number.
    b (int or float): The second number.
    Returns:
```

```
    int or float: The product of a and b.
    """
    return a * b
def divide(a, b):
    """
    Return the division of a by b.
    Parameters:
    a (int or float): The numerator.
    b (int or float): The denominator.
    Returns:
    float: The result of the division.
    Raises:
    ValueError: If b is zero.
    """
    if b == 0:
        raise ValueError("Cannot divide by zero.")
    return a / b
# Optional test block to run when this module is executed directly
if __name__ == "__main__":
    print("Testing utilities module:")
    print("5 + 3 =", add(5, 3))
    print("10 - 4 =", subtract(10, 4))
```

```
print("6 * 7 =", multiply(6, 7))

print("8 / 2 =", divide(8, 2))
```

**Explanation:**

- The module starts with a module-level docstring that describes its purpose.
- Four functions (add, subtract, multiply, and divide) are defined, each with its own docstring explaining parameters, return values, and behavior.
- The divide function includes error handling to prevent division by zero.
- The if __name__ == "__main__": block allows you to run basic tests when the module is executed directly but prevents the test code from running when the module is imported.

**2. Creating a String Operations Module**

Next, we'll create another module named string_ops.py that offers utility functions for common string operations, such as reversing a string and capitalizing words.

**Step 1: Create the Module File**

Create a file named string_ops.py with the following code:

```
# string_ops.py

"""

A reusable module for string operations.

Provides functions for reversing a string and capitalizing each word in a string.

"""
```

```
def reverse_string(s):
    """
    Return the reversed version of the input string s.
    Parameters:
    s (str): The string to be reversed.
    Returns:
    str: The reversed string.
    """
    return s[::-1]
def capitalize_words(s):
    """
    Return the string with the first letter of each word capitalized.

    Parameters:
    s (str): The input string.
    Returns:
    str: The string with each word capitalized.
    """
    return s.title()
# Optional test block to run when this module is executed directly
if __name__ == "__main__":
    test_str = "hello world, this is python"
```

```
    print("Original String:", test_str)
    print("Reversed String:", reverse_string(test_str))
    print("Capitalized String:", capitalize_words(test_str))
```

**Explanation:**

- Similar to the previous module, string_ops.py begins with a module-level docstring.
- Two functions are defined:
  - reverse_string(s): Returns the string in reverse order.
  - capitalize_words(s): Uses the built-in title() method to capitalize the first letter of each word.
- The test block at the end allows for simple verification when running the module independently.

3. Importing and Using Your Reusable Modules

Now that you have created your modules, you can import and use them in your main application script. Create a file named main.py in the same project directory.

Example: Using Modules in main.py

```
# main.py
# Importing specific functions from the utilities module
from utilities import add, divide
# Importing the entire string_ops module
import string_ops
def main():
    # Using math utility functions
```

```
    sum_result = add(10, 5)
    division_result = divide(20, 4)
    print("Sum of 10 and 5:", sum_result)
    print("Division of 20 by 4:", division_result)
    # Using string operations functions
    original_text = "python programming is fun"
    reversed_text = string_ops.reverse_string(original_text)
    capitalized_text = string_ops.capitalize_words(original_text)
    print("Original Text:", original_text)
    print("Reversed Text:", reversed_text)
    print("Capitalized Text:", capitalized_text)
if __name__ == "__main__":
    main()
```

**Explanation:**

- The script uses from utilities import add, divide to import specific functions from utilities.py, which simplifies function calls.
- The entire string_ops module is imported, and its functions are accessed with the module name as a prefix.
- The main() function demonstrates how to use both math and string utility functions to perform tasks and print the results.
- The check if __name__ == "__main__": ensures that the main() function runs only when main.py is executed directly.

## 4. Best Practices for Creating Reusable Modules

- **Modularity:**
  Organize your code by grouping related functions and classes into separate modules. This improves clarity and makes maintenance easier.

- **Documentation:**
  Include meaningful docstrings at both the module and function levels. This helps users understand the purpose and usage of each component.

- **Testing:**
  Use the if __name__ == "__main__": block to include simple tests in your modules. This practice helps verify functionality during development without interfering with the module's reusability.

- **Error Handling:**
  Implement proper error handling within your functions to manage edge cases and invalid inputs gracefully.

- **Consistent Naming:**
  Use clear and consistent naming conventions for modules, functions, and variables to enhance readability and maintainability.

### In Summary

By creating reusable modules, you enhance the modularity and maintainability of your code. In this exercise, we created two modules:

- **utilities.py:**
  Contains math functions (add, subtract, multiply, and divide) with proper documentation and error handling.

- **string_ops.py:**
  Provides string manipulation functions (reverse_string and capitalize_words) to process and transform text.

We then demonstrated how to import these modules into a main application script (main.py) and use their functions to perform various tasks. Following best practices such as modular design, documentation, and testing, you can build robust, scalable projects that are easy to maintain and extend.

# Section VI: Object-Oriented Programming (OOP)
# Chapter 13: Classes and Objects

## Defining Classes and Objects

Object-oriented programming (OOP) is a programming paradigm that organizes code into "objects," which are instances of "classes." Classes serve as blueprints for objects, encapsulating data (attributes) and behaviors (methods) into reusable components. By defining classes, you can model real-world entities, organize your code better, and promote reusability and maintainability.

### 1. Defining a Class

A class in Python is defined using the class keyword followed by the class name and a colon. The class body contains method definitions and class-level variables.

**Example: Basic Class Definition**

```
class Person:
    """
    A class representing a person with a name and an age.
    """
    # The __init__ method initializes new objects (instances) of the class.
    def __init__(self, name, age):
        """
        Initialize a new Person instance.
        Parameters:
        name (str): The name of the person.
```

```
        age (int): The age of the person.
        """
        self.name = name  # Instance variable for the person's name
        self.age = age    # Instance variable for the person's age
    # A method to print a greeting from the person.
    def greet(self):
        """
        Print a greeting message that includes the person's name and
age.
        """
        print(f"Hello, my name is {self.name} and I am {self.age} years
old.")
```

**Explanation:**

- **Class Declaration:**
  The class Person: statement defines a new class named Person.
- **The __init__ Method:**
  The __init__ method is a special constructor method that initializes a new instance of the class.
  - self refers to the instance itself.
  - The parameters name and age are used to initialize instance variables (self.name and self.age).
- **Instance Method:**
  The greet method is an instance method that uses the object's attributes (self.name and self.age) to print a greeting.

## 2. Creating Objects (Instances)

Once a class is defined, you can create objects (instances) of that class by calling the class as if it were a function. This process is known as instantiation.

### Example: Creating and Using Objects

```
# Creating instances of the Person class

person1 = Person("Alice", 30)

person2 = Person("Bob", 25)

# Calling methods on the objects

person1.greet()  # Output: Hello, my name is Alice and I am 30 years old.

person2.greet()  # Output: Hello, my name is Bob and I am 25 years old.
```

### Explanation:

- **Instantiation:**
  The expressions Person("Alice", 30) and Person("Bob", 25) create two separate objects of the Person class.
- **Accessing Methods:**
  Each object can call its own greet() method, which prints a personalized greeting using the instance's attributes.

## 3. Instance Variables vs. Class Variables

In Python, variables defined inside the __init__ method are **instance variables**; they are unique to each instance of the class. You can also define **class variables** directly inside the class (but outside any methods) which are shared across all instances.

**Example: Class Variables**

```
class Person:
    # Class variable shared by all instances
    species = "Homo sapiens"
    def __init__(self, name, age):
        self.name = name
        self.age = age
    def greet(self):
        print(f"Hello, my name is {self.name}, I am {self.age} years old, and I am a {Person.species}.")
# Creating instances
person1 = Person("Alice", 30)
person2 = Person("Bob", 25)
person1.greet() # Output: Hello, my name is Alice, I am 30 years old, and I am a Homo sapiens.
person2.greet() # Output: Hello, my name is Bob, I am 25 years old, and I am a Homo sapiens.
```

**Explanation:**

**Class Variable (species):**
Defined at the class level, species is shared by all instances. It can be accessed using either the class name (e.g., Person.species) or through an instance (e.g., self.species).

## 4. Best Practices for Defining and Using Classes

- **Use Descriptive Names:**
  Choose clear and descriptive names for classes and methods. Class names should follow the CamelCase convention.

- **Include Docstrings:**
  Add docstrings to classes and methods to explain their purpose, parameters, and return values. This improves code readability and maintainability.

- **Encapsulation:**
  Use instance variables to store data that is specific to each object, and use methods to operate on that data.

- **Keep It Simple:**
  Design each class to have a single responsibility. If a class grows too complex, consider breaking it down into smaller, more focused classes.

- **Avoid Global Variables:**
  Prefer passing variables as arguments or using instance variables to avoid the pitfalls of global state.

### In Summary

Defining classes and creating objects are fundamental to object-oriented programming in Python. Key takeaways include:

- **Class Definition:**
  - Use the class keyword to define a new class.
  - The __init__ method initializes instance variables.
- **Creating Objects:**
  - Instantiate objects by calling the class.
  - Access object methods using dot notation.

- **Instance vs. Class Variables:**
  - Instance variables are unique to each object.
  - Class variables are shared across all instances.
- **Best Practices:**
  - Use descriptive names and include docstrings.
  - Encapsulate functionality within classes.
  - Keep classes focused and avoid unnecessary complexity.

By mastering these concepts, you build a solid foundation for object-oriented programming, enabling you to create modular, reusable, and maintainable code.

## Instance Variables, Class Variables, and Methods

Object-Oriented Programming (OOP) in Python enables you to model real-world entities by encapsulating data and behaviors into classes. In this paradigm, **instance variables**, **class variables**, and **methods** are key concepts that help organize and structure your code effectively. This section provides an in-depth look at these concepts with explanations and code examples.

### 1. Instance Variables

**Instance variables** are attributes that belong to an individual object (instance) of a class. They are defined within methods (typically in the __init__ method) and are accessed using the self keyword. Each instance has its own copy of these variables, which can hold unique values.

#### Example: Defining and Using Instance Variables

```
class Car:

    def __init__(self, make, model, year):
```

```
        # Instance variables: unique to each Car object
        self.make = make
        self.model = model
        self.year = year
    def display_info(self):
        """Display information about the car."""
        print(f"Car: {self.year} {self.make} {self.model}")
# Creating two instances of Car
car1 = Car("Toyota", "Corolla", 2020)
car2 = Car("Honda", "Civic", 2021)
# Each object has its own instance variables
car1.display_info()  # Output: Car: 2020 Toyota Corolla
car2.display_info()  # Output: Car: 2021 Honda Civic
```

**Explanation:**

- The __init__ method initializes each new instance with its own make, model, and year values.
- The display_info method accesses these instance variables via self and prints the car details.
- Different instances (car1 and car2) maintain their own independent states.

**2. Class Variables**

**Class variables** are attributes that are shared among all instances of a class. They are defined within the class body but outside of any instance methods. These variables are used to store data that should be consistent across all objects, such as constants or default values.

**Example: Defining and Using Class Variables**

```
class Car:
    # Class variable: shared by all instances of Car
    wheels = 4
    def __init__(self, make, model, year):
        # Instance variables
        self.make = make
        self.model = model
        self.year = year
    def display_info(self):
        """Display information about the car along with the number of wheels."""
        print(f"Car: {self.year} {self.make} {self.model}, Wheels: {Car.wheels}")
# Creating instances of Car
car1 = Car("Toyota", "Corolla", 2020)
car2 = Car("Honda", "Civic", 2021)
# Accessing class variable via instances or directly through the class name
car1.display_info()  # Output: Car: 2020 Toyota Corolla, Wheels: 4
car2.display_info()  # Output: Car: 2021 Honda Civic, Wheels: 4
# Changing the class variable (affects all instances)
```

```
Car.wheels = 6
print("\nAfter modifying class variable:")
car1.display_info()  # Output: Car: 2020 Toyota Corolla, Wheels: 6
car2.display_info()  # Output: Car: 2021 Honda Civic, Wheels: 6
```

**Explanation:**

- wheels is defined as a class variable, meaning all Car objects share the same number of wheels.
- When you update Car.wheels, the change is reflected in all instances because they reference the same variable.
- Class variables are accessed either via the class name (Car.wheels) or through an instance (e.g., self.wheels), though using the class name is often clearer for shared values.

### 3. Methods

**Methods** are functions defined within a class that describe the behaviors of the objects. They can access both instance variables (using self) and class variables (using the class name or self). Methods allow objects to perform actions and manipulate their internal state.

**Types of Methods:**

**Instance Methods:**
Regular methods that operate on an instance of the class. They automatically receive the instance (self) as the first parameter.

**Example:**

```
class Car:
    wheels = 4  # Class variable
    def __init__(self, make, model, year):
```

```
        self.make = make  # Instance variable

        self.model = model  # Instance variable

        self.year = year  # Instance variable

    def display_info(self):

        """Display information about the car."""

        print(f"Car: {self.year} {self.make} {self.model}, Wheels:
{Car.wheels}")

    def update_year(self, new_year):

        """Update the car's year."""

        self.year = new_year

        print(f"Updated year: {self.year}")

# Create an instance and use its methods

car = Car("Ford", "Mustang", 1969)

car.display_info()        # Output: Car: 1969 Ford Mustang, Wheels: 4

car.update_year(1970)     # Output: Updated year: 1970

car.display_info()        # Output: Car: 1970 Ford Mustang, Wheels: 4
```

**Class Methods:**
Methods that operate on the class itself rather than an instance. They are defined using the @classmethod decorator and take the class (cls) as the first parameter.

**Example:**

```
class Car:

    wheels = 4

    def __init__(self, make, model, year):
```

```
        self.make = make
        self.model = model
        self.year = year
    @classmethod
    def set_wheels(cls, number):
        """Set the number of wheels for all cars."""
        cls.wheels = number
# Before modifying class variable
car1 = Car("Toyota", "Corolla", 2020)
print("Initial wheels:", car1.wheels)  # Output: 4
# Modify class variable using a class method
Car.set_wheels(6)
print("Updated wheels:", car1.wheels)  # Output: 6
```

**Static Methods:**

Methods that do not depend on instance or class-specific data. They are defined using the @staticmethod decorator. These functions behave like regular functions but belong to the class's namespace.

**Example:**

```
class Car:
    @staticmethod
    def is_motorized():
        """Return True since cars are motorized vehicles."""
        return True
```

```
print("Are cars motorized?", Car.is_motorized())  # Output: True
```

### 4. Best Practices for Classes and Methods

- **Encapsulation:**
  Keep data (attributes) and behavior (methods) bundled together. Avoid exposing internal data structures unless necessary.
- **Clear Naming:**
  Use descriptive names for classes, methods, and variables. Follow naming conventions (CamelCase for classes and lowercase_with_underscores for methods and variables).
- **Documentation:**
  Include docstrings in your classes and methods to explain their purpose, parameters, and return values. This aids in code readability and maintenance.
- **Single Responsibility Principle:**
  Each class should have a single, clear purpose. If a class is handling too many responsibilities, consider refactoring it into smaller, more focused classes.

### In Summary

Understanding instance variables, class variables, and methods is essential for working with classes and objects in Python. Key points include:

- **Instance Variables:**

  - Belong to individual objects and are defined within methods (usually __init__).
  - Each object has its own copy, allowing unique data storage.

- **Class Variables:**

  - Shared by all instances of a class.

- Useful for storing data that should be consistent across all objects.

- **Methods:**

  - **Instance Methods:** Operate on individual objects and access instance variables.
  - **Class Methods:** Operate on the class itself and modify class variables.
  - **Static Methods:** Belong to the class's namespace but do not access class or instance-specific data.

By mastering these concepts, you can effectively design and implement classes that model real-world entities, promote code reusability, and make your programs easier to maintain.

## Special Methods (__init__, __str__, etc.)

Special methods, often referred to as "magic methods" or "dunder methods" (because they begin and end with double underscores), provide a way to define or customize the behavior of your objects. These methods allow you to integrate your classes with Python's built-in operations and functions. Some of the most commonly used special methods include __init__, __str__, __repr__, __eq__, and many others.

### 1. The __init__ Method

The __init__ method is the constructor of a class. It is automatically called when a new object (instance) of the class is created. The purpose of __init__ is to initialize the object's attributes with values.

**Example: Using __init__**

```
class Person:

    def __init__(self, name, age):
```

```
        """
        Initialize a new Person instance.
        Parameters:
        name (str): The person's name.
        age (int): The person's age.
        """
        self.name = name  # Instance variable for name
        self.age = age    # Instance variable for age
# Creating an instance of Person
person1 = Person("Alice", 30)
print("Name:", person1.name)  # Output: Name: Alice
print("Age:", person1.age)    # Output: Age: 30
```

**Explanation:**

- The __init__ method sets up the initial state of a Person instance by assigning values to self.name and self.age.
- Each instance of Person can have its own unique name and age.

## 2. The __str__ Method

The __str__ method defines the "informal" or nicely printable string representation of an object. It is called by the str() built-in function and by the print() function to convert the object to a string.

**Example: Implementing __str__**

```
class Person:
    def __init__(self, name, age):
```

```
        self.name = name
        self.age = age
    def __str__(self):
        """
        Return a user-friendly string representation of the object.
        """
        return f"Person(name={self.name}, age={self.age})"
# Creating an instance of Person
person1 = Person("Bob", 25)
print(person1)  # Output: Person(name=Bob, age=25)
```

**Explanation:**

- When print(person1) is executed, Python calls person1.__str__(), which returns a formatted string representing the object.
- This method improves readability, especially when printing objects during debugging or logging.

### 3. The __repr__ Method

The __repr__ method is meant to provide an "official" string representation of an object that, ideally, could be used to recreate the object if fed back to Python's interpreter. It is used by the repr() function and in the interactive shell.

**Example: Implementing __repr__**

```
class Person:
    def __init__(self, name, age):
        self.name = name
```

```
        self.age = age
    def __repr__(self):
        """
        Return an official string representation of the object.
        """
        return f"Person(name='{self.name}', age={self.age})"
# Creating an instance of Person
person2 = Person("Charlie", 35)
print(repr(person2))  # Output: Person(name='Charlie', age=35)
```

**Explanation:**

- The __repr__ method is used to provide a more precise representation that is useful for debugging.
- Ideally, the string returned by __repr__ should be a valid Python expression that could be used to recreate the object (if possible).

### 4. Other Common Special Methods

Special methods extend far beyond just __init__, __str__, and __repr__. Here are a few additional ones that can be very useful:

#### 4.1 The __eq__ Method

The __eq__ method defines behavior for the equality operator ==. It allows you to specify when two objects of your class should be considered equal.

```
class Person:
    def __init__(self, name, age):
        self.name = name
```

```
        self.age = age
    def __eq__(self, other):
        """
        Return True if two Person objects are equal based on name and
age.
        """
        if isinstance(other, Person):
            return self.name == other.name and self.age == other.age
        return False
# Creating two Person instances
person1 = Person("Alice", 30)
person2 = Person("Alice", 30)
person3 = Person("Bob", 25)
print(person1 == person2)  # Output: True
print(person1 == person3)  # Output: False
```

### 4.2 The __len__ Method

The __len__ method defines behavior for the built-in len() function. It allows you to specify the "length" of an object.

```
class Sentence:
    def __init__(self, text):
        self.text = text
        self.words = self.text.split()
    def __len__(self):
```

```
        """
        Return the number of words in the sentence.
        """
        return len(self.words)

# Creating an instance of Sentence
sentence = Sentence("Hello, world! Welcome to Python programming.")
print("Number of words:", len(sentence))  # Output: Number of words: 6
```

**Explanation:**

- The __len__ method allows the object to be used with the built-in len() function.
- In this example, it returns the number of words in a sentence.

**5. Best Practices for Special Methods**

- **Consistency:**
  Ensure that the string representations provided by __str__ and __repr__ are consistent and meaningful. Use __repr__ for debugging and __str__ for end-user display.
- **Clarity:**
  Write clear and concise docstrings for special methods to explain their purpose, especially if the behavior is non-standard or complex.
- **Return Types:**
  Special methods should always return a value of the expected type. For example, __len__ must return an integer, and __repr__ should return a string.

- **Implement Equality:**
  If your class instances will be compared or used in collections that require hashing (like sets or dictionary keys), implement __eq__ (and possibly __hash__) appropriately.

**In Summary**

Special methods (or magic methods) are an integral part of Python's object model, allowing you to define custom behavior for your objects. Key points include:

- **__init__:**
  Initializes new instances of a class.

- **__str__:**
  Returns a user-friendly string representation of an object, used by print() and str().

- **__repr__:**
  Provides an official string representation, useful for debugging, and ideally can be used to recreate the object.

- **Additional Methods (__eq__, __len__, etc.):**
  Allow you to customize comparison, measure object length, and more.

By effectively using these special methods, you can make your classes more intuitive, easier to debug, and seamlessly integrated with Python's built-in functions and operations.

## Example Exercises

Building simple classes is an excellent way to learn and practice object-oriented programming concepts in Python. In these exercises, we will create two sample classes - **Car** and **BankAccount** - to illustrate how to define classes, create objects (instances), and implement methods and attributes to model real-world entities.

## 1. Building a Car Class

A **Car** class can model attributes like the make, model, and year, as well as behaviors like starting the engine or displaying the car's information.

### Step 1: Define the Car Class

```
class Car:
    """
    A simple class representing a car.
    Attributes:
        make (str): The manufacturer of the car.
        model (str): The model of the car.
        year (int): The year the car was made.
        speed (float): The current speed of the car (default is 0).
    """
    def __init__(self, make, model, year):
        """
        Initialize a new Car instance.
        Parameters:
            make (str): The manufacturer.
            model (str): The model.
            year (int): The production year.
        """
        self.make = make
```

```
        self.model = model
        self.year = year
        self.speed = 0  # Instance variable to track the current speed of the car
    def accelerate(self, increment):
        """
        Increase the car's speed.
        Parameters:
            increment (float): The amount to increase the speed.
        """
        self.speed += increment
        print(f"The car has accelerated. New speed: {self.speed} km/h")
    def brake(self, decrement):
        """
        Decrease the car's speed.
        Parameters:
            decrement (float): The amount to decrease the speed.
        """
        self.speed = max(0, self.speed - decrement)
        print(f"The car has slowed down. New speed: {self.speed} km/h")
    def display_info(self):
```

```
        """
        Display the car's details.
        """
        print(f"Car Info: {self.year} {self.make} {self.model}")
# Creating and using Car objects
car1 = Car("Toyota", "Corolla", 2020)
car1.display_info()        # Output: Car Info: 2020 Toyota Corolla
car1.accelerate(50)        # Output: The car has accelerated. New
speed: 50 km/h
car1.brake(20)             # Output: The car has slowed down. New
speed: 30 km/h
```

**Explanation:**

- **Attributes:**
  The Car class includes instance variables such as make, model, year, and speed. The speed attribute is initialized to 0.
- **Methods:**
  - The __init__ method initializes the attributes when a new Car object is created.
  - accelerate and brake methods adjust the speed attribute.
  - display_info prints the details of the car.
- **Usage:**
  An instance of Car is created and its methods are called to simulate real-world behavior like accelerating and braking.

## 2. Building a BankAccount Class

A **BankAccount** class can simulate basic banking operations. It might include attributes such as the account holder's name and balance, and methods for depositing and withdrawing funds.

### Step 1: Define the BankAccount Class

```
class BankAccount:
    """
    A simple class representing a bank account.
    Attributes:
        owner (str): The account holder's name.
        balance (float): The current balance in the account.
    """
    def __init__(self, owner, balance=0.0):
        """
        Initialize a new BankAccount instance.
        Parameters:
            owner (str): The account holder's name.
            balance (float): The initial balance (default is 0.0).
        """
        self.owner = owner
        self.balance = balance
    def deposit(self, amount):
        """
```

```
        Deposit money into the account.

        Parameters:

            amount (float): The amount to deposit.

        """

        if amount <= 0:

            print("Deposit amount must be positive.")

            return

        self.balance += amount

        print(f"Deposited ${amount:.2f}. New balance:
${self.balance:.2f}")

    def withdraw(self, amount):

        """

        Withdraw money from the account.

        Parameters:

            amount (float): The amount to withdraw.

        """

        if amount <= 0:

            print("Withdrawal amount must be positive.")

            return

        if amount > self.balance:

            print("Insufficient funds!")

        else:

            self.balance -= amount
```

```
        print(f"Withdrew ${amount:.2f}. New balance:
${self.balance:.2f}")

    def display_balance(self):
        """
        Display the current account balance.
        """
        print(f"{self.owner}'s account balance: ${self.balance:.2f}")

# Creating and using BankAccount objects
account1 = BankAccount("Alice", 1000.0)
account1.display_balance()    # Output: Alice's account balance:
$1000.00
account1.deposit(500.0)       # Output: Deposited $500.00. New
balance: $1500.00
account1.withdraw(200.0)      # Output: Withdrew $200.00. New
balance: $1300.00
account1.withdraw(1500.0)     # Output: Insufficient funds!
```

**Explanation:**

- **Attributes:**
  The BankAccount class uses instance variables owner and balance. The balance is initialized to a default value of 0.0 unless specified.
- **Methods:**
  - The __init__ method initializes the bank account.
  - deposit adds money to the account after checking that the amount is positive.

  - withdraw subtracts money if sufficient funds exist; otherwise, it prints an error message.
  - display_balance outputs the current balance in a formatted manner.

- **Usage:**
  An instance of BankAccount is created and methods are called to simulate deposits and withdrawals, demonstrating basic bank account operations.

### 3. Best Practices for Building Simple Classes

- **Encapsulation:**
  Keep data (attributes) and behaviors (methods) together. Use instance variables for data that should belong to an object and methods to manipulate that data.

- **Input Validation:**
  Validate inputs within your methods (e.g., check for negative deposit amounts or withdrawals that exceed the balance).

- **Documentation:**
  Include clear docstrings for classes and methods. Document the purpose of each method, the parameters it expects, and what it returns.

- **Simplicity:**
  Ensure each class has a single, clear responsibility. If a class starts to handle too many tasks, consider breaking it down into smaller, more focused classes.

### In Summary

Creating simple classes such as **Car** and **BankAccount** helps illustrate the core principles of object-oriented programming in Python:

- **Defining Classes:**
  Use the class keyword to define a blueprint for objects.
- **Instance Variables:**
  Hold data unique to each instance.
- **Methods:**
  Define the behaviors of the class, allowing you to manipulate instance variables and perform operations.
- **Object Instantiation:**
  Create objects (instances) from your class and call methods to interact with these objects.

By building and experimenting with these simple classes, you gain hands-on experience with OOP concepts, making it easier to design and implement more complex systems.

# Chapter 14: Inheritance, Polymorphism, and Encapsulation

## Single and Multiple Inheritance

Inheritance is a key concept in object-oriented programming (OOP) that allows you to create a new class (derived or child class) that is based on an existing class (base or parent class). This mechanism promotes code reuse and establishes a natural hierarchy between classes. Inheritance also plays a central role in enabling polymorphism and encapsulation.

### 1. Inheritance Overview

- **Inheritance** allows a new class to inherit attributes and methods from an existing class.
- **Polymorphism** lets objects of different classes be treated as objects of a common superclass, particularly when methods are overridden.
- **Encapsulation** bundles data and methods operating on that data within one unit (the class) and restricts access to some of the object's components.

### 2. Single Inheritance

In **single inheritance**, a class (child) inherits from one parent class. This is the most straightforward form of inheritance.

**Example: Single Inheritance with a Car Class**

```
class Vehicle:
    """
    A base class representing a generic vehicle.
    """
    def __init__(self, make, model):
```

```
        self.make = make
        self.model = model
    def display_info(self):
        """Display information about the vehicle."""
        print(f"Vehicle: {self.make} {self.model}")
# Derived class inheriting from Vehicle
class Car(Vehicle):
    """
    A Car class that inherits from Vehicle and adds additional attributes.
    """
    def __init__(self, make, model, year):
        # Call the constructor of the base class
        super().__init__(make, model)
        self.year = year
    def display_info(self):
        """Display information about the car, including the year."""
        print(f"Car: {self.year} {self.make} {self.model}")
# Create an instance of Car
my_car = Car("Toyota", "Corolla", 2020)
my_car.display_info()  # Output: Car: 2020 Toyota Corolla
```

**Explanation:**

- The Vehicle class is the base class containing common attributes and methods.
- The Car class inherits from Vehicle using single inheritance. It extends Vehicle by adding a year attribute and overriding the display_info() method.
- The super() function is used to call the parent class's constructor to initialize inherited attributes.

**3. Multiple Inheritance**

In **multiple inheritance**, a class inherits from more than one parent class. This can be useful when you need to combine behaviors from multiple sources. However, it may also introduce complexity, such as the "diamond problem," where a derived class inherits from two classes that both inherit from a common base class.

**Example: Multiple Inheritance with a Hybrid Class**

```
class Electric:
    """
    A base class representing electric-powered features.
    """
    def __init__(self, battery_capacity):
        self.battery_capacity = battery_capacity
    def display_battery(self):
        print(f"Battery capacity: {self.battery_capacity} kWh")
class Gasoline:
    """
```

```
    A base class representing gasoline-powered features.
    """
    def __init__(self, fuel_tank_size):
        self.fuel_tank_size = fuel_tank_size
    def display_fuel(self):
        print(f"Fuel tank size: {self.fuel_tank_size} liters")
# HybridVehicle inherits from both Electric and Gasoline
class HybridVehicle(Electric, Gasoline):
    """
    A class representing a hybrid vehicle that uses both electric and gasoline power.
    """
    def __init__(self, make, model, battery_capacity, fuel_tank_size):
        # Initialize attributes from both parent classes
        Electric.__init__(self, battery_capacity)
        Gasoline.__init__(self, fuel_tank_size)
        self.make = make
        self.model = model
    def display_info(self):
        print(f"Hybrid Vehicle: {self.make} {self.model}")
        self.display_battery()
        self.display_fuel()
```

```
# Create an instance of HybridVehicle
hybrid = HybridVehicle("Toyota", "Prius", 8.8, 43)
hybrid.display_info()
# Expected output:
# Hybrid Vehicle: Toyota Prius
# Battery capacity: 8.8 kWh
# Fuel tank size: 43 liters
```

**Explanation:**

- Two base classes, Electric and Gasoline, are defined, each with its own attributes and methods.
- The HybridVehicle class inherits from both base classes, thus combining electric and gasoline features.
- Each parent class's constructor is explicitly called within the HybridVehicle constructor.
- The display_info() method of HybridVehicle aggregates information from both parent classes.

**4. Polymorphism and Encapsulation in Inheritance**

**Polymorphism** allows objects of different classes to be treated interchangeably if they share a common interface. In the examples above, both Vehicle and Car have a display_info() method, and Car overrides this method to provide additional details.

**Encapsulation** is the bundling of data (attributes) and methods (functions) that operate on the data into a single unit or class. By controlling access to data through methods, you can protect the internal state of an object. In both single and multiple inheritance examples, the internal attributes are managed through constructors and methods, demonstrating encapsulation.

### 5. Best Practices for Inheritance

- **Prefer Composition Over Inheritance When Appropriate:**
  While inheritance is powerful, it's sometimes better to use composition (i.e., including instances of other classes as attributes) to achieve flexibility.
- **Keep the Inheritance Hierarchy Simple:**
  Avoid overly complex multiple inheritance hierarchies. Ensure that each class has a clear purpose.
- **Use super() in Single Inheritance:**
  In single inheritance, prefer using super() to call parent class methods, as it helps maintain consistency and supports cooperative multiple inheritance when necessary.
- **Explicit is Better Than Implicit:**
  When using multiple inheritance, explicitly call parent class constructors to ensure that each base class is properly initialized.
- **Document Class Hierarchies:**
  Use docstrings and comments to explain the relationships between classes, which is especially important in complex inheritance structures.

### In Summary

Inheritance is a cornerstone of OOP that allows you to create a hierarchical organization of classes:

- **Single Inheritance:**
  A child class inherits from one parent class, extending or overriding functionality.
- **Multiple Inheritance:**
  A child class inherits from multiple parent classes, combining

behaviors from each. This approach offers great flexibility but requires careful management to avoid complexity.

- **Polymorphism:**
  Enables methods to be overridden in derived classes, allowing objects of different classes to be treated uniformly based on shared behavior.

- **Encapsulation:**
  Ensures that data and the methods that manipulate it are bundled together, promoting modularity and protecting internal state.

By understanding and applying these principles, you can design robust, reusable, and maintainable systems that mirror real-world relationships and behaviors.

## Overriding Methods

Method overriding is a fundamental concept in object-oriented programming that allows a subclass (child class) to provide a specific implementation for a method that is already defined in its superclass (parent class). Overriding methods is one of the primary ways to achieve polymorphism, enabling objects of different classes to be treated interchangeably based on shared behavior while still having their own unique implementations.

### 1. What Is Method Overriding?

When a subclass defines a method with the same name, parameters, and return type as a method in its parent class, the method in the subclass **overrides** the one in the parent. This means that when the method is called on an instance of the subclass, the overridden version in the subclass is executed, rather than the one defined in the parent class.

**Key Points:**

- **Polymorphism:**
  Overriding allows different classes to implement methods that are conceptually similar but behave differently. This enables polymorphism where a common interface is shared but the internal workings differ.

- **Encapsulation:**
  By overriding methods, subclasses can hide or modify the behavior inherited from the parent class, thus encapsulating specific functionality.

- **Use of super():**
  In many cases, a subclass method may want to extend the functionality of the parent method rather than completely replacing it. The super() function allows you to call the parent class's version of the method from the overriding method.

## 2. Basic Example of Overriding Methods

Let's illustrate method overriding with a simple example involving a parent class Animal and a subclass Dog.

**Example: Animal and Dog Classes**

```
class Animal:
    def __init__(self, name):
        self.name = name
    def speak(self):
        """Return a generic sound."""
        return "Some generic sound"
    def __str__(self):
```

```
        """Return a string representation of the Animal."""
        return f"Animal: {self.name}"
class Dog(Animal):
    def __init__(self, name, breed):
        super().__init__(name)  # Initialize the name using the parent
class's constructor
        self.breed = breed
    def speak(self):
        """Return a dog-specific sound, overriding the parent's speak
method."""
        return "Woof!"
    def __str__(self):
        """Return a string representation of the Dog, including its
breed."""
        # Optionally, we can use the parent's __str__ method via
super()
        parent_str = super().__str__()
        return f"{parent_str}, Breed: {self.breed}"
# Creating instances of Animal and Dog
generic_animal = Animal("GenericAnimal")
dog = Dog("Buddy", "Golden Retriever")
print(generic_animal.speak())  # Output: Some generic sound
print(dog.speak())             # Output: Woof!
print(generic_animal)          # Output: Animal: GenericAnimal
```

```
print(dog)                # Output: Animal: Buddy, Breed: Golden
Retriever
```

**Explanation:**

- **Parent Class (Animal):**
  The Animal class defines a method speak() that returns a generic sound and a __str__ method for its string representation.
- **Subclass (Dog):**
  The Dog class inherits from Animal and overrides the speak() method to return a dog-specific sound ("Woof!").
  - The Dog class also defines its own __str__ method. It calls super().__str__() to reuse the parent class's string representation and then appends additional information (the breed).
- **Polymorphism in Action:**
  When calling speak() on an Animal instance, the generic sound is returned. When calling speak() on a Dog instance, the overridden version is executed, demonstrating polymorphism.

### 3. Extending Functionality with super()

Sometimes, you may want to extend rather than completely override a method. You can use the super() function to call the method from the parent class within the overriding method.

**Example: Extending a Method**

```
class Employee:

    def __init__(self, name, salary):

        self.name = name

        self.salary = salary

    def display_info(self):
```

```
        """Display employee's name and salary."""
        return f"Employee: {self.name}, Salary: ${self.salary}"
class Manager(Employee):
    def __init__(self, name, salary, department):
        super().__init__(name, salary)
        self.department = department
    def display_info(self):
        """Display manager's information, extending the employee info."""
        base_info = super().display_info()  # Get the information from the Employee class
        return f"{base_info}, Department: {self.department}"
# Creating instances
employee = Employee("Alice", 50000)
manager = Manager("Bob", 80000, "Sales")
print(employee.display_info())
# Output: Employee: Alice, Salary: $50000
print(manager.display_info())
# Output: Employee: Bob, Salary: $80000, Department: Sales
```

**Explanation:**

- The Manager class extends the Employee class. It overrides display_info() to include department information.

- The super().display_info() call retrieves the string representation from the parent class, which is then enhanced with additional details.

**4. Best Practices for Overriding Methods**

- **Clarity and Consistency:**
  Clearly document overridden methods using docstrings. Ensure that the overriding method's signature matches the parent class's method.

- **Use super() Wisely:**
  When extending functionality, use super() to call the parent method. This maintains the chain of method calls, especially important in multiple inheritance scenarios.

- **Maintain Expected Behavior:**
  Overridden methods should generally adhere to the expected behavior of the parent method, unless there is a compelling reason to change it. This ensures that objects remain substitutable (the Liskov Substitution Principle).

- **Avoid Unnecessary Overriding:**
  Only override a method when you need to change or extend its behavior. If the parent class's method is sufficient, reuse it instead of duplicating code.

**In Summary**

Overriding methods is a powerful aspect of object-oriented programming that enables:

- **Polymorphism:**
  Different classes can implement methods with the same name but distinct behaviors.

- **Encapsulation and Extension:**
  Subclasses can override methods to provide specialized behavior

while still leveraging common functionality from parent classes using super().

By effectively overriding methods, you can create more flexible, reusable, and maintainable code that accurately models real-world scenarios.

## Access Modifiers and Encapsulation in Python

Encapsulation is a core principle of object-oriented programming that involves bundling data (attributes) and methods (functions) operating on that data within a class, and restricting direct access to some of the object's components. In many programming languages, access modifiers (such as public, protected, and private) enforce encapsulation. While Python does not have strict access modifiers like some other languages, it follows conventions to indicate the intended level of access for class members.

### 1. Access Modifiers in Python

#### 1.1 Public Attributes and Methods

- **Definition:**
  Public members are accessible from anywhere, both inside and outside the class. In Python, all class attributes and methods are public by default.
- **Usage:**
  Use public members for the interface that you expect users of the class to access.

**Example:**

```
class PublicExample:
    def __init__(self, value):
        self.value = value  # Public attribute
    def display(self):
```

```
        # Public method
        print(f"Value is: {self.value}")
# Creating an instance and accessing public members
obj = PublicExample(42)
print(obj.value)  # Accessing public attribute
obj.display()    # Calling public method
```

### 1.2 Protected Attributes and Methods

- **Definition:**
  Protected members are intended for internal use within the class and its subclasses. By convention, these members are prefixed with a single underscore (_).
- **Usage:**
  Although not enforced by Python, the single underscore is a signal to developers that these attributes or methods should not be accessed directly from outside the class hierarchy.

**Example:**

```
class ProtectedExample:
    def __init__(self, value):
        self._internal_value = value  # Protected attribute
    def _compute(self):
        # Protected method
        return self._internal_value * 2
class DerivedExample(ProtectedExample):
    def show_computation(self):
```

```
        # Accessing a protected method from a subclass
        result = self._compute()
        print(f"Computed result: {result}")

# Creating an instance and using the protected member via a subclass method
derived_obj = DerivedExample(10)
derived_obj.show_computation()  # Output: Computed result: 20

# Although possible, accessing _internal_value directly is discouraged
print("Direct access (not recommended):", derived_obj._internal_value)
```

### 1.3 Private Attributes and Methods

- **Definition:**
  Private members are intended to be inaccessible from outside the class. In Python, private members are denoted by prefixing the attribute or method name with double underscores (__). This triggers name mangling, where the interpreter changes the attribute name to include the class name, reducing the likelihood of accidental access or overriding.
- **Usage:**
  Use private members to hide the internal implementation details of a class.

**Example:**

```
class PrivateExample:
    def __init__(self, value):
        self.__hidden_value = value  # Private attribute
    def __secret_method(self):
```

```
        # Private method
        return self.__hidden_value * 3
    def reveal_secret(self):
        # Public method that accesses a private member
        return self.__secret_method()
# Creating an instance and attempting to access private members
private_obj = PrivateExample(5)
# The following lines would raise AttributeError if uncommented:
# print(private_obj.__hidden_value)
# print(private_obj.__secret_method())
# Correct way to access private members through a public method
print("Revealed secret:", private_obj.reveal_secret())  # Output: Revealed secret: 15
# However, name mangling allows access (not recommended in practice)
print("Access via name mangling:", private_obj._PrivateExample__hidden_value)  # Output: 5
```

**Explanation:**

- The attribute __hidden_value and the method __secret_method are intended to be private. They are not directly accessible using their given names outside the class.
- The public method reveal_secret() provides controlled access to the private method.

- While Python's name mangling allows access using _ClassName__attribute, this is discouraged and should be avoided in well-designed code.

## 2. Encapsulation in Python

Encapsulation is achieved by:

- **Bundling Data and Methods:**
  A class encapsulates its data (attributes) and methods (functions) that operate on that data. This organization helps manage complexity and promotes code reusability.
- **Restricting Direct Access:**
  Using naming conventions (single or double underscores), you signal to other developers which parts of your class are intended for internal use versus public use. This minimizes accidental modifications and enforces a clear interface.
- **Providing Public Interfaces:**
  Even if some attributes or methods are private, you can provide public methods (getters/setters) to allow controlled access to the internal state. This is part of the principle of encapsulation that helps maintain the integrity of the data.

**Example: Controlled Access with Getters and Setters**

```
class BankAccount:
    def __init__(self, owner, balance=0):
        self.owner = owner  # Public attribute
        self.__balance = balance  # Private attribute
    def deposit(self, amount):
        """Deposit money into the account."""
        if amount > 0:
```

```
            self.__balance += amount
            print(f"Deposited ${amount}. New balance: ${self.__balance}.")
        else:
            print("Deposit amount must be positive.")

    def withdraw(self, amount):
        """Withdraw money from the account if sufficient funds exist."""
        if 0 < amount <= self.__balance:
            self.__balance -= amount
            print(f"Withdrew ${amount}. New balance: ${self.__balance}.")
        else:
            print("Insufficient funds or invalid withdrawal amount.")

    def get_balance(self):
        """Return the current account balance."""
        return self.__balance

# Creating an instance of BankAccount
account = BankAccount("Alice", 1000)
account.deposit(200)
account.withdraw(150)
print("Current balance (accessed via getter):", account.get_balance())
```

**Explanation:**

- The BankAccount class encapsulates the account balance as a private attribute (__balance).
- Public methods (deposit, withdraw, and get_balance) provide controlled access to modify and retrieve the balance.
- This design ensures that the balance cannot be altered directly, preserving the integrity of the account's state.

**3. Best Practices for Using Access Modifiers and Encapsulation**

- **Follow Conventions:**
  Adhere to Python's naming conventions for protected (_var) and private (__var) members. This helps other developers understand the intended usage of your class members.
- **Minimize Direct Exposure:**
  Avoid exposing internal data directly. Use getter and setter methods if necessary, so that you can validate or process data before it is modified or returned.
- **Document Your Code:**
  Clearly document which attributes and methods are intended for internal use and which are part of the public interface. This improves code maintainability and usability.
- **Encapsulate Logic:**
  Group related functionalities within classes, and restrict access to the inner workings by using private and protected members. This leads to a cleaner, more modular design.

**In Summary**

In Python, encapsulation and access control are primarily achieved through naming conventions rather than strict language-enforced access modifiers. Key points include:

- **Public Members:**
  Accessible from anywhere; no special prefix is required.
- **Protected Members:**
  Indicated by a single underscore (e.g., _var), these members are intended for internal use within the class and its subclasses.
- **Private Members:**
  Indicated by double underscores (e.g., __var), these members are subject to name mangling, making them inaccessible from outside the class by their given names.
- **Encapsulation:**
  Encapsulation is achieved by bundling data and methods together in a class and restricting direct access to the internal state through controlled interfaces (getters and setters).

By following these principles and best practices, you can design robust, maintainable, and modular Python classes that encapsulate data effectively and protect it from unintended modifications.

**Example Exercises**

Designing a class hierarchy for geometric shapes is a classic exercise to illustrate the core OOP concepts of inheritance, polymorphism, and encapsulation. In this example, we will create a base class Shape that defines the common interface for all shapes, and then extend this base class with specific shapes like Rectangle and Circle. These derived classes will override methods to provide their own implementations for calculating area and perimeter. Additionally, we will use encapsulation to protect the internal state of each object.

### 1. Designing the Base Class

The base class Shape defines the common interface for all geometric shapes. It includes methods for calculating area and perimeter, which are intended to be overridden by subclasses. We can use abstract methods (by raising NotImplementedError) to indicate that subclasses must provide their own implementations.

```
class Shape:
    """
    A base class for geometric shapes.
    This class defines the interface for calculating area and perimeter.
    Subclasses should override the area() and perimeter() methods.
    """
    def area(self):
        """
        Calculate the area of the shape.
        This method should be overridden by subclasses.
        """
        raise NotImplementedError("Subclasses must implement this
method.")

    def perimeter(self):
        """
        Calculate the perimeter of the shape.
        This method should be overridden by subclasses.
        """
        raise NotImplementedError("Subclasses must implement this
method.")
```

```
    def __str__(self):
        """
        Return a string representation of the shape.
        """
        return "Shape"
# Example usage:
# shape = Shape()
# shape.area()  # This would raise NotImplementedError
```

**Explanation:**

- The Shape class acts as an abstract base class.
- The area() and perimeter() methods are defined to signal that they must be implemented by any subclass.
- The __str__ method provides a default string representation.

**2. Implementing Derived Classes**

**2.1 The Rectangle Class**

The Rectangle class inherits from Shape and represents a rectangle. It encapsulates its dimensions (width and height) as private attributes.

```
class Rectangle(Shape):
    """
    A class representing a rectangle.

    Attributes:
        __width (float): The width of the rectangle.
```

```
        __height (float): The height of the rectangle.
    """

    def __init__(self, width, height):
        self.__width = width    # Private attribute for width
        self.__height = height  # Private attribute for height
    def area(self):
        """Return the area of the rectangle."""
        return self.__width * self.__height

    def perimeter(self):
        """Return the perimeter of the rectangle."""
        return 2 * (self.__width + self.__height)
    def __str__(self):
        """Return a string representation of the rectangle."""
        return f"Rectangle(width={self.__width},
height={self.__height})"

# Testing the Rectangle class
rect = Rectangle(4, 5)
print(rect)                    # Output: Rectangle(width=4, height=5)
print("Area:", rect.area())    # Output: Area: 20
print("Perimeter:", rect.perimeter())  # Output: Perimeter: 18
```

**Explanation:**

- The Rectangle class defines its own constructor __init__ to initialize width and height.
- Private attributes (__width and __height) encapsulate the dimensions.
- The methods area() and perimeter() override the abstract methods from Shape.
- The __str__ method is overridden to provide a readable string representation.

### 2.2 The Circle Class

The Circle class also inherits from Shape and models a circle. It encapsulates the radius as a private attribute.

```
import math
class Circle(Shape):
    """
    A class representing a circle.
    Attributes:
        __radius (float): The radius of the circle.
    """
    def __init__(self, radius):
        self.__radius = radius  # Private attribute for radius
    def area(self):
        """Return the area of the circle."""
        return math.pi * self.__radius ** 2
```

```
    def perimeter(self):
        """Return the perimeter (circumference) of the circle."""
        return 2 * math.pi * self.__radius
    def __str__(self):
        """Return a string representation of the circle."""
        return f"Circle(radius={self.__radius})"
# Testing the Circle class
circle = Circle(3)
print(circle)                    # Output: Circle(radius=3)
print("Area:", circle.area())    # Output: Area: 28.274333882308138 (approx.)
print("Perimeter:", circle.perimeter()) # Output: Perimeter: 18.84955592153876 (approx.)
```

**Explanation:**

- The Circle class initializes the radius in its constructor.
- The area() and perimeter() methods compute the respective values using math.pi.
- The private attribute __radius is used to encapsulate the circle's state.
- The __str__ method provides a clear representation of a circle object.

**3. Polymorphism with the Shape Hierarchy**

Polymorphism allows you to write code that can work with objects of different types through a common interface. In our hierarchy, both

Rectangle and Circle implement the area() and perimeter() methods, so we can treat them uniformly as shapes.

**Example: Polymorphic Behavior**

```
# List of shapes (polymorphic collection)
shapes = [
    Rectangle(4, 5),
    Circle(3),
    Rectangle(2, 3),
    Circle(5)
]
# Iterating over the shapes and displaying their information
for shape in shapes:
    print(shape)                    # Calls the overridden __str__ method
    print("Area:", shape.area())    # Polymorphic call to area()
    print("Perimeter:", shape.perimeter())  # Polymorphic call to
perimeter()
    print("-" * 30)
```

**Explanation:**

- The list shapes contains objects of different types (Rectangle and Circle), but all are treated as instances of Shape.
- The loop calls area() and perimeter() on each object, and the correct overridden method is executed, demonstrating polymorphism.

- This approach allows you to add new shapes to your hierarchy without modifying the code that processes them.

### 4. Encapsulation in Action

Encapsulation is demonstrated by the use of private attributes (__width, __height, and __radius) in our classes. These attributes are not accessible directly from outside the class, ensuring that the internal state of an object can only be modified through its public methods. This protects the object's data and maintains integrity.

---

### 5. Summary

Creating a class hierarchy for geometric shapes is an excellent exercise to illustrate core OOP concepts:

- **Inheritance:**
  - The Rectangle and Circle classes inherit from the Shape base class, reusing and extending its interface.
- **Polymorphism:**
  - Both subclasses override the area() and perimeter() methods. This allows code that works with the base class (Shape) to operate seamlessly with any derived class.
- **Encapsulation:**
  - Private attributes (e.g., __width, __height, __radius) protect the internal state of each object.
  - Public methods provide controlled access to these attributes and define the behavior of the objects.

By mastering these concepts, you can design robust and maintainable systems that accurately model real-world entities.

# Chapter 15: Advanced OOP Concepts

## Abstract Base Classes (abc module)

Abstract Base Classes (ABCs) provide a way to define interfaces when creating a class hierarchy. They allow you to specify methods and properties that derived classes **must** implement, ensuring a consistent API. Python's abc module provides the infrastructure for defining abstract base classes. This approach enforces a contract for subclasses and promotes robust and maintainable code design.

### 1. Why Use Abstract Base Classes?

- **Interface Enforcement:**
  ABCs allow you to declare methods that must be implemented by any concrete subclass, ensuring consistency across your code.
- **Preventing Instantiation:**
  Abstract classes cannot be instantiated on their own. This prevents the creation of incomplete objects.
- **Polymorphism:**
  They support polymorphic behavior by allowing different classes to implement the same abstract methods while behaving differently.

### 2. Defining an Abstract Base Class

To create an abstract base class in Python, you inherit from abc.ABC and decorate methods that must be overridden with @abstractmethod. You can also use @abstractproperty (or @property in combination with @abstractmethod in Python 3) for abstract properties.

### Example: A Base Class for Geometric Shapes

In this example, we'll define an abstract base class Shape that requires any subclass to implement the area() and perimeter() methods.

```
from abc import ABC, abstractmethod
class Shape(ABC):
    """
    Abstract base class representing a generic geometric shape.
    Any subclass must implement the area() and perimeter() methods.
    """
    @abstractmethod
    def area(self):
        """
        Calculate the area of the shape.
        Must be implemented by subclasses.
        """
        pass
    @abstractmethod
    def perimeter(self):
        """
        Calculate the perimeter of the shape.
        Must be implemented by subclasses.
        """
        pass
    def __str__(self):
        """
```

```
        Return a string representation of the shape.
        """
        return f"{self.__class__.__name__} with area: {self.area()} and perimeter: {self.perimeter()}"

# Attempting to instantiate Shape will raise an error:
# shape = Shape()  # Raises TypeError: Can't instantiate abstract class Shape with abstract methods area, perimeter
```

**Explanation:**

- The Shape class inherits from ABC, marking it as an abstract base class.
- The @abstractmethod decorator is applied to area() and perimeter(), making them mandatory for any subclass.
- The __str__ method provides a common string representation that uses the abstract methods. This method can be inherited by subclasses.

**3. Implementing Concrete Subclasses**

Concrete subclasses of Shape must override all abstract methods. Let's implement two subclasses: Rectangle and Circle.

**Example: Rectangle Subclass**

```
class Rectangle(Shape):
    def __init__(self, width, height):
        self.width = width
        self.height = height
    def area(self):
        """Return the area of the rectangle."""
```

```
        return self.width * self.height
    def perimeter(self):
        """Return the perimeter of the rectangle."""
        return 2 * (self.width + self.height)
# Testing Rectangle
rect = Rectangle(4, 5)
print(rect)  # Output: Rectangle with area: 20 and perimeter: 18
```

Example: Circle Subclass

```
import math
class Circle(Shape):
    def __init__(self, radius):
        self.radius = radius
    def area(self):
        """Return the area of the circle."""
        return math.pi * self.radius ** 2
    def perimeter(self):
        """Return the circumference of the circle."""
        return 2 * math.pi * self.radius
# Testing Circle
circle = Circle(3)
print(circle)  # Output: Circle with area: 28.27... and perimeter: 18.85...
```

**Explanation:**

- Both Rectangle and Circle implement the area() and perimeter() methods as required by the abstract base class.
- Now, instances of Rectangle and Circle can be created, and their overridden methods will be used.

**4. Advanced Usage: Abstract Properties**

You can also define abstract properties to require that subclasses provide specific data attributes with getter (and optionally setter) methods.

**Example: Abstract Property for a Name Attribute**

```
from abc import ABC, abstractmethod

class NamedShape(ABC):

    @property

    @abstractmethod

    def name(self):

        """

        Abstract property to get the name of the shape.

        """

        pass

class Square(NamedShape):

    def __init__(self, side_length):

        self.side_length = side_length

    @property

    def name(self):
```

```
        return "Square"

    def area(self):

        return self.side_length ** 2

    def perimeter(self):

        return 4 * self.side_length

# Testing Square with abstract property

square = Square(5)

print(f"{square.name} with area: {square.area()} and perimeter: {square.perimeter()}")

# Output: Square with area: 25 and perimeter: 20
```

**Explanation:**

- The NamedShape abstract base class defines an abstract property name.
- The Square class implements the name property along with its own area() and perimeter() methods.
- This ensures that every subclass of NamedShape provides a name attribute.

**5. Best Practices for Using Abstract Base Classes**

- **Design for Extensibility:**
  Define abstract methods and properties to enforce a common interface across all subclasses. This helps maintain consistency and predictability.
- **Document Abstract Methods:**
  Use clear docstrings for abstract methods and properties, so that developers know what is expected when subclassing.

- **Use ABCs to Prevent Instantiation:**
  Use abstract base classes to prevent the creation of incomplete objects by ensuring that all necessary methods are implemented in subclasses.

- **Leverage super():**
  When overriding methods in subclasses, consider using super() to call the base class's implementation if it provides useful default behavior.

**In Summary**

Abstract Base Classes (ABCs) in Python, provided by the abc module, enable you to:

- **Enforce Interfaces:**
  Define a set of methods and properties that all subclasses must implement.

- **Prevent Instantiation:**
  Abstract classes cannot be instantiated directly, ensuring that only complete implementations are used.

- **Support Polymorphism:**
  By providing a common interface, ABCs allow different classes to be used interchangeably.

- **Enhance Code Quality:**
  Using ABCs helps catch implementation errors early, leading to more robust and maintainable code.

By integrating abstract base classes into your design, you can build a more structured, consistent, and extensible class hierarchy.

## Mixins and Interfaces

Advanced OOP techniques such as **mixins** and **interfaces** enable you to design flexible and reusable code architectures. While both concepts contribute to code reuse and modularity, they serve different purposes:

- **Mixins:** Provide a way to add reusable functionality to classes through multiple inheritance. They are not meant to stand alone; instead, they "mix in" extra behavior into a class.
- **Interfaces:** Define a contract or a set of methods that a class must implement. In Python, interfaces are typically created using abstract base classes (ABCs) with abstract methods, ensuring that any subclass provides concrete implementations.

## 1. Mixins

### 1.1 What Are Mixins?

A **mixin** is a class that offers additional functionality to a class through inheritance. Mixins are designed to be combined with other classes and are not intended to be instantiated on their own. They allow you to "mix in" specific behaviors into multiple classes without forming a deep or rigid inheritance hierarchy.

### 1.2 Characteristics of Mixins

- **Focused Functionality:**
  A mixin typically provides a single piece of functionality.
- **Non-Standalone:**
  Mixins are not meant to be instantiated independently.
- **Combinable:**
  They are designed to be used with other classes, often via multiple inheritance.

### 1.3 Example: A LoggingMixin

Consider a scenario where you want several classes to have logging capabilities. You can create a LoggingMixin that provides a simple logging method, then mix it into any class that requires logging.

```
class LoggingMixin:
    """
    A mixin that provides logging functionality.
    This class is not intended to be instantiated on its own.
    """
    def log(self, message):
        print(f"[LOG] {message}")
# Example of a class using LoggingMixin
class DataProcessor(LoggingMixin):
    def process(self, data):
        self.log("Starting data processing.")
        # Imagine processing data here...
        self.log("Finished data processing.")
        return data
# Using the DataProcessor class
processor = DataProcessor()
result = processor.process("sample data")
```

**Explanation:**

- The LoggingMixin class defines a log() method.
- The DataProcessor class inherits from LoggingMixin (and possibly other classes), gaining the logging capability.
- When processor.process() is called, it logs messages before and after processing data.

## 2. Interfaces

### 2.1 What Are Interfaces?

An **interface** defines a contract that a class must follow by specifying methods and properties that must be implemented. Although Python does not have built-in interfaces like some other languages (e.g., Java), you can achieve a similar effect using abstract base classes (ABCs) provided by the abc module.

### 2.2 Creating an Interface with Abstract Base Classes

To create an interface-like structure in Python, define an abstract base class with abstract methods that subclasses are required to implement.

```
from abc import ABC, abstractmethod

class Shape(ABC):

    """

    An abstract base class representing a geometric shape.

    All concrete shape classes must implement the area and perimeter methods.

    """

    @abstractmethod

    def area(self):

        """Calculate and return the area of the shape."""

        pass

    @abstractmethod

    def perimeter(self):

        """Calculate and return the perimeter of the shape."""
```

```
        pass
# Example: Implementing the Shape interface
class Rectangle(Shape):
    def __init__(self, width, height):
        self.width = width
        self.height = height
    def area(self):
        return self.width * self.height
    def perimeter(self):
        return 2 * (self.width + self.height)
# Testing the implementation
rect = Rectangle(4, 5)
print("Rectangle Area:", rect.area())        # Output: 20
print("Rectangle Perimeter:", rect.perimeter())  # Output: 18
```

**Explanation:**

- The Shape class inherits from ABC and uses the @abstractmethod decorator to declare methods that must be implemented by any subclass.
- The Rectangle class implements the area() and perimeter() methods, fulfilling the contract of the Shape interface.
- Attempting to instantiate Shape directly would result in a TypeError, ensuring that only fully implemented subclasses are used.

### 3. Combining Mixins and Interfaces

Mixins and interfaces can be used together to create classes that adhere to a specific interface while also gaining additional functionality.

#### Example: A Hybrid Class with an Interface and a Mixin

Consider a scenario where you have a Shape interface and a ColorMixin that provides color functionality.

```
from abc import ABC, abstractmethod

# Define the interface using an abstract base class

class Shape(ABC):

    @abstractmethod

    def area(self):

        pass

    @abstractmethod

    def perimeter(self):

        pass

# Define a mixin to add color functionality

class ColorMixin:

    def set_color(self, color):

        self.color = color

    def get_color(self):

        return getattr(self, 'color', 'No color set')

# Concrete class that implements the Shape interface and uses ColorMixin
```

```
class ColoredRectangle(Shape, ColorMixin):
    def __init__(self, width, height):
        self.width = width
        self.height = height
    def area(self):
        return self.width * self.height
    def perimeter(self):
        return 2 * (self.width + self.height)
# Testing the hybrid class
colored_rect = ColoredRectangle(3, 4)
colored_rect.set_color("red")
print("Area:", colored_rect.area())            # Output: 12
print("Perimeter:", colored_rect.perimeter())    # Output: 14
print("Color:", colored_rect.get_color())        # Output: red
```

**Explanation:**

- The Shape interface requires any subclass to implement area() and perimeter().
- The ColorMixin provides methods to set and get a color.
- The ColoredRectangle class inherits from both Shape and ColorMixin, thus combining the responsibilities of providing a geometric shape with the ability to have a color.
- This design demonstrates how mixins can enhance classes that implement interfaces without interfering with the required method implementations.

### 4. Best Practices for Using Mixins and Interfaces

- **Keep Mixins Focused:**
  Mixins should provide a single, specific piece of functionality (e.g., logging, coloring, serialization) and should not become a catch-all for unrelated features.
- **Use Abstract Base Classes for Interfaces:**
  Utilize Python's abc module to define interfaces. This enforces a contract for subclasses, ensuring consistency across your codebase.
- **Clear Hierarchies:**
  Design your class hierarchies thoughtfully. When using multiple inheritance, ensure that the mixins and interfaces are well-defined and do not conflict.
- **Documentation:**
  Clearly document the purpose of your interfaces and mixins. Explain which methods need to be implemented and how the mixin methods are expected to interact with the rest of the class.
- **Test Thoroughly:**
  With the flexibility of multiple inheritance, it's important to write tests to ensure that mixins and interfaces interact as expected.

### In Summary

Mixins and interfaces are advanced OOP concepts that greatly enhance the modularity and reusability of your code:

- **Mixins:**
  - Provide additional functionality through multiple inheritance.
  - Are not meant to be instantiated on their own.
- **Interfaces:**
  - Define a contract using abstract base classes.

- Ensure that derived classes implement specific methods, promoting consistency and polymorphism.

- **Combining Both:**
  - You can mix interfaces and mixins in a single class to achieve a rich set of behaviors while adhering to a defined API.

By effectively utilizing mixins and interfaces, you can design robust and scalable systems that promote code reuse and maintainability.

## Decorators and Metaclasses

In advanced OOP, decorators and metaclasses are powerful tools that allow you to modify and extend the behavior of classes and functions. Although they may seem complex at first, understanding these concepts can greatly enhance your ability to write modular, reusable, and expressive Python code.

### 1. Decorators

#### 1.1 What Are Decorators?

Decorators are a design pattern in Python that allow you to wrap a function, method, or class with another function to modify or extend its behavior without changing its source code. Essentially, a decorator is a callable that takes a function as input and returns a new function as output.

#### 1.2 Basic Syntax and Example

The typical syntax for using a decorator is the @decorator_name syntax placed directly above the function definition. Consider the following simple example—a logging decorator that prints a message before and after a function call:

```
def log_decorator(func):
    """
```

```
    A simple decorator that logs the execution of the function.
    """
    def wrapper(*args, **kwargs):
        print(f"[LOG] Calling function '{func.__name__}' with arguments {args} {kwargs}")
        result = func(*args, **kwargs)
        print(f"[LOG] Function '{func.__name__}' returned {result}")
        return result
    return wrapper
@log_decorator
def add(a, b):
    """Return the sum of a and b."""
    return a + b
# Calling the decorated function
print("Result:", add(3, 5))
```

**Explanation:**

- **Decorator Function (log_decorator):**
  - Accepts a function func as its argument.
  - Defines an inner function wrapper that wraps the execution of func, printing log messages before and after calling func.
  - Returns the wrapper function, effectively replacing the original function with the enhanced version.

- **Usage:**
  - The @log_decorator syntax applies the decorator to the add function.
  - When add(3, 5) is called, it executes the wrapper, which logs the call and then executes the original add function.

### 1.3 Decorators with Arguments

Decorators can also be parameterized by writing a decorator factory - a function that returns a decorator.

```
def repeat(num_times):
    """
    A decorator factory that repeats the execution of the decorated function.
    """
    def decorator(func):
        def wrapper(*args, **kwargs):
            result = None
            for _ in range(num_times):
                result = func(*args, **kwargs)
            return result
        return wrapper
    return decorator
@repeat(3)
def greet(name):
    """Print a greeting message."""
```

```
    print(f"Hello, {name}!")
# Calling the decorated function; greet will be executed 3 times.
greet("Alice")
```

**Explanation:**

- **Decorator Factory (repeat):**
  - Accepts a parameter num_times and returns a decorator.
- **Decorator Function (decorator):**
  - Wraps the target function, executing it num_times before returning the final result.
- **Usage:**
  - The @repeat(3) syntax repeats the execution of greet("Alice") three times.

## 2. Metaclasses

### 2.1 What Are Metaclasses?

Metaclasses are the "classes of classes" — they define the behavior and structure of classes themselves. In Python, a metaclass is a class that controls the creation of other classes. Although metaclasses are an advanced feature and are used less frequently, they provide a powerful mechanism for customizing class creation and enforcing class-level constraints.

### 2.2 Basic Syntax and Example

To define a metaclass, you subclass type and override methods such as __new__() or __init__(). The following example demonstrates a simple metaclass that logs the creation of a class:

```
class LoggingMeta(type):
```

```
    """
    A metaclass that logs class creation.
    """
    def __new__(cls, name, bases, namespace):
        print(f"Creating class {name} with bases {bases}")
        # You can modify the namespace here if needed
        return super().__new__(cls, name, bases, namespace)
# Using LoggingMeta as the metaclass for a new class
class MyClass(metaclass=LoggingMeta):
    def __init__(self, value):
        self.value = value
    def display(self):
        print(f"MyClass value: {self.value}")
# Creating an instance of MyClass triggers the metaclass
instance = MyClass(10)
instance.display()
```

**Explanation:**

- **Defining a Metaclass (LoggingMeta):**
  - Subclasses type.
  - Overrides __new__() to log the creation of a class.
- **Using a Metaclass:**
  - The MyClass class is created with LoggingMeta as its metaclass.

- When MyClass is defined, the metaclass's __new__() method is called, printing a log message.

- **Behavior:**

- The metaclass doesn't change the behavior of MyClass other than logging its creation, but more complex modifications could be applied.

### 2.3 When to Use Metaclasses

Metaclasses are particularly useful when you need to:

- Enforce certain patterns or constraints on classes.
- Automatically register classes in a system (e.g., plugins, serializers).
- Modify or extend class attributes and methods during class creation.

**Note:**
Metaclasses are an advanced feature. For most common use cases, decorators, mixins, and abstract base classes provide sufficient flexibility.

## 3. Best Practices

- **Keep It Simple:**
  Use decorators for function/method modifications whenever possible. Reserve metaclasses for cases where you need to control class creation.

- **Readability:**
  Document your decorators and metaclasses thoroughly. Their behavior can be non-obvious, so clear comments and docstrings are essential.

- **Prefer Composition Over Inheritance:**
  In many scenarios, decorators and mixins can provide the needed functionality without the complexity of metaclasses.

- **Use Metaclasses Sparingly:**
  Because metaclasses add a layer of complexity, use them only when necessary to enforce class-level behavior or constraints.

**In Summary**

- **Decorators:**

  - Allow you to modify or extend the behavior of functions and methods without altering their code.
  - Are defined using the @decorator_name syntax and can be parameterized.
  - Useful for logging, validation, caching, and more.

- **Metaclasses:**

  - Define how classes are created and can be used to enforce class-level constraints.
  - Are more advanced and are typically used in framework development or when a uniform interface across many classes is required.
  - Provide powerful customization of class creation, though they should be used sparingly.

By mastering decorators and metaclasses, you gain powerful tools to enhance and streamline your Python code, making it more flexible, modular, and expressive. These advanced concepts open up new possibilities for code reuse and dynamic behavior, contributing to robust and maintainable software design.

## Example Exercises: Plugin Systems

A plugin system is a powerful architectural pattern that enables extensibility and modularity in software design. By decoupling core functionality from additional features, plugin systems allow new capabilities to be added dynamically without modifying the core application code. This is particularly useful for large projects and frameworks, where you may want to extend functionality or allow third-party developers to contribute plugins.

### 1. Designing the Plugin Interface

The first step in creating a plugin system is to define a common interface that all plugins must adhere to. In Python, this is typically done using an abstract base class (ABC) from the abc module.

**Code: Defining the Plugin Interface**

```
from abc import ABC, abstractmethod

class Plugin(ABC):
    """
    Abstract base class for plugins.
    All plugin classes must implement the execute() method.
    """
    @abstractmethod
    def execute(self, data):
        """
        Process the given data.
        Parameters:
            data (str): The data to process.
```

```
    """
    Pass
```

**Explanation:**

- The Plugin class inherits from ABC, marking it as an abstract base class.
- The execute() method is decorated with @abstractmethod, enforcing that any subclass of Plugin must implement this method.
- This ensures a consistent interface across all plugins.

**2. Implementing the Plugin Manager**

A plugin manager is responsible for registering and coordinating the execution of plugins. It maintains a collection of plugins and provides methods to register new plugins and run all registered plugins.

**Code: Creating the Plugin Manager**

```
class PluginManager:
    """
    A manager for registering and executing plugins.
    """
    def __init__(self):
        self.plugins = []
    def register_plugin(self, plugin):
        """
        Register a plugin instance.
        Parameters:
```

```
            plugin (Plugin): An instance of a Plugin subclass.
        """
        self.plugins.append(plugin)

    def run_plugins(self, data):
        """
        Execute the execute() method of all registered plugins.

        Parameters:
            data (str): The data to be processed by each plugin.
        """
        for plugin in self.plugins:
            plugin.execute(data)
# Create a global plugin manager instance
plugin_manager = PluginManager()
```

**Explanation:**

- The PluginManager class maintains a list of plugins.
- The register_plugin() method adds a plugin to the list.
- The run_plugins() method iterates over the registered plugins and calls their execute() method, passing along any necessary data.

**3. Registering Plugins with a Decorator**

To simplify plugin registration, we can create a decorator that automatically registers a plugin with the plugin manager when the plugin class is defined. This reduces boilerplate code and ensures consistency.

**Code: Creating the Registration Decorator**

```
def register_plugin(cls):
    """
    A decorator that registers a plugin class with the global plugin manager.

    Parameters:
        cls (type): The plugin class to register.

    Returns:
        type: The original plugin class.
    """
    # Create an instance of the plugin and register it
    instance = cls()
    plugin_manager.register_plugin(instance)
    return cls
```

**Explanation:**

- The register_plugin decorator takes a class cls as an argument.
- It creates an instance of the class and registers it with the plugin_manager.
- Finally, it returns the class unchanged, allowing it to be used normally.

**4. Creating Concrete Plugin Classes**

Now, we implement a few plugin classes that inherit from the Plugin interface. Each plugin will provide its own implementation of the execute() method.

**Example 1: Plugin for Uppercase Conversion**

```
@register_plugin

class UppercasePlugin(Plugin):

    def execute(self, data):

        print("Uppercase Plugin:", data.upper())
```

Example 2: Plugin for Lowercase Conversion

```
@register_plugin

class LowercasePlugin(Plugin):

    def execute(self, data):

        print("Lowercase Plugin:", data.lower())
```

Example 3: Plugin for Reversing the String

```
@register_plugin

class ReversePlugin(Plugin):

    def execute(self, data):

        print("Reverse Plugin:", data[::-1])
```

**Explanation:**

- Each plugin class is decorated with @register_plugin, ensuring that an instance is automatically created and registered with the plugin manager.
- The plugins implement the execute() method in different ways, showcasing polymorphism.

### 5. Running the Plugin System

Finally, we create a main script that triggers the execution of all registered plugins.

**Code: Running Plugins in a Main Script**

```
if __name__ == "__main__":
    # Data to be processed by plugins
    sample_data = "Hello, Plugin Systems!"
    print("Running all plugins with sample data:")
    plugin_manager.run_plugins(sample_data)
```

Expected Output:

```
Running all plugins with sample data:
Uppercase Plugin: HELLO, PLUGIN SYSTEMS!
Lowercase Plugin: hello, plugin systems!
Reverse Plugin: !smetsyS nigulP ,olleH
```

**Explanation:**

- The if __name__ == "__main__": block ensures that the plugin system runs only when the script is executed directly.
- The plugin_manager.run_plugins(sample_data) call iterates over each registered plugin and executes its execute() method using the provided sample data.

**In Summary**

In this exercise, we built a simple plugin system that demonstrates key advanced OOP concepts:

- **Abstract Base Classes (Interfaces):**
  We defined a Plugin interface that requires an execute() method.
- **Plugin Manager:**
  A centralized manager registers and runs plugins.
- **Decorators for Registration:**
  A decorator (register_plugin) automates plugin registration, reducing boilerplate and ensuring consistency.
- **Polymorphism:**
  Different plugins implement the execute() method differently, but they can all be invoked through the common interface provided by the Plugin class.

By designing your system with these principles, you create a modular and extensible architecture that can be easily expanded with new plugins. This approach not only promotes code reuse but also enhances maintainability and flexibility in your projects.

# Section VII: Error Handling, Testing, and Debugging
# Chapter 16: Error and Exception Handling

## Introduction to Exceptions

In Python, exceptions are events that occur during the execution of a program that disrupt the normal flow of the program's instructions. They are used to handle errors gracefully, allowing a program to continue running or exit cleanly without crashing unexpectedly. Understanding exceptions and how to handle them is critical for writing robust and reliable code.

### 1. What Are Exceptions?

Exceptions are errors detected during execution. Common examples include:

- **Syntax Errors:** Mistakes in the code's syntax (detected before runtime).
- **Runtime Errors:** Issues that occur during program execution, such as division by zero, invalid type operations, or accessing a non-existent file.

When an error occurs, Python raises an exception. If the exception is not handled, the program will terminate and display a traceback.

**Example: Division by Zero**

```
# This code will raise a ZeroDivisionError

result = 10 / 0
```

**Explanation:**

Attempting to divide 10 by 0 triggers a ZeroDivisionError, causing the program to halt if not caught.

### 2. Handling Exceptions with try-except Blocks

The primary mechanism for handling exceptions in Python is the try-except block. This construct allows you to "try" a block of code and "catch" exceptions if they occur, thereby preventing the program from crashing.

**Basic Syntax:**

```
try:
    # Code that might raise an exception
    risky_operation()
except ExceptionType:
    # Code that runs if the specified exception occurs
    handle_exception()
```

Example: Catching a ZeroDivisionError

```
try:
    numerator = 10
    denominator = 0
    result = numerator / denominator
    print("Result:", result)
except ZeroDivisionError:
    print("Error: Cannot divide by zero!")
```

**Explanation:**

- The code inside the try block is executed.
- If a ZeroDivisionError is raised, the except block catches it and executes its code, printing an error message.

### 3. Using Multiple except Clauses

You can handle different types of exceptions by specifying multiple except clauses. This enables you to provide specific responses based on the error type.

#### Example: Handling Different Exceptions

```
try:
    value = int(input("Enter an integer: "))
    result = 100 / value
    print("Result:", result)
except ZeroDivisionError:
    print("Error: Division by zero is not allowed.")
except ValueError:
    print("Error: Please enter a valid integer.")
```

**Explanation:**

- If the user enters a non-integer value, a ValueError is raised.
- If the user enters 0, a ZeroDivisionError is raised.
- Each except clause handles a specific error type, ensuring that the program provides an appropriate message for each scenario.

### 4. The try-except-else-finally Structure

Python provides additional clauses to further refine exception handling:

- **else:**
  Executed if no exceptions occur in the try block.

- **finally:**
  Executed regardless of whether an exception occurred, typically used for cleanup actions.

**Example: Using else and finally**

```
try:
    value = int(input("Enter an integer: "))
except ValueError:
    print("Error: Invalid input.")
else:
    print("You entered:", value)
finally:
    print("Execution completed.")
```

**Explanation:**

- If int(input(...)) executes without raising a ValueError, the else block runs, printing the entered value.
- The finally block runs in all cases, ensuring that "Execution completed." is printed whether an exception was raised or not.

**5. Best Practices for Exception Handling**

**Catch Specific Exceptions:**
Avoid using a bare except: clause. Catch specific exceptions to prevent masking unexpected errors.

```
# Instead of this:
try:
    # code
```

```
except:
    # handle error
# Do this:
try:
    # code
except ValueError:
    # handle ValueError specifically
```

- **Use Else and Finally:**
  Use the else block to run code that should execute only if no exceptions occurred, and the finally block for cleanup actions.
- **Keep try Blocks Small:**
  Limit the scope of the try block to only the code that might raise an exception. This makes it easier to pinpoint which operation caused the error.
- **Log Exceptions:**
  For larger applications, consider logging exceptions using Python's logging module. This is useful for debugging and maintaining your code.
- **Don't Overuse Exceptions for Flow Control:**
  Use exceptions for error handling, not as a regular control flow mechanism.

**In Summary**

Exceptions are a fundamental part of Python, enabling you to handle errors gracefully and keep your programs running even when unexpected issues arise. Key concepts include:

- **try-except Blocks:**
  Allow you to attempt a block of code and handle specific exceptions if they occur.
- **Multiple except Clauses:**
  Enable handling of different exception types with tailored responses.
- **Else and Finally Clauses:**
  Provide additional control: else runs if no exceptions occur, while finally executes regardless of the outcome.
- **Best Practices:**
  Catch specific exceptions, keep try blocks small, and use logging for better error management.

By mastering these techniques, you can write more robust, maintainable, and user-friendly Python code.

## Using try/except/else/finally Blocks

Python's exception handling mechanism allows you to gracefully manage runtime errors and ensure that your programs continue to run or exit cleanly when unexpected conditions occur. The try/except/else/finally structure provides a flexible way to handle errors, execute fallback actions, and perform cleanup tasks.

### 1. The try Block

The try block contains the code that might raise an exception. This is where you place operations that are potentially error-prone.

**Example:**

```
try:
    # Code that may raise an exception
    result = 10 / 2
```

```
    print("Result:", result)
except Exception as e:
    # This block will not execute if no exception occurs
    print("An error occurred:", e)
```

**Explanation:**

- The code within the try block is executed.
- If no exception occurs, the code runs normally.
- In this example, division is safe, so the output will be Result: 5.0.

**2. The except Block**

The except block catches and handles exceptions that occur in the try block. You can specify the type of exception to catch and handle it accordingly.

**Example: Catching a Specific Exception**

```
try:
    result = 10 / 0  # This will raise a ZeroDivisionError
except ZeroDivisionError:
    print("Error: Cannot divide by zero!")
```

**Explanation:**

- When division by zero occurs, a ZeroDivisionError is raised.
- The except ZeroDivisionError block catches this specific exception and executes the corresponding error-handling code.

**Example: Catching Multiple Exceptions**

```
try:
```

```
    value = int("not_a_number")  # This will raise a ValueError
    result = 10 / value
except ZeroDivisionError:
    print("Error: Division by zero!")
except ValueError:
    print("Error: Invalid integer conversion!")
```

**Explanation:**

- Here, if the conversion to an integer fails, a ValueError is raised and caught by the corresponding except block.
- If a ZeroDivisionError occurred instead, it would be caught by its dedicated block.

**3. The else Block**

The else block runs if the try block does **not** raise an exception. It is useful for code that should execute only when no errors occur.

**Example: Using else**

```
try:
    value = int("123")
except ValueError:
    print("Error: Invalid input!")
else:
    # This block runs only if the try block succeeds without raising an
exception.
    print("Conversion successful. Value is:", value)
```

**Explanation:**

- If the conversion to an integer is successful (which it is in this case), the else block is executed.
- The else block is a good place to put code that depends on the successful completion of the try block.

### 4. The finally Block

The finally block contains code that is always executed, regardless of whether an exception occurred or not. It is typically used for cleanup tasks such as closing files or releasing resources.

**Example: Using finally**

```
try:
    file = open("sample.txt", "r")
    data = file.read()
    print("File data:", data)
except FileNotFoundError:
    print("Error: File not found!")
else:
    print("File read successfully!")
finally:
    # This block will execute regardless of the try/except outcome.
    file.close()
    print("File closed.")
```

**Explanation:**

- The try block attempts to open and read a file.

- If the file is not found, the except FileNotFoundError block handles the error.
- If no error occurs, the else block confirms the successful read.
- The finally block executes in either case, ensuring that the file is properly closed.

**5. Combining try/except/else/finally**

You can combine all these blocks to create robust error-handling structures that not only catch exceptions but also handle post-processing and cleanup tasks.

**Comprehensive Example: Data Processing with Cleanup**

```
def process_data(filename):
    try:
        file = open(filename, "r")
        data = file.read()
    except FileNotFoundError as e:
        print(f"Error: {e}")
    else:
        # Process data only if file reading was successful
        print("Data processing started.")
        processed_data = data.upper()  # Example processing: convert
data to uppercase
        print("Processed Data:", processed_data)
    finally:
        # Ensure the file is closed if it was opened
```

```
    try:
        file.close()
        print("File closed successfully.")
    except NameError:
        # 'file' was not defined because open() failed
        print("No file to close.")

# Testing the function
process_data("sample.txt")
```

**Explanation:**

- **try:** Attempts to open and read the file.
- **except:** Catches a FileNotFoundError and prints an error message.
- **else:** Processes the data (converts it to uppercase) if reading is successful.
- **finally:** Ensures that the file is closed whether an exception occurred or not. The inner try/except in finally handles the case where file was never assigned due to an earlier error.

**6. Best Practices for Using try/except/else/finally**

- **Catch Specific Exceptions:**
  Avoid catching all exceptions with a bare except: clause. Catch specific exceptions to handle errors appropriately.
- **Keep try Blocks Small:**
  Limit the code inside a try block to only the operations that

might raise an exception. This makes it easier to identify the source of an error.

- **Use else for Dependent Code:**
  Place code that should only run if no exception occurred in the else block, enhancing clarity.
- **Always Clean Up with finally:**
  Use the finally block to perform cleanup actions such as closing files, releasing locks, or resetting state, regardless of whether an exception occurred.
- **Log Exceptions:**
  In larger applications, consider logging exceptions to help with debugging and monitoring.

**In Summary**

- **try Block:**
  Contains the code that may raise an exception.
- **except Block:**
  Catches and handles exceptions, allowing the program to continue or fail gracefully.
- **else Block:**
  Executes only if the try block does not raise any exceptions.
- **finally Block:**
  Contains cleanup code that always executes, regardless of whether an exception occurred.

By effectively using try/except/else/finally blocks, you can write robust Python programs that handle errors gracefully, perform necessary cleanup, and maintain a smooth user experience even in the face of unexpected conditions.

## Custom Exceptions

Custom exceptions are user-defined exception classes that allow you to signal specific error conditions in your programs. By creating your own exception types, you can provide more informative error messages, better control error handling in your code, and improve the clarity of your code's error management. In Python, custom exceptions are typically created by subclassing the built-in Exception class (or one of its subclasses).

### 1. Why Use Custom Exceptions?

- **Expressiveness:**
  Custom exceptions allow you to convey specific error conditions that are unique to your application. Instead of raising a generic Exception, you can define exceptions like InvalidInputError, DataNotFoundError, or InsufficientFundsError that make the error context clear.

- **Granular Error Handling:**
  When your code raises custom exceptions, you can catch and handle them separately from built-in exceptions. This enables more targeted recovery strategies.

- **Improved Debugging:**
  Custom exceptions can include additional information (via attributes) about the error, which aids in debugging.

### 2. Defining Custom Exceptions

Custom exceptions are defined by subclassing Python's built-in Exception class. You can also add custom attributes or methods to enrich the exception's behavior.

### 2.1 Basic Custom Exception Example

```
class MyCustomError(Exception):

    """A custom exception for specific error conditions."""
```

```
    pass

# Example usage:

def divide(a, b):

    if b == 0:

        raise MyCustomError("Division by zero is not allowed.")

    return a / b

try:

    result = divide(10, 0)

except MyCustomError as e:

    print("Custom Exception Caught:", e)
```

**Explanation:**

- **Defining the Exception:**
  The class MyCustomError subclasses Exception and includes a docstring. It doesn't add any new functionality beyond the base class.
- **Raising the Exception:**
  The divide function raises MyCustomError when an invalid operation (division by zero) is attempted.
- **Handling the Exception:**
  The try/except block catches MyCustomError and prints an informative message.

### 2.2 Custom Exception with Additional Information

Custom exceptions can be extended to carry more contextual information about the error.

```
class InsufficientFundsError(Exception):
```

```
    """Exception raised when an account has insufficient funds for a withdrawal."""
    def __init__(self, balance, amount, message="Insufficient funds for the requested withdrawal."):
        self.balance = balance
        self.amount = amount
        self.message = message
        super().__init__(self.message)
    def __str__(self):
        return f"{self.message} (Balance: ${self.balance:.2f}, Withdrawal: ${self.amount:.2f})"
# Example usage:
def withdraw(balance, amount):
    if amount > balance:
        raise InsufficientFundsError(balance, amount)
    return balance - amount
try:
    new_balance = withdraw(100, 150)
except InsufficientFundsError as e:
    print("Error:", e)
```

**Explanation:**

- **Custom Attributes:**
  The InsufficientFundsError class stores the current balance and attempted withdrawal amount as attributes.

- **Constructor (__init__):**
  It initializes these attributes and calls the base class constructor with a default or provided message.

- **String Representation (__str__):**
  The __str__ method is overridden to provide a detailed error message that includes relevant context.

- **Usage:**
  The withdraw function raises the custom exception if the withdrawal amount exceeds the balance. The try/except block catches the exception and prints a detailed error message.

**3. Best Practices for Custom Exceptions**

- **Inherit from Exception:**
  Always subclass from Exception (or one of its appropriate subclasses) rather than directly from BaseException, to ensure that your exceptions integrate properly with Python's exception handling framework.

- **Be Specific:**
  Define distinct exception classes for different error conditions. This makes your error handling more precise and your code easier to debug.

- **Include Descriptive Docstrings:**
  Document your custom exceptions with clear descriptions of when they are raised and what information they carry.

- **Implement __str__ or __repr__:**
  Overriding these methods provides a meaningful string representation of the exception, which aids in debugging and logging.

- **Raise Exceptions Early:**
  Validate input and state early in your functions to raise exceptions

as soon as an error condition is detected, rather than letting errors propagate later in the code.

**In Summary**

Custom exceptions are a powerful tool in Python for creating specific error conditions that make your code more expressive and easier to debug. Key points include:

- **Defining Custom Exceptions:**
  Subclass Exception and add any additional attributes or methods as needed.
- **Raising Custom Exceptions:**
  Use the raise statement to signal specific error conditions.
- **Handling Custom Exceptions:**
  Use targeted except clauses to catch and handle your custom exceptions appropriately.
- **Best Practices:**
  Write clear, specific exception classes, include meaningful documentation, and implement helpful string representations.

By incorporating custom exceptions into your code, you can create more robust, maintainable, and user-friendly applications that clearly communicate error conditions and support effective debugging.

**Example Exercises**

Graceful error recovery is a crucial aspect of robust software design. Instead of allowing a program to crash when an error occurs, graceful recovery aims to handle errors smoothly, provide meaningful feedback, and keep the application running or exit in a controlled manner. This involves anticipating possible failures, catching exceptions, logging the error details, and implementing fallback or retry mechanisms. Below, we present several example exercises that illustrate strategies for graceful error recovery in Python using try/except/else/finally constructs.

### 1. Example Exercise: Handling User Input with Fallback Values

In this exercise, we write a function that prompts the user for an integer. If the user provides invalid input, the function will catch the exception and use a default value, allowing the program to continue gracefully.

```
def get_integer(prompt, default=0):
    """
    Prompt the user to enter an integer. If the input is invalid,
    catch the exception and return a default value.
    Parameters:
    - prompt (str): The message displayed to the user.
    - default (int, optional): The default value to return in case of invalid input.
    Returns:
    - int: The valid integer entered by the user or the default value.
    """
    try:
        user_input = input(prompt)
        value = int(user_input)
    except ValueError:
        print(f"Warning: Invalid input. Using default value: {default}")
```

```
        value = default
    else:
        print("Input accepted successfully.")
    finally:
        print("Input processing complete.\n")
    return value
# Testing the function
num = get_integer("Enter an integer: ", default=10)
print("Resulting integer:", num)
```

**Explanation:**

- **try:** Attempts to convert the user's input to an integer.
- **except:** Catches a ValueError if the conversion fails, printing a warning and using a default value.
- **else:** Executes if no exception occurs, confirming successful input.
- **finally:** Executes regardless of the outcome, signaling that input processing is complete.
- This approach prevents the program from crashing due to invalid input and ensures continuity.

**2. Example Exercise: Graceful File Handling**

In file operations, errors such as missing files or read/write issues can occur. In this exercise, we attempt to read a file. If the file is not found, the program recovers gracefully by using fallback data and ensures that resources are properly cleaned up.

```
def read_file_content(filename, fallback="Default content"):
```

```
"""
Attempt to read the content of a file. If the file is not found,
catch the exception and return fallback content.
Parameters:
- filename (str): The path to the file.
- fallback (str, optional): Fallback content if the file cannot be read.
Returns:
- str: The content of the file or the fallback content.
"""
try:
    file = open(filename, "r")
    content = file.read()
except FileNotFoundError:
    print(f"Error: File '{filename}' not found. Using fallback
content.")
    content = fallback
except Exception as e:
    print(f"An unexpected error occurred: {e}. Using fallback
content.")
    content = fallback
else:
    print(f"File '{filename}' read successfully.")
finally:
```

```
        try:
            file.close()
            print("File closed.")
        except NameError:
            print("No file to close.")
        print("File processing complete.\n")
    return content
# Testing the function
file_content = read_file_content("non_existent_file.txt")
print("File Content:\n", file_content)
```

**Explanation:**

- **try:** Attempts to open and read a file.
- **except FileNotFoundError:** Catches the error if the file does not exist, then uses fallback content.
- **except Exception:** Catches any other unexpected errors.
- **else:** Executes if the file is read without error.
- **finally:** Ensures that the file is closed if it was opened, even if an error occurred.
- This structure ensures that the program handles file-related errors gracefully without crashing.

**3. Example Exercise: Recovering from Calculation Errors**

In mathematical computations, errors such as division by zero may occur. In this exercise, we design a function that performs a division operation but recovers gracefully by returning a default value when a division error is encountered.

```
def safe_divide(a, b, default=None):
    """
    Perform a division of a by b, recovering gracefully from division by zero.
    Parameters:
    - a (float): The numerator.
    - b (float): The denominator.
    - default (any, optional): The default value to return if division by zero occurs.
    Returns:
    - float or any: The result of the division, or the default value if b is zero.
    """
    try:
        result = a / b
    except ZeroDivisionError:
        print("Error: Division by zero. Returning default value.")
        result = default
    else:
        print("Division performed successfully.")
    finally:
        print("Division operation complete.\n")
```

```
    return result

# Testing the function
print("Result of safe_divide(10, 2):", safe_divide(10, 2))
print("Result of safe_divide(10, 0):", safe_divide(10, 0,
default="Undefined"))
```

**Explanation:**

- **try:** Performs the division.
- **except ZeroDivisionError:** Catches a division by zero error and returns a default value.
- **else:** Confirms successful division when no exception occurs.
- **finally:** Prints a message indicating the operation is complete.
- This function gracefully handles division errors and provides a fallback mechanism.

**4. Best Practices for Graceful Error Recovery**

- **Catch Specific Exceptions:**
  Always target specific exceptions (e.g., ValueError, FileNotFoundError) rather than using a bare except: clause. This prevents masking other unforeseen errors.
- **Use Fallbacks Wisely:**
  When providing fallback values, choose defaults that make sense within the context of your application.
- **Clean Up Resources:**
  Always use the finally block (or context managers) to ensure resources like file handles are properly released.

- **Log Errors:**
  In production systems, consider logging exceptions to a file or logging system to help with debugging and monitoring.
- **Keep try Blocks Focused:**
  Limit the code within a try block to only the statements that might raise exceptions. This makes it easier to isolate and fix issues.

**In Summary**

Graceful error recovery is a fundamental technique for building robust Python applications. By using the try/except/else/finally structure, you can:

- **Prevent Crashes:**
  Handle exceptions without terminating the program abruptly.
- **Provide Fallbacks:**
  Use default values or alternative behaviors when errors occur.
- **Ensure Cleanup:**
  Use the finally block to clean up resources regardless of whether an error occurred.

Through these exercises - handling user input, file operations, and calculation errors - you learn to design error-handling strategies that keep your applications resilient and user-friendly

# Chapter 17: Testing and Debugging

## The Importance of Testing

Testing is a critical aspect of software development that helps ensure your code behaves as expected, prevents regressions, and makes maintenance easier over time. In the context of error handling and debugging, thorough testing allows you to:

- **Catch Bugs Early:**
  Unit tests and integration tests help identify issues in isolated components before they affect the entire application.
- **Ensure Robustness:**
  Testing verifies that your error handling works correctly, so that your application can recover gracefully from unexpected conditions.
- **Facilitate Refactoring:**
  With a robust test suite, you can confidently modify or extend your code, knowing that any changes that break functionality will be caught.
- **Improve Code Quality:**
  Writing tests encourages better design, modularity, and clarity in your code. It forces you to think about the expected behavior of your functions and classes.
- **Document Behavior:**
  Tests serve as a form of living documentation, illustrating how the code is supposed to work and what its edge cases are.

### 1. Types of Testing

- **Unit Testing:**
  Focuses on testing individual functions or methods in isolation.

Unit tests validate that each part of your code behaves correctly on its own.

- **Integration Testing:**
  Ensures that different modules or services work together as expected. Integration tests verify the interactions between components.
- **System Testing:**
  Validates the complete and integrated software to ensure it meets the specified requirements.
- **Regression Testing:**
  After making changes to the code, regression tests ensure that new changes do not break existing functionality.

## 2. Tools for Testing in Python

Python offers several frameworks for testing, with unittest (built-in) and pytest (third-party) being among the most popular.

### 2.1 Using unittest

The unittest module provides a test framework inspired by Java's JUnit. It allows you to create test cases by subclassing unittest.TestCase and defining test methods.

**Example: Unit Test for a Division Function**

Consider a simple division function that handles division by zero gracefully:

```
def safe_divide(a, b):
    """
    Perform division of a by b.
```

```
    Parameters:
        a (float): Numerator.
        b (float): Denominator.
    Returns:
        float: The result of the division.
    Raises:
        ValueError: If b is zero.
    """
    if b == 0:
        raise ValueError("Cannot divide by zero.")
    return a / b
```

Now, we write unit tests for safe_divide:

```
import unittest
class TestSafeDivide(unittest.TestCase):
    def test_division_normal(self):
        # Test normal division
        self.assertAlmostEqual(safe_divide(10, 2), 5.0)
        self.assertAlmostEqual(safe_divide(9, 3), 3.0)
    def test_division_by_zero(self):
        # Test division by zero should raise ValueError
        with self.assertRaises(ValueError):
            safe_divide(10, 0)
```

```
    def test_division_result_type(self):
        # Test that the result is of type float
        result = safe_divide(10, 3)
        self.assertIsInstance(result, float)

if __name__ == "__main__":
    unittest.main()
```

**Explanation:**

- **Test Class:**
  TestSafeDivide subclasses unittest.TestCase.
- **Test Methods:**
  - test_division_normal checks that normal division returns the correct result using assertAlmostEqual for floating-point comparisons.
  - test_division_by_zero verifies that a ValueError is raised when attempting to divide by zero.
  - test_division_result_type ensures that the result of the division is a float.
- **Running Tests:**
  The if __name__ == "__main__": block allows the tests to run when the script is executed directly.

### 2.2 Using pytest

pytest is a popular third-party testing framework that offers a simpler and more powerful syntax. Here's an example using pytest for the same function:

```
import pytest
def safe_divide(a, b):
    if b == 0:
        raise ValueError("Cannot divide by zero.")
    return a / b
def test_division_normal():
    assert safe_divide(10, 2) == 5.0
    assert safe_divide(9, 3) == 3.0
def test_division_by_zero():
    with pytest.raises(ValueError):
        safe_divide(10, 0)
def test_division_result_type():
    result = safe_divide(10, 3)
    assert isinstance(result, float)
# To run these tests, use the command: pytest <script_name>.py
```

**Explanation:**

- **Function-Based Tests:**
  pytest allows you to write tests as simple functions.
- **Assertions:**
  Standard assert statements are used for checking expected outcomes.
- **Exception Testing:**
  The with pytest.raises(ValueError) context manager is used to verify that a ValueError is raised for division by zero.

### 3. The Role of Debugging

Testing is closely tied to debugging:

- **Early Detection:**
  Tests catch errors early, before they make it into production.
- **Reproducibility:**
  Failing tests provide a consistent way to reproduce issues, making debugging easier.
- **Isolation:**
  Unit tests isolate functionality, helping pinpoint the exact location and cause of a problem.
- **Continuous Integration:**
  Automated tests can be integrated into your development workflow to catch regressions.

Debugging tools such as Python's built-in pdb module can be used in conjunction with tests to step through code and inspect variable values.

**Example: Using pdb for Debugging**

```
import pdb

def faulty_function(x):

    result = x * 2

    pdb.set_trace()  # Execution will pause here

    result += 5

    return result

# When you call faulty_function, the debugger will start at
pdb.set_trace()

print(faulty_function(10))
```

**Explanation:**

- The pdb.set_trace() call initiates a breakpoint, allowing you to inspect the state of your program and step through subsequent lines of code.

**4. Best Practices for Testing and Debugging**

- **Write Tests Early:**
  Incorporate testing into your development process early. Test-driven development (TDD) is a methodology where tests are written before code.
- **Keep Tests Small and Focused:**
  Each test should focus on a single functionality or behavior.
- **Automate Testing:**
  Use continuous integration tools to run tests automatically on code changes.
- **Use Debuggers:**
  Utilize tools like pdb or IDE-integrated debuggers to step through code and inspect variables when tests fail.
- **Maintain Clear Documentation:**
  Document the expected behavior of functions and classes in your tests to serve as additional documentation for your codebase.

**In Summary**

Testing is essential for building robust, reliable, and maintainable software. It allows you to catch errors early, debug more effectively, and ensure that your code continues to function as expected as it evolves. Key points include:

- **try/except/else/finally Blocks:**
  Handle errors gracefully and perform necessary cleanup.

- **Custom Exceptions:**
  Create meaningful error messages and manage specific error conditions.
- **Testing Frameworks:**
  Use unittest or pytest to write tests that validate the behavior of your code.
- **Debugging:**
  Incorporate debugging tools to inspect and resolve issues detected by your tests.

By embracing thorough testing and debugging practices, you improve the quality and resilience of your code, making it easier to maintain and extend over time.

## unittest vs. pytest: Basic Usage

Testing is an indispensable part of software development that ensures your code behaves as expected and remains robust as it evolves. In Python, two popular frameworks for writing tests are unittest (a built-in module inspired by Java's JUnit) and pytest (a powerful third-party framework). Both have their strengths and can be used effectively for unit testing and debugging. Below, we compare their basic usage with illustrative code examples.

### 1. Using unittest

unittest is included in Python's standard library. It is based on a class-based approach where test cases are created by subclassing unittest.TestCase. Each test is a method within this subclass that should start with test_.

### Example: Testing a Simple Function with unittest

Let's consider a simple function safe_divide(a, b) that performs division but raises a ValueError if an attempt is made to divide by zero.

```
# safe_divide.py
def safe_divide(a, b):
    """
    Divide a by b and return the result.
    Parameters:
        a (float): Numerator.
        b (float): Denominator.
    Returns:
        float: Result of division.
    Raises:
        ValueError: If b is zero.
    """
    if b == 0:
        raise ValueError("Cannot divide by zero.")
    return a / b
```

Now, we create a test module using unittest to validate the behavior of safe_divide.

```
# test_safe_divide.py
import unittest
from safe_divide import safe_divide
class TestSafeDivide(unittest.TestCase):
    def test_division_normal(self):
        """Test normal division."""
```

```
        self.assertAlmostEqual(safe_divide(10, 2), 5.0)
        self.assertAlmostEqual(safe_divide(9, 3), 3.0)
    def test_division_by_zero(self):
        """Test division by zero raises ValueError."""
        with self.assertRaises(ValueError):
            safe_divide(10, 0)
    def test_result_type(self):
        """Test that the result is of type float."""
        result = safe_divide(10, 3)
        self.assertIsInstance(result, float)
if __name__ == "__main__":
    unittest.main()
```

**Explanation:**

- **Test Class:**
  TestSafeDivide subclasses unittest.TestCase and contains multiple test methods.
- **Test Methods:**
  Each method tests a specific aspect of safe_divide. Methods starting with test_ are automatically discovered and run by unittest.
- **Assertions:**

  - assertAlmostEqual is used for comparing floating-point numbers.
  - assertRaises checks that a ValueError is raised when expected.
  - assertIsInstance confirms the type of the result.

- **Running Tests:**
  Running the script directly will execute all tests via unittest.main().

**2. Using pytest**

pytest is a third-party testing framework that offers a simpler, more flexible syntax. Tests in pytest are written as standalone functions, and assertions are made with simple assert statements.

**Example: Testing the Same Function with pytest**

```
# test_safe_divide_pytest.py

import pytest

from safe_divide import safe_divide

def test_division_normal():

    assert safe_divide(10, 2) == 5.0

    assert safe_divide(9, 3) == 3.0

def test_division_by_zero():

    with pytest.raises(ValueError):

        safe_divide(10, 0)

def test_result_type():

    result = safe_divide(10, 3)

    assert isinstance(result, float)

# To run these tests, simply execute the command:

# pytest test_safe_divide_pytest.py
```

**Explanation:**

- **Function-Based Tests:**
  Each test is defined as a function whose name starts with test_.
- **Assertions:**
  Standard Python assert statements are used, which are more straightforward than unittest assertions.
- **Exception Testing:**
  The pytest.raises context manager is used to check that safe_divide raises a ValueError when dividing by zero.
- **Running Tests:**
  To run tests with pytest, execute the command pytest test_safe_divide_pytest.py in your terminal.

**3. Comparison: unittest vs. pytest**

- **Syntax and Simplicity:**
  - **unittest:**
    - Uses a class-based approach.
    - Requires boilerplate code such as subclassing unittest.TestCase and using specialized assertion methods.
  - **pytest:**
    - Uses simple, function-based tests.
    - Allows the use of plain assert statements, making tests concise and easier to read.
- **Discoverability and Flexibility:**
  - **unittest:**
    - Part of the standard library; no external dependencies.

    - Structured and familiar to developers with backgrounds in other xUnit frameworks.
  - **pytest:**
    - More flexible and extensible with a rich ecosystem of plugins.
    - Automatically discovers tests without the need for boilerplate code.

- **Error Reporting:**
  - **pytest:**
    - Provides detailed and user-friendly error reports.
    - Highlights failed assertions with useful context.

**4. Best Practices for Testing**

- **Write Clear and Focused Tests:**
  Each test should focus on a single aspect of the functionality.
- **Use Meaningful Test Names:**
  Descriptive test names help indicate the purpose of each test.
- **Isolate Tests:**
  Ensure tests are independent; one test's outcome should not affect another.
- **Run Tests Frequently:**
  Integrate tests into your development process using continuous integration tools.

**In Summary**

Testing is essential to ensure the reliability and robustness of your code. Both unittest and pytest offer effective frameworks for writing and running tests:

- **unittest:**

  - Built-in to Python.
  - Uses a class-based approach with a comprehensive set of assertion methods.
- **pytest:**
  - Simpler syntax with function-based tests.
  - More flexible and provides rich, detailed error reports.

By understanding and utilizing these testing frameworks, you can catch bugs early, improve code quality, and maintain a robust and reliable codebase.

## Debugging Techniques

Debugging is a crucial part of the development process. When your code doesn't work as expected, effective debugging techniques help you quickly identify and fix issues. Two common debugging approaches in Python are **print debugging** and using the built-in **Python Debugger (pdb)**.

### 1. Print Debugging

Print debugging is the simplest form of debugging. It involves inserting print statements at strategic locations in your code to output the values of variables, the flow of execution, or the state of the program at specific points.

### 1.1 How to Use Print Debugging

- **Trace Variable Values:**
  Print variable values at various points to verify they hold the expected data.
- **Check Execution Flow:**
  Insert print statements to confirm that certain parts of the code are being executed.

- **Display Error Information:**
  Print error messages or diagnostic information when catching exceptions.

**Example: Print Debugging in Action**

```
def compute_average(numbers):
    # Print the input list for verification
    print("Input numbers:", numbers)
    if not numbers:
        print("Warning: Empty list provided.")
        return None
    total = 0
    for num in numbers:
        total += num
        # Print the running total after adding each number
        print(f"Adding {num}, running total: {total}")
    average = total / len(numbers)
    # Print the final computed average
    print(f"Computed average: {average}")
    return average
# Testing the function with print debugging
result = compute_average([10, 20, 30, 40, 50])
print("Average:", result)
```

**Explanation:**

- Print statements are added to trace the flow of execution and variable values.
- They help verify that the list is processed correctly and that the computed average is as expected.
- Although print debugging is straightforward and quick to implement, it can become cumbersome in larger codebases or in situations where the issue is intermittent.

## 2. Python Debugger (pdb)

For more advanced debugging, Python provides the pdb module—a powerful interactive source code debugger. pdb allows you to pause program execution, inspect variables, step through code line-by-line, and evaluate expressions in real-time.

### 2.1 How to Use pdb

To use pdb, insert pdb.set_trace() at the point in your code where you want to start debugging. When the interpreter reaches this line, it will enter an interactive debugging session.

**Example: Basic Usage of pdb**

```
import pdb

def faulty_function(x):

    result = x * 2

    pdb.set_trace()  # Execution will pause here

    result += 5

    return result

# Run the function to start debugging
```

```
print("Final Result:", faulty_function(10))
```

**Explanation:**

- The pdb.set_trace() call pauses the program execution, and the interactive debugger prompt ((Pdb)) appears.
- In the interactive session, you can:
  - **Inspect Variables:** Use commands like p result to print variable values.
  - **Step Through Code:** Use n (next) to execute the next line, or s (step) to step into function calls.
  - **Continue Execution:** Use c (continue) to resume normal execution until the next breakpoint.
  - **Exit Debugger:** Use q (quit) to exit the debugger and terminate the program.

**2.2 Common pdb Commands**

- **l (list):**
  Display the source code around the current line.
- **p (print):**
  Print the value of an expression (e.g., p x).
- **n (next):**
  Execute the next line of code.
- **s (step):**
  Step into a function call.
- **c (continue):**
  Continue execution until the next breakpoint.
- **q (quit):**
  Exit the debugger and abort the program.

**Example: Debugging with pdb in a Loop**

```
import pdb

def sum_of_list(numbers):
    total = 0
    for num in numbers:
        total += num
        pdb.set_trace()  # Pause here to inspect values during each iteration
    return total

result = sum_of_list([1, 2, 3, 4])
print("Sum of list:", result)
```

**Explanation:**

- This example pauses execution during each iteration of the loop.
- You can inspect the current value of num, total, and other variables to understand the behavior of the loop.

**3. Best Practices for Debugging**

- **Start Simple:**
  Use print debugging for quick checks and small scripts. When issues are more complex or intermittent, switch to using pdb.
- **Remove Debug Statements:**
  Once the issue is resolved, remove or comment out print statements and pdb breakpoints to keep the code clean.
- **Use Logging for Production:**
  For larger projects or production systems, consider using

Python's logging module to record diagnostic information instead of using print statements.

- **Learn pdb Commands:**
  Familiarize yourself with the most common pdb commands to make your debugging sessions more efficient.

- **Isolate Issues:**
  When debugging, try to isolate the problematic code. This may involve writing small test functions or using interactive debugging sessions to narrow down the source of the error.

**In Summary**

Effective debugging is essential for developing robust and reliable software. In Python, you can employ a variety of techniques to diagnose and resolve issues:

- **Print Debugging:**
  A simple, quick method for tracing variable values and execution flow. Best suited for smaller code segments and initial troubleshooting.

- **Python Debugger (pdb):**
  A powerful tool that allows you to interactively inspect, step through, and modify program execution. Ideal for complex bugs or when print debugging becomes unwieldy.

By combining these techniques and following best practices, you can streamline your debugging process, catch errors early, and maintain a high-quality codebase.

**Example Exercises**

Unit tests are an essential part of the software development process. They allow you to verify that individual functions or methods work as expected and help catch bugs early in development. In this section, we'll walk through several example exercises that demonstrate how to write unit tests for small functions. We will use Python's built-in unittest framework, though similar concepts apply when using other testing frameworks like pytest.

### 1. The Importance of Unit Testing

- **Early Bug Detection:**
  Unit tests help catch bugs as soon as they are introduced.
- **Documentation:**
  Tests serve as executable documentation that shows how functions are supposed to behave.
- **Facilitates Refactoring:**
  A comprehensive suite of tests gives you the confidence to change and improve code without introducing new errors.
- **Improves Code Quality:**
  Writing tests encourages modular design and clear function interfaces.

### 2. Writing Unit Tests with the unittest Framework

The unittest framework is included in Python's standard library. To write unit tests with unittest, you need to:

- Create a test module (a Python file starting with test_ is common).
- Import the functions you want to test.
- Create a test class that inherits from unittest.TestCase.
- Define test methods (methods whose names start with test_) that contain assertions.

#### Example Function: safe_divide

Consider a simple function that divides two numbers and handles division by zero by raising a ValueError.

```
# safe_divide.py
def safe_divide(a, b):
    """
    Divide a by b and return the result.
    Parameters:
        a (float): Numerator.
        b (float): Denominator.
    Returns:
        float: The result of the division.
    Raises:
        ValueError: If b is zero.
    """
    if b == 0:
        raise ValueError("Cannot divide by zero.")
    return a / b
```

**Writing Unit Tests for safe_divide Using unittest**

Create a test file (e.g., test_safe_divide.py) with the following content:

```
# test_safe_divide.py
import unittest
from safe_divide import safe_divide
class TestSafeDivide(unittest.TestCase):
    def test_division_normal(self):
```

```
        """Test normal division behavior."""
        self.assertAlmostEqual(safe_divide(10, 2), 5.0)
        self.assertAlmostEqual(safe_divide(9, 3), 3.0)
    def test_division_by_zero(self):
        """Test that division by zero raises ValueError."""
        with self.assertRaises(ValueError):
            safe_divide(10, 0)
    def test_division_result_type(self):
        """Test that the result is a float."""
        result = safe_divide(10, 3)
        self.assertIsInstance(result, float)
if __name__ == "__main__":
    unittest.main()
```

**Explanation:**

- **Test Class:**
  The class TestSafeDivide inherits from unittest.TestCase. Each method whose name starts with test_ is automatically run as a test.
- **Assertions:**
  - assertAlmostEqual is used to compare floating-point values because of precision issues.
  - assertRaises ensures that a ValueError is raised when dividing by zero.
  - assertIsInstance verifies that the returned value is of type float.

- **Running Tests:**
  When you run python test_safe_divide.py from the command line, unittest will execute all tests and report the results.

### 3. Writing Unit Tests with pytest

pytest is another popular testing framework in Python that simplifies writing tests. Its syntax is more concise and relies on Python's built-in assert statement.

**Example: Testing safe_divide with pytest**

Create a test file (e.g., test_safe_divide_pytest.py) with the following content:

```
# test_safe_divide_pytest.py

import pytest

from safe_divide import safe_divide

def test_division_normal():

    assert safe_divide(10, 2) == 5.0

    assert safe_divide(9, 3) == 3.0

def test_division_by_zero():

    with pytest.raises(ValueError):

        safe_divide(10, 0)

def test_division_result_type():

    result = safe_divide(10, 3)

    assert isinstance(result, float)
```

**Explanation:**

- **Function-Based Tests:**
  Each test is a standalone function whose name starts with test_.
- **Assertions:**
  Standard assert statements check the expected outcomes.
- **Exception Testing:**
  The pytest.raises context manager checks that safe_divide(10, 0) raises a ValueError.
- **Running Tests:**
  To run these tests, simply execute pytest in the directory containing the test file.

**4. Best Practices for Writing Unit Tests**

- **Isolate Tests:**
  Each test should focus on a single functionality or edge case.
- **Clear Test Names:**
  Use descriptive names for test methods or functions to indicate what is being tested.
- **Avoid Dependencies:**
  Tests should be independent of each other. One test should not rely on the output or state of another.
- **Use Setup and Teardown:**
  For more complex tests, use setUp() and tearDown() methods (in unittest) or fixtures (in pytest) to prepare and clean up the test environment.
- **Continuous Integration:**
  Integrate your tests into your development process using continuous integration (CI) tools to ensure that code changes do not introduce regressions.

## In Summary

Unit tests are a critical component of robust software development. They:

- **Verify Correctness:**
  Ensure individual functions work as expected.
- **Catch Bugs Early:**
  Identify errors before they propagate into larger systems.
- **Document Behavior:**
  Serve as a form of documentation by showing how functions are intended to be used.
- **Facilitate Refactoring:**
  Provide a safety net that allows you to modify code with confidence.

Both unittest and pytest offer powerful frameworks for writing tests in Python. While unittest is built into the standard library and uses a class-based approach, pytest provides a simpler, function-based syntax with more detailed reporting. By incorporating unit tests into your development workflow, you can improve the reliability, maintainability, and overall quality of your code.

# Section VIII: Working with Files, Data, and the Web
# Chapter 18: File I/O and Data Serialization

## Reading and Writing Files

File input/output (I/O) is a fundamental aspect of many Python applications, enabling you to persist data, read configurations, log information, and process text or binary data.

### 1. Opening Files

In Python, you can open a file using the built-in open() function, which returns a file object. The basic syntax is:

```
file_object = open("filename", "mode")
```

**Common File Modes:**

- "r": Read mode (default). Opens the file for reading.
- "w": Write mode. Opens the file for writing, truncating the file first if it exists.
- "a": Append mode. Opens the file for writing, appending to the end of the file if it exists.
- "b": Binary mode. Can be appended to other modes (e.g., "rb" or "wb") for binary files.
- "x": Exclusive creation mode. Fails if the file already exists.

**Example:**

```
# Open a file in read mode

file = open("example.txt", "r")
```

*Note:* Always ensure that the file exists when opening in read mode to avoid a FileNotFoundError.

## 2. Reading from Files

There are several ways to read the contents of a file:

### 2.1 Using read()

The read() method reads the entire contents of a file as a single string.

```
with open("example.txt", "r") as file:
    content = file.read()
    print("File Content:\n", content)
```

**Explanation:**

- The with statement automatically manages the file resource, ensuring it is properly closed after reading.
- read() returns the complete contents of the file.

### 2.2 Using readline()

The readline() method reads the next line from the file each time it is called.

```
with open("example.txt", "r") as file:
    first_line = file.readline()
    print("First Line:", first_line)
```

**Explanation:**

- readline() reads a single line (including the newline character) from the file.
- Subsequent calls to readline() will read the next lines.

### 2.3 Using readlines()

The readlines() method reads all lines of a file into a list, where each element is a line.

```
with open("example.txt", "r") as file:
    lines = file.readlines()
    print("Lines:", lines)
```

**Explanation:**

- Each element in the list lines represents a line from the file.
- This method is useful for processing files line-by-line.

### 3. Writing to Files

Writing data to files is just as important as reading. Python provides several methods to write text or binary data to files.

#### 3.1 Using write()

The write() method writes a string to the file. If you open a file in "w" mode, it will truncate the file if it already exists.

```
with open("output.txt", "w") as file:
    file.write("Hello, World!\n")
    file.write("This is a test file.\n")
```

**Explanation:**

- Opening the file in "w" mode creates or truncates the file.
- write() writes the specified string to the file.

#### 3.2 Using writelines()

The writelines() method writes a list of strings to the file without adding newlines automatically.

```
lines = ["First line\n", "Second line\n", "Third line\n"]
with open("output.txt", "w") as file:
```

```
    file.writelines(lines)
```

**Explanation:**

- writelines() iterates over the list and writes each string to the file.
- Ensure that each string includes a newline character (\n) if you want each to appear on a separate line.

### 3.3 Appending to Files

To add data to an existing file without truncating it, use the append mode "a".

```
with open("output.txt", "a") as file:
    file.write("This line is appended.\n")
```

**Explanation:**

- The file is opened in append mode, so new content is added to the end of the file without erasing existing content.

## 4. Best Practices for File I/O

- **Use the with Statement:**
  The with statement is highly recommended because it automatically closes the file, even if an error occurs. This prevents resource leaks and ensures that files are properly managed.
- **Handle Exceptions:**
  Use try/except blocks to handle potential errors (e.g., FileNotFoundError, IOError) gracefully.
- **Specify File Encoding:**
  When dealing with text files, especially those that may contain non-ASCII characters, specify the encoding (e.g., encoding="utf-8") to avoid encoding-related issues.

- **Work with Binary Data:**
  When reading or writing binary files (e.g., images, executables), open the file in binary mode ("rb", "wb").

**Example: Handling FileNotFoundError**

```
try:
    with open("nonexistent.txt", "r", encoding="utf-8") as file:
        content = file.read()
except FileNotFoundError:
    print("Error: The file 'nonexistent.txt' was not found.")
```

**In Summary**

Reading and writing files are fundamental operations for many Python programs. Key points include:

- **Opening Files:**
  Use the open() function with appropriate modes ("r", "w", "a", "rb", "wb").
- **Reading Files:**
  - read() to get the entire content as a string.
  - readline() to get one line at a time.
  - readlines() to obtain a list of lines.
- **Writing Files:**
  - write() to write a string to the file.
  - writelines() to write a list of strings.
  - Use append mode ("a") to add content without erasing existing data.

- **Best Practices:**
  Always use the with statement to ensure files are properly closed, handle exceptions to manage errors gracefully, and consider specifying encoding for text files.

By mastering these file I/O operations, you can effectively manage data persistence and perform data serialization, forming a solid foundation for more complex file and data processing tasks.

## Working with CSV, JSON, and XML

Data serialization and file I/O are crucial for many applications, enabling you to store, exchange, and process structured data. Python provides robust support for working with common data formats such as CSV, JSON, and XML.

### 1. Working with CSV Files

CSV (Comma-Separated Values) is a widely used format for storing tabular data. Python's built-in csv module makes it straightforward to read from and write to CSV files.

### 1.1 Reading CSV Files

To read a CSV file, use the csv.reader class. This converts each row of the CSV file into a list of strings.

**Example: Reading a CSV File**

```
import csv

filename = "data.csv"

with open(filename, mode="r", newline='', encoding="utf-8") as file:

    csv_reader = csv.reader(file)

    header = next(csv_reader)  # Read header row (if present)

    print("Header:", header)
```

```
    for row in csv_reader:
        print("Row:", row)
```

**Explanation:**

- The file is opened in read mode ("r") with proper encoding and newline handling.
- csv.reader(file) creates a reader object that iterates over lines in the CSV file.
- The next() function is used to skip the header row, if one exists.
- Each subsequent row is printed as a list of strings.

### 1.2 Writing CSV Files

To write data to a CSV file, use the csv.writer class. This allows you to write rows of data (as lists) to the file.

**Example: Writing to a CSV File**

```
import csv

data = [
    ["Name", "Age", "City"],
    ["Alice", "30", "New York"],
    ["Bob", "25", "Los Angeles"],
    ["Charlie", "35", "Chicago"]
]

filename = "output.csv"

with open(filename, mode="w", newline='', encoding="utf-8") as file:
    csv_writer = csv.writer(file)
```

```
    csv_writer.writerows(data)
print("Data written to", filename)
```

**Explanation:**

- The file is opened in write mode ("w") so that it is created or truncated.
- csv.writer(file) creates a writer object.
- The writerows() method writes all rows from the data list to the file.
- Ensure that each row is a list of strings (or convertible types) for proper CSV formatting.

## 2. Working with JSON Files

JSON (JavaScript Object Notation) is a popular format for data exchange, particularly in web applications. Python's built-in json module makes it easy to serialize (convert objects to JSON) and deserialize (convert JSON back to objects) data.

### 2.1 Reading JSON Files

Use the json.load() function to parse a JSON file into a Python object (typically a dictionary or list).

**Example: Reading a JSON File**

```
import json
filename = "data.json"
with open(filename, mode="r", encoding="utf-8") as file:
    data = json.load(file)
print("JSON Data:", data)
```

**Explanation:**

- The file is opened in read mode with the proper encoding.
- json.load(file) parses the JSON content and returns the corresponding Python data structure.

### 2.2 Writing JSON Files

Use the json.dump() function to serialize a Python object to JSON and write it to a file.

**Example: Writing to a JSON File**

```
import json

data = {
    "name": "Alice",
    "age": 30,
    "city": "New York",
    "hobbies": ["reading", "cycling", "hiking"]
}

filename = "output.json"

with open(filename, mode="w", encoding="utf-8") as file:
    json.dump(data, file, indent=4)

print("JSON data written to", filename)
```

**Explanation:**

- The file is opened in write mode.
- json.dump(data, file, indent=4) serializes the data dictionary into JSON format, with an indentation of 4 spaces for readability.

### 2.3 Converting JSON Strings

You can also convert between JSON strings and Python objects using json.loads() and json.dumps().

**Example: Converting JSON String to Python Object**

```
json_string = '{"name": "Bob", "age": 25, "city": "Los Angeles"}'

data = json.loads(json_string)

print("Parsed JSON:", data)
```

Example: Converting Python Object to JSON String

```
data = {"name": "Charlie", "age": 35, "city": "Chicago"}

json_string = json.dumps(data, indent=4)

print("JSON String:\n", json_string)
```

**Explanation:**

- json.loads(json_string) parses the JSON string into a Python dictionary.
- json.dumps(data, indent=4) serializes the Python dictionary into a formatted JSON string.

## 3. Working with XML Files

XML (eXtensible Markup Language) is another widely used format for structured data, particularly in legacy systems and certain data exchange scenarios. Python's xml.etree.ElementTree module provides tools for parsing and creating XML data.

### 3.1 Parsing XML Files

Use xml.etree.ElementTree to parse XML data into an element tree, which you can then traverse.

**Example: Parsing an XML File**

```
import xml.etree.ElementTree as ET

filename = "data.xml"

# Parse the XML file

tree = ET.parse(filename)

root = tree.getroot()

print("Root tag:", root.tag)

# Iterate through child elements and print their tags and attributes

for child in root:

    print("Child tag:", child.tag, "Attributes:", child.attrib)
```

**Explanation:**

- The XML file is parsed with ET.parse(filename), which returns an ElementTree object.
- getroot() retrieves the root element of the XML.
- You can iterate over the child elements to inspect their tags and attributes.

### 3.2 Creating XML Files

You can also build an XML tree from scratch and write it to a file.

**Example: Creating an XML File**

```
import xml.etree.ElementTree as ET

# Create the root element

root = ET.Element("library")

# Create a sub-element for a book

book1 = ET.SubElement(root, "book", attrib={"id": "1"})
```

```
title1 = ET.SubElement(book1, "title")
title1.text = "Python Programming"
author1 = ET.SubElement(book1, "author")
author1.text = "John Doe"
# Create another book element
book2 = ET.SubElement(root, "book", attrib={"id": "2"})
title2 = ET.SubElement(book2, "title")
title2.text = "Learning XML"
author2 = ET.SubElement(book2, "author")
author2.text = "Jane Smith"
# Create an ElementTree object and write to a file
tree = ET.ElementTree(root)
tree.write("library.xml", encoding="utf-8", xml_declaration=True)
print("XML file 'library.xml' created successfully.")
```

**Explanation:**

- ET.Element("library") creates the root element.
- ET.SubElement() is used to create child elements with optional attributes.
- The tree.write() method writes the XML tree to a file, including an XML declaration.

**4. Best Practices for Working with Data Serialization**

- **Use Context Managers:**
  Always use the with statement when working with file I/O to ensure files are properly closed, even if an error occurs.

- **Handle Exceptions:**
  Wrap file operations in try/except blocks to gracefully handle errors such as missing files or parsing errors.
- **Validate Data:**
  When reading data from external sources, validate that the data is in the expected format before processing.
- **Format Output for Readability:**
  Use parameters like indent in json.dump() or json.dumps() to produce human-readable output when appropriate.
- **Choose the Right Format:**
  Use CSV for tabular data, JSON for hierarchical or web-based data interchange, and XML for structured data where a more verbose and flexible format is needed.

## In Summary

Python's built-in modules for file I/O and data serialization—csv, json, and xml.etree.ElementTree—provide robust tools for handling different data formats:

- **CSV Files:**
  Use the csv module to read and write tabular data.
- **JSON Files:**
  Use the json module to serialize and deserialize data, making it ideal for web applications and configuration files.
- **XML Files:**
  Use xml.etree.ElementTree to parse and create XML data, which is useful for legacy systems and certain data exchange standards.

By mastering these modules and following best practices, you can efficiently manage data persistence, interchange, and processing in your Python applications.

## Example Exercises

In many real-world applications, you need to process and transform data stored in files. Whether you're cleaning data, filtering records, or computing summaries, having a suite of simple data processing tools is invaluable.

### 1. Exercise: CSV Data Filtering and Transformation

**Objective:**

Create a simple tool that reads data from a CSV file, filters rows based on a specific condition, and writes the filtered data to a new CSV file.

**Scenario:**

Suppose you have a CSV file employees.csv with the following content:

```
Name,Department,Salary
Alice,Engineering,90000
Bob,Marketing,55000
Charlie,Engineering,105000
David,HR,48000
Eve,Engineering,98000
```

You want to extract only the rows for employees in the "Engineering" department and write the filtered data to a new CSV file called engineering_employees.csv.

**Implementation:**

```
import csv

def filter_employees_by_department(input_file, output_file, department):
```

```
"""
Read employee data from a CSV file, filter rows by department,
and write the filtered data to a new CSV file.
Parameters:
    input_file (str): Path to the input CSV file.
    output_file (str): Path to the output CSV file.
    department (str): The department to filter by.
"""
try:
    with open(input_file, mode="r", newline='', encoding="utf-8")
as infile:
        reader = csv.DictReader(infile)
        filtered_rows = [row for row in reader if row["Department"]
== department]

    with open(output_file, mode="w", newline='', encoding="utf-
8") as outfile:
        if filtered_rows:
            # Use fieldnames from the first row to maintain header
consistency
            fieldnames = filtered_rows[0].keys()
            writer = csv.DictWriter(outfile, fieldnames=fieldnames)
            writer.writeheader()
            writer.writerows(filtered_rows)
```

```
        else:
            print("No records found for department:", department)
    except Exception as e:
        print("An error occurred:", e)
# Usage example:
filter_employees_by_department("employees.csv",
"engineering_employees.csv", "Engineering")
print("Filtered data has been written to
'engineering_employees.csv'.")
```

**Explanation:**

- The function filter_employees_by_department reads the CSV file using csv.DictReader, which maps each row to a dictionary using the header row as keys.
- It filters rows where the "Department" value matches the specified department.
- The filtered data is then written to a new CSV file using csv.DictWriter, preserving the header.
- Exceptions are caught and printed, ensuring graceful error handling.

**2. Exercise: JSON Data Transformation and Aggregation**

**Objective:**

Develop a tool that reads data from a JSON file, performs a transformation (e.g., sorting and aggregating), and writes the processed data back to another JSON file.

**Scenario:**

Assume you have a JSON file products.json with a list of products and their prices:

```
[
    {"name": "Laptop", "price": 1200},
    {"name": "Smartphone", "price": 800},
    {"name": "Tablet", "price": 500},
    {"name": "Headphones", "price": 150}
]
```

You want to sort the products by price and calculate the total value of all products. Then, output the sorted list along with the total value to a new JSON file called processed_products.json.

**Implementation:**

```
import json
def process_products(input_file, output_file):
    """
    Read product data from a JSON file, sort products by price, calculate the total price,
    and write the results to a new JSON file.
    Parameters:
        input_file (str): Path to the input JSON file.
        output_file (str): Path to the output JSON file.
    """
    try:
```

```
        # Read data from the JSON file
        with open(input_file, "r", encoding="utf-8") as infile:
            products = json.load(infile)
        # Sort products by price (ascending order)
        sorted_products = sorted(products, key=lambda x: x["price"])
        # Calculate total price
        total_value = sum(product["price"] for product in products)
        # Prepare output data
        output_data = {
            "sorted_products": sorted_products,
            "total_value": total_value
        }
        # Write processed data to the output JSON file
        with open(output_file, "w", encoding="utf-8") as outfile:
            json.dump(output_data, outfile, indent=4)
        print("Processed data has been written to", output_file)
    except Exception as e:
        print("An error occurred while processing the products:", e)
# Usage example:
process_products("products.json", "processed_products.json")
```

**Explanation:**

- The function process_products reads a JSON file containing product data.

- Products are sorted by their "price" using the sorted() function with a lambda as the key.
- The total value is computed by summing the "price" for each product.
- The sorted list and the total value are written to a new JSON file with proper formatting using indent=4.
- Exception handling ensures that errors during file I/O or JSON parsing are caught and reported.

### 3. Exercise: Text File Analysis and Reporting

#### Objective:

Write a tool that reads a text file, performs simple text analysis (such as word count and line count), and writes a summary report to a new text file.

#### Scenario:

You have a text file document.txt containing multiple lines of text. Your task is to:

- Count the total number of lines.
- Count the total number of words.
- Write a summary report to a file called report.txt.

#### Implementation:

```
def analyze_text(input_file, report_file):
    """
    Analyze a text file to count the number of lines and words,
    and write a summary report to another file.
```

```
    Parameters:
        input_file (str): Path to the input text file.
        report_file (str): Path to the output report file.
    """
    try:
        with open(input_file, "r", encoding="utf-8") as infile:
            lines = infile.readlines()
        line_count = len(lines)
        word_count = sum(len(line.split()) for line in lines)
        # Create a summary report
        report = (
            f"Text Analysis Report\n"
            f"--------------------\n"
            f"Total Lines: {line_count}\n"
            f"Total Words: {word_count}\n"
        )
        # Write the report to the output file
        with open(report_file, "w", encoding="utf-8") as outfile:
            outfile.write(report)
        print("Report generated successfully in", report_file)
    except Exception as e:
        print("An error occurred while analyzing the text:", e)
```

```
# Usage example:
analyze_text("document.txt", "report.txt")
```

**Explanation:**

- The function analyze_text reads the entire content of the input file using readlines().
- It calculates the number of lines by measuring the length of the list returned.
- The total word count is computed by splitting each line into words and summing their counts.
- A summary report string is constructed and written to the output file.
- Exception handling ensures that any errors during file operations are handled gracefully.

**In Summary**

These example exercises demonstrate how to build simple data processing tools using Python's file I/O and data serialization capabilities:

- **CSV Processing:**
  - Read data from a CSV file.
  - Filter rows based on a condition.
  - Write the filtered data back to a new CSV file.
- **JSON Processing:**
  - Read and parse a JSON file.
  - Sort data and compute aggregates.
  - Serialize and write the processed data to a new JSON file.

- **Text Analysis:**
  - Read a text file.
  - Count lines and words.
  - Generate and write a summary report to another file.

By mastering these techniques, you can create robust tools for data processing and analysis, which are essential for handling real-world data in your Python applications.

# Chapter 19: Network and Web Services

## HTTP Requests

Interacting with web services is a fundamental aspect of modern applications. Python's requests library simplifies the process of sending HTTP requests and handling responses, making it a popular choice for network programming and web data retrieval.

### 1. Introduction to the requests Library

The requests library provides an easy-to-use API for sending HTTP/1.1 requests. It abstracts many of the complexities of HTTP requests behind a simple interface, allowing you to focus on the logic of your application.

#### Installation

If you haven't installed the requests library yet, you can do so using pip:

```
pip install requests
```

Importing the Library

```
import requests
```

### 2. Making HTTP GET Requests

A GET request is used to retrieve information from a server. With requests, making a GET request is straightforward.

#### Example: Basic GET Request

```
import requests

# Send a GET request to a URL

response = requests.get("https://api.github.com")
```

```
# Check the status code of the response
print("Status Code:", response.status_code)
# Print the response content (as text)
print("Response Content:", response.text)
```

**Explanation:**

- The requests.get() function sends a GET request to the specified URL.
- The response object contains information such as the status code and the content returned by the server.
- The status code helps determine if the request was successful (e.g., 200) or if an error occurred.

**Example: GET Request with Query Parameters**

```
import requests
# Define query parameters as a dictionary
params = {
    "q": "python programming",  # Search query
    "sort": "stars",
    "order": "desc"
}
# Send a GET request with query parameters
response =
requests.get("https://api.github.com/search/repositories",
params=params)
# Parse the JSON response
```

```
data = response.json()
print("Total repositories found:", data.get("total_count"))
```

**Explanation:**

- Query parameters are passed as a dictionary to the params argument in requests.get().
- The server returns a JSON response, which can be parsed using the .json() method.
- This example demonstrates searching for repositories related to "python programming" on GitHub and printing the total count.

### 3. Making HTTP POST Requests

A POST request is used to send data to a server, often resulting in a change in state or side effects on the server.

**Example: Basic POST Request**

```
import requests
# Data to be sent in the POST request (can be a dictionary)
data = {
    "username": "example_user",
    "password": "securepassword123"
}
# Send a POST request to a hypothetical login endpoint
response = requests.post("https://httpbin.org/post", data=data)
# Parse and print the JSON response
print("Response JSON:", response.json())
```

**Explanation:**

- The requests.post() function sends data to the specified URL.
- In this example, data is sent as form data.
- The server (httpbin.org in this case) echoes the request in its JSON response, which is parsed using .json().

**Example: POST Request with JSON Data**

```
import requests

import json

# Data to be sent as JSON

json_data = {

    "title": "Sample Post",

    "body": "This is a sample post created using the requests library.",

    "userId": 1

}

# Send a POST request with JSON payload

response =
requests.post("https://jsonplaceholder.typicode.com/posts",
json=json_data)

# Print the JSON response from the server

print("Created Post:", response.json())
```

**Explanation:**

- Using the json parameter in requests.post(), the data is automatically serialized to JSON.

- The response is parsed as JSON and printed, simulating the creation of a new post.

### 4. Customizing Requests with Headers

Sometimes, you need to send additional metadata with your requests, such as authentication tokens or content type information. This is achieved by specifying HTTP headers.

**Example: GET Request with Custom Headers**

```
import requests

headers = {

    "User-Agent": "MyApp/1.0",

    "Accept": "application/json"

}

response = requests.get("https://api.github.com", headers=headers)

print("Response Headers:", response.headers)
```

**Explanation:**

- The headers parameter allows you to include custom HTTP headers in your request.
- The example sets a custom User-Agent and specifies that the client expects a JSON response.

### 5. Error Handling with Requests

Proper error handling is crucial for robust network communication. The requests library provides a way to check for HTTP errors using the raise_for_status() method and exception handling.

**Example: Handling HTTP Errors**

```
import requests
```

```
url = "https://api.github.com/nonexistent_endpoint"
try:
    response = requests.get(url)
    # Raise an HTTPError if the HTTP request returned an unsuccessful status code
    response.raise_for_status()
    print("Response JSON:", response.json())
except requests.exceptions.HTTPError as http_err:
    print(f"HTTP error occurred: {http_err}")
except Exception as err:
    print(f"Other error occurred: {err}")
```

**Explanation:**

- The raise_for_status() method checks the response status code and raises an HTTPError for bad responses (4xx or 5xx status codes).
- The try/except block catches the exception and prints an informative message.
- This approach ensures that your program handles errors gracefully and provides meaningful feedback to the user.

**6. Best Practices for Using the requests Library**

- **Use Context Managers:**
  While the requests library handles connections automatically, using context managers (via the with statement) when dealing with file uploads or streaming responses can help ensure resources are properly managed.

- **Set Timeouts:**
  Always specify a timeout for your requests to prevent your application from hanging indefinitely if the server does not respond.

```
response = requests.get("https://api.github.com", timeout=5) # Timeout after 5 seconds
```

- **Handle Exceptions:**
  Catch specific exceptions such as requests.exceptions.HTTPError or requests.exceptions.ConnectionError to provide detailed error handling.
- **Use Secure Connections:**
  Always use HTTPS to ensure that your data is transmitted securely over the network.

**In Summary**

The requests library is a powerful tool for making HTTP requests in Python. Key points include:

- **GET Requests:**
  Retrieve data from a server, with support for query parameters.
- **POST Requests:**
  Send data to a server, supporting both form data and JSON payloads.
- **Custom Headers:**
  Add metadata to your requests via the headers parameter.
- **Error Handling:**
  Use raise_for_status() and exception handling to manage HTTP errors gracefully.

- **Best Practices:**
  Set timeouts, use secure connections, and handle exceptions to create robust network applications.

By mastering these techniques, you can build applications that interact with web services effectively, process data from remote sources, and handle errors gracefully.

## Consuming and Creating API

APIs (Application Programming Interfaces) allow different software systems to communicate with each other. REST (Representational State Transfer) is one of the most popular architectural styles for designing networked applications. In RESTful APIs, resources are identified via URLs and manipulated using standard HTTP methods such as GET, POST, PUT, and DELETE.

### 1. Consuming REST APIs

Consuming an API means sending HTTP requests to a web service and processing the responses. Python's requests library is a powerful tool for this purpose.

### 1.1 Making a GET Request

A GET request is used to retrieve information from a server. Here's an example of making a GET request to a public API (e.g., the GitHub API):

```
import requests

# URL of the API endpoint

url = "https://api.github.com"

# Sending a GET request

response = requests.get(url)

# Check if the request was successful
```

```
if response.status_code == 200:
    # Parsing the JSON response
    data = response.json()
    print("API Response:")
    print(data)
else:
    print(f"Request failed with status code: {response.status_code}")
```

**Explanation:**

- The requests.get() function sends a GET request to the specified URL.
- If the response status code is 200, indicating success, the response is parsed as JSON.
- The resulting data is printed; otherwise, an error message is displayed.

### 1.2 Making a POST Request

A POST request sends data to the server. Often, this is used to create a new resource. Below is an example using a test API provided by httpbin.org.

```
import requests
# URL for a test POST request
url = "https://httpbin.org/post"
# Data to be sent in the request (as form data)
payload = {
    "username": "test_user",
```

```
    "password": "securepassword"
}
# Sending a POST request with data
response = requests.post(url, data=payload)
# Parsing the JSON response
if response.status_code == 200:
    data = response.json()
    print("POST Response JSON:")
    print(data)
else:
    print(f"POST request failed with status code: {response.status_code}")
```

**Explanation:**

- The requests.post() function sends data (here as form data) to the specified URL.
- The server echoes back the data in JSON format, which we parse and print.

### 1.3 Setting Headers and Parameters

Sometimes, APIs require additional headers (such as authentication tokens) or query parameters. Here's an example:

```
import requests
# URL of an API endpoint that accepts query parameters
url = "https://api.github.com/search/repositories"
```

```
# Query parameters as a dictionary
params = {
    "q": "python programming",
    "sort": "stars",
    "order": "desc"
}
# Custom headers
headers = {
    "User-Agent": "MyApp/1.0",
    "Accept": "application/vnd.github.v3+json"
}
# Sending the GET request with headers and parameters
response = requests.get(url, params=params, headers=headers)
if response.status_code == 200:
    data = response.json()
    print("Search Results:")
    print(data)
else:
    print(f"Search request failed with status code:
{response.status_code}")
```

**Explanation:**

- Query parameters and custom headers are passed to the get() function.

- The API responds with data based on the specified search criteria.

## 2. Creating REST APIs

Creating a REST API allows you to expose your application's functionality over the web. Frameworks like Flask make it easy to build APIs in Python. Below is an example of creating a simple REST API using Flask.

### 2.1 Installing Flask

If you don't have Flask installed, you can install it using pip:

```
pip install Flask
```

### 2.2 Creating a Simple Flask API

Create a file named app.py with the following content:

```
from flask import Flask, request, jsonify

app = Flask(__name__)

# In-memory data store for demonstration purposes

items = [

    {"id": 1, "name": "Item One", "price": 9.99},

    {"id": 2, "name": "Item Two", "price": 19.99},

    {"id": 3, "name": "Item Three", "price": 29.99}

]

@app.route('/items', methods=['GET'])

def get_items():

    """Retrieve all items."""

    return jsonify(items), 200
```

```
@app.route('/items/<int:item_id>', methods=['GET'])
def get_item(item_id):
    """Retrieve an item by its ID."""
    item = next((item for item in items if item["id"] == item_id),
None)
    if item:
        return jsonify(item), 200
    else:
        return jsonify({"error": "Item not found"}), 404
@app.route('/items', methods=['POST'])
def create_item():
    """Create a new item."""
    new_item = request.get_json()
    new_item["id"] = len(items) + 1
    items.append(new_item)
    return jsonify(new_item), 201
if __name__ == "__main__":
    app.run(debug=True)
```

**Explanation:**

- **Flask Application Setup:**
  The Flask application is created using Flask(__name__).
- **Routes:**

- /items (GET): Returns all items in JSON format.
- /items/<int:item_id> (GET): Retrieves a specific item based on its ID.
- /items (POST): Accepts JSON data to create a new item, assigns a new ID, and appends it to the list.

- **JSON Responses and HTTP Status Codes:**
  The API returns JSON responses with appropriate HTTP status codes (e.g., 200 for success, 404 for not found, 201 for created).

- **Running the API:**
  When you run app.py, Flask starts a development server, and you can interact with your API using tools like curl, Postman, or your web browser.

### 2.3 Testing Your API

You can test your API using the requests library or tools like Postman. Here's an example of how to test your API with Python's requests library:

```
import requests

# URL of the running Flask API (assuming it runs on localhost:5000)

base_url = "http://127.0.0.1:5000"

# Test GET /items

response = requests.get(f"{base_url}/items")

print("GET /items:", response.json())

# Test GET /items/1

response = requests.get(f"{base_url}/items/1")

print("GET /items/1:", response.json())
```

```
# Test POST /items to create a new item
new_item = {"name": "Item Four", "price": 39.99}
response = requests.post(f"{base_url}/items", json=new_item)
print("POST /items:", response.json())
```

**Explanation:**

- The testing script sends GET and POST requests to your API and prints the JSON responses.
- This demonstrates how the API can be consumed by client applications.

**3. Best Practices for Consuming and Creating REST APIs**

- **Use Clear and Consistent Endpoints:**
  Design your API endpoints to be intuitive and consistent. Use standard HTTP methods (GET, POST, PUT, DELETE) to represent actions.
- **Properly Handle HTTP Status Codes:**
  Return meaningful HTTP status codes that accurately reflect the outcome of a request (e.g., 200 for success, 201 for resource creation, 404 for not found).
- **Validate and Sanitize Data:**
  Always validate input data on the server side to prevent errors and potential security issues.
- **Use JSON for Data Exchange:**
  JSON is lightweight and widely supported. Ensure your API consistently uses JSON for both requests and responses.
- **Secure Your API:**
  Implement authentication and authorization as needed, and use HTTPS to secure data transmission.

## In Summary

Interacting with web services through REST APIs is a critical skill in modern software development. Python's requests library simplifies consuming APIs, while frameworks like Flask make it easy to create your own APIs. Key points include:

- **Consuming APIs:**
  - Use GET, POST, and other HTTP methods to interact with web services.
  - Handle query parameters, headers, and errors effectively.
- **Creating APIs:**
  - Design clear and consistent endpoints using Flask.
  - Return JSON responses with appropriate HTTP status codes.
- **Best Practices:**
  - Validate and sanitize input data.
  - Secure your API using HTTPS and proper authentication.

By mastering these techniques, you can build applications that effectively interact with external services and expose your own functionality via RESTful APIs.

## Example Exercises

Interacting with public APIs is a common task in modern software development. Public APIs allow you to retrieve and use data from external sources, enabling your applications to integrate with various web services. In Python, the requests library simplifies the process of sending HTTP requests and handling responses.

### 1. Understanding Public APIs

A public API is an interface provided by a service that allows developers to access data or functionality over the web. Common tasks when consuming an API include:

- **Sending HTTP requests** (typically GET, POST, etc.)
- **Parsing responses** (usually in JSON format)
- **Handling errors** and exceptions that may occur during the request

In this example, we will use the Coindesk API to fetch the current Bitcoin price.

### 2. Fetching Data Using the requests Library

#### Step 1: Import the requests Library

Before making HTTP requests, ensure you have the requests library installed. If not, install it using:

```
pip install requests
```

Then, import it in your script:

```
import requests
```

#### Step 2: Define a Function to Fetch Data

We will define a function that:

- Sends a GET request to the API endpoint.
- Checks the response status.
- Parses the JSON response.
- Extracts and returns specific data (e.g., the current Bitcoin price in USD and the update time).

```
def fetch_bitcoin_price():
    """
    Fetch the current Bitcoin price in USD from the Coindesk API.

    Returns:
        tuple: A tuple containing the Bitcoin price as a string and the
updated time, or None if an error occurs.
    """
    url = "https://api.coindesk.com/v1/bpi/currentprice.json"
    try:
        # Send a GET request to the API endpoint with a timeout of 5
seconds.
        response = requests.get(url, timeout=5)
        # Raise an HTTPError for bad responses (status codes 4xx or
5xx)
        response.raise_for_status()
    except requests.exceptions.RequestException as e:
        # Handle any request-related errors (connection issues,
timeouts, invalid responses)
        print(f"Error fetching data: {e}")
        return None
    else:
        # Parse the JSON response
        data = response.json()
```

```
        # Extract the current Bitcoin price in USD and the updated
time
        bitcoin_price = data["bpi"]["USD"]["rate"]
        updated_time = data["time"]["updated"]
        return bitcoin_price, updated_time
# Testing the function
result = fetch_bitcoin_price()
if result:
    price, updated = result
    print(f"Current Bitcoin price: ${price}")
    print(f"Updated at: {updated}")
```

**Explanation:**

- **Request Execution:**
  The function sends a GET request to the Coindesk API. A timeout is specified to avoid waiting indefinitely.
- **Error Handling:**
  The try block attempts to fetch data. If any exception occurs (e.g., network issues, HTTP errors), it is caught by the except block, and a meaningful error message is printed.
- **Response Processing:**
  On a successful request, response.raise_for_status() ensures the response status is OK (200). The response JSON is parsed, and the required data (Bitcoin price and update time) is extracted.
- **Return Value:**
  The function returns a tuple with the extracted data. If an error occurs, it returns None.

### 3. Best Practices for Fetching Data from Public APIs

- **Set a Timeout:**
  Always specify a timeout to prevent your application from hanging if the API is slow to respond.
- **Check Response Status:**
  Use response.raise_for_status() to catch HTTP errors immediately.
- **Handle Exceptions Gracefully:**
  Use try/except blocks to manage potential errors, and provide informative error messages to aid debugging.
- **Parse Responses Carefully:**
  Verify that the expected keys exist in the JSON response to avoid KeyError exceptions.
- **Document Your Code:**
  Include docstrings and comments explaining the purpose of your function, the API endpoint being used, and any assumptions made about the data format.

### In Summary

Fetching data from public APIs is a fundamental skill for integrating external data sources into your Python applications. Key steps include:

- **Sending HTTP Requests:**
  Use the requests library to send GET requests to API endpoints.
- **Error Handling:**
  Implement robust error handling using try/except blocks and response.raise_for_status() to manage network errors and bad responses.

- **Parsing and Extracting Data:**
  Parse the JSON response and extract relevant information for use in your application.

- **Best Practices:**
  Always set a timeout, check the response status, and handle exceptions gracefully.

By mastering these techniques, you can build applications that consume web services reliably and efficiently.

# Chapter 20: Databases and Persistence

## SQLite with Python

SQLite is a lightweight, file-based relational database that is built into Python via the sqlite3 module. It is ideal for small to medium-sized applications, prototyping, and applications that require an embedded database without the overhead of a separate database server.

### 1. Introduction to SQLite in Python

SQLite is a self-contained, serverless, zero-configuration, transactional SQL database engine. In Python, the sqlite3 module provides a straightforward interface for interacting with SQLite databases. When you connect to an SQLite database file, if the file does not exist, SQLite automatically creates it.

### 2. Connecting to an SQLite Database

To start working with SQLite, you first need to establish a connection to a database file using sqlite3.connect(). It is best practice to use a context manager (with statement) to ensure that the connection is properly closed.

**Example: Connecting to a Database**

```
import sqlite3

# Connect to an SQLite database (or create it if it doesn't exist)

connection = sqlite3.connect("example.db")

# Create a cursor object to execute SQL commands

cursor = connection.cursor()

# Always remember to close the connection when done

connection.close()
```

**Explanation:**

- The sqlite3.connect("example.db") call connects to the database file example.db. If it doesn't exist, SQLite creates it.
- A cursor object is created using connection.cursor() to execute SQL commands.
- Finally, closing the connection is essential to free up resources.

### 3. Creating Tables

Once connected, you can create tables using SQL commands. Here's an example of creating a simple table to store employee information.

**Example: Creating a Table**

```
import sqlite3

with sqlite3.connect("example.db") as conn:
    cursor = conn.cursor()
    # Create a table named 'employees'
    cursor.execute("""
        CREATE TABLE IF NOT EXISTS employees (
            id INTEGER PRIMARY KEY AUTOINCREMENT,
            name TEXT NOT NULL,
            department TEXT,
            salary REAL
        )
    """)
    conn.commit()  # Commit the changes to the database
```

```
print("Table 'employees' created successfully.")
```

**Explanation:**

- The CREATE TABLE IF NOT EXISTS SQL statement creates the employees table if it does not already exist.
- The table includes an auto-incrementing primary key (id), a non-null text field for name, and fields for department and salary.
- The conn.commit() call ensures that the changes are saved.

**4. Inserting Data**

Inserting data into the database is done using the INSERT SQL command. Parameter substitution should be used to prevent SQL injection attacks.

**Example: Inserting Data into a Table**

```
import sqlite3

with sqlite3.connect("example.db") as conn:

    cursor = conn.cursor()

    # Define employee data

    employee_data = [

        ("Alice", "Engineering", 90000),

        ("Bob", "Marketing", 55000),

        ("Charlie", "Engineering", 105000),

        ("David", "HR", 48000)

    ]
```

```
    # Insert multiple rows using executemany()
    cursor.executemany("""
        INSERT INTO employees (name, department, salary)
        VALUES (?, ?, ?)
    """, employee_data)
    conn.commit()
print("Employee data inserted successfully.")
```

**Explanation:**

- executemany() is used to insert multiple rows efficiently.
- The question marks (?) are placeholders for the actual data, which are supplied as a tuple for each row.
- This method helps prevent SQL injection and ensures data is safely inserted.

### 5. Querying Data

Querying data involves executing a SELECT statement to retrieve data from the database. The results can be fetched using methods like fetchone() or fetchall().

**Example: Querying the Database**

```
import sqlite3
with sqlite3.connect("example.db") as conn:
    cursor = conn.cursor()
    # Execute a SELECT query
    cursor.execute("SELECT id, name, department, salary FROM employees WHERE department = ?", ("Engineering",))
```

```
    # Fetch all matching rows
    rows = cursor.fetchall()
print("Engineering Department Employees:")
for row in rows:
    print(f"ID: {row[0]}, Name: {row[1]}, Department: {row[2]}, Salary: ${row[3]:,.2f}")
```

**Explanation:**

- The SELECT statement retrieves data from the employees table where the department is "Engineering".
- fetchall() returns a list of all matching rows.
- The results are then printed in a formatted manner.

**6. Updating and Deleting Data**

Updating and deleting records are essential operations for managing your data. These operations use the UPDATE and DELETE SQL commands.

**Example: Updating Data**

```
import sqlite3
with sqlite3.connect("example.db") as conn:
    cursor = conn.cursor()
    # Update the salary of a specific employee
    cursor.execute("""
        UPDATE employees
        SET salary = ?
        WHERE name = ?
```

```
    """, (95000, "Alice"))
    conn.commit()
print("Employee salary updated successfully.")
```

Example: Deleting Data

```
import sqlite3
with sqlite3.connect("example.db") as conn:
    cursor = conn.cursor()
    # Delete an employee record
    cursor.execute("DELETE FROM employees WHERE name = ?",
("David",))
    conn.commit()
print("Employee record deleted successfully.")
```

**Explanation:**

- The UPDATE statement modifies existing records, while the DELETE statement removes records.
- Parameter substitution is used in both cases to safely pass data to the SQL statements.
- Changes are committed to the database using conn.commit().

**7. Best Practices for Working with SQLite in Python**

- **Use Context Managers:**
  Always use the with statement when working with file I/O or databases. This ensures that connections are properly closed, even if errors occur.

- **Parameter Substitution:**
  Use parameterized queries (using ? placeholders) to prevent SQL injection and ensure data integrity.
- **Commit Changes:**
  Always call commit() after executing statements that modify the database to persist changes.
- **Handle Exceptions:**
  Wrap database operations in try/except blocks to catch and handle potential errors (e.g., connection issues, SQL syntax errors).
- **Modularize Database Operations:**
  Organize your database code into functions or classes for better reusability and maintenance.

**In Summary**

Working with SQLite in Python allows you to efficiently manage persistent data using a lightweight, file-based database. Key operations include:

- **Connecting to a Database:**
  Use sqlite3.connect() with context managers for safe resource handling.
- **Creating Tables:**
  Use SQL CREATE TABLE statements to define the structure of your data.
- **Inserting Data:**
  Use parameterized queries with executemany() or execute() for safe data insertion.
- **Querying Data:**
  Retrieve data using SQL SELECT statements and fetch methods.

- **Updating and Deleting Data:**
  Modify and remove records using UPDATE and DELETE statements.
- **Best Practices:**
  Use context managers, parameter substitution, error handling, and modularization to build robust and maintainable database applications.

By mastering these file I/O and data serialization techniques with SQLite, you lay a strong foundation for building applications that require persistent data storage and complex data processing.

## Introduction to ORMs

Object-Relational Mapping (ORM) is a programming technique that allows developers to interact with databases using object-oriented paradigms instead of writing raw SQL queries. ORMs map database tables to classes and rows to objects, enabling you to work with persistent data in a more intuitive and Pythonic way. Two of the most popular ORMs in the Python ecosystem are **SQLAlchemy** and the **Django ORM**.

### 1. What is an ORM?

An ORM abstracts the database interactions into objects and methods. This approach offers several advantages:

- **Productivity:** Write database queries using Python code, reducing boilerplate and avoiding manual SQL syntax.
- **Maintainability:** The code is easier to read and maintain, as it adheres to the principles of object-oriented programming.
- **Portability:** ORMs often allow you to switch database backends (e.g., SQLite, PostgreSQL, MySQL) with minimal code changes.
- **Security:** Parameterized queries are automatically used, which helps prevent SQL injection attacks.

## 2. SQLAlchemy

SQLAlchemy is a powerful and flexible ORM for Python. It provides both a high-level ORM interface and a low-level SQL expression language for those who need more control over their queries.

### 2.1 Setting Up SQLAlchemy

First, install SQLAlchemy using pip:

```
pip install sqlalchemy
```

### 2.2 Basic Example with SQLAlchemy

In this example, we will:

- Define a database model for a simple User table.
- Create the database (using SQLite for simplicity).
- Insert and query data using SQLAlchemy's ORM interface.

```
from sqlalchemy import create_engine, Column, Integer, String
from sqlalchemy.ext.declarative import declarative_base
from sqlalchemy.orm import sessionmaker
# Define the base class for declarative models
Base = declarative_base()
# Define the User model
class User(Base):
    __tablename__ = 'users'
    id = Column(Integer, primary_key=True)
    name = Column(String)
    age = Column(Integer)
```

```
    def __repr__(self):
        return f"<User(name='{self.name}', age={self.age})>"
# Create an SQLite engine
engine = create_engine('sqlite:///example.db', echo=True)
# Create all tables in the database
Base.metadata.create_all(engine)
# Create a session for interacting with the database
Session = sessionmaker(bind=engine)
session = Session()
# Inserting data: Create new User instances
user1 = User(name='Alice', age=30)
user2 = User(name='Bob', age=25)
session.add(user1)
session.add(user2)
session.commit()
# Querying data: Retrieve all users
users = session.query(User).all()
print("All Users:", users)
# Querying data: Filter users by age
young_users = session.query(User).filter(User.age < 30).all()
print("Users under 30:", young_users)
```

```
# Close the session

session.close()
```

**Explanation:**

- **Declarative Base:**
  declarative_base() creates a base class for all our ORM models.
- **Model Definition:**
  The User class represents a table in the database. Attributes such as id, name, and age are mapped to columns.
- **Engine Creation:**
  The engine connects to an SQLite database (example.db). The echo=True parameter logs generated SQL statements.
- **Session Management:**
  A session is created to interact with the database. Data is inserted by adding instances to the session and committing.
- **Querying:**
  SQLAlchemy's ORM interface allows querying using Python expressions.
- **Cleanup:**
  The session is closed after operations are complete.

### 3. Django ORM

Django ORM is part of the Django web framework and provides a high-level abstraction for database interactions. It allows developers to define database models as Python classes and automatically generates SQL queries.

### 3.1 Setting Up Django (Simplified Overview)

First, install Django:

```
pip install Django
```

Create a Django project and an app:

```
django-admin startproject myproject

cd myproject

python manage.py startapp myapp
```

### 3.2 Defining a Model with Django ORM

Inside your Django app (myapp), define a model in models.py:

```
# myapp/models.py

from django.db import models

class User(models.Model):

    name = models.CharField(max_length=100)

    age = models.IntegerField()

    def __str__(self):

        return f"{self.name} ({self.age})"
```

**Explanation:**

- **Model Definition:**
  The User class inherits from models.Model, which tells Django to treat it as a database model.
- **Field Types:**
  CharField and IntegerField are used to define columns in the database.
- **String Representation:**
  The __str__ method provides a readable string representation for instances.

### 3.3 Running Migrations and Interacting with the Database

After defining your model, run migrations to create the corresponding table in your database.

```
python manage.py makemigrations

python manage.py migrate
```

You can then interact with the database using Django's shell:

```
python manage.py shell
```

Within the Django shell, execute the following:

```
from myapp.models import User

# Create new User instances

user1 = User(name="Alice", age=30)

user2 = User(name="Bob", age=25)

user1.save()

user2.save()

# Query the database

all_users = User.objects.all()

print("All Users:", list(all_users))

young_users = User.objects.filter(age__lt=30)

print("Users under 30:", list(young_users))
```

**Explanation:**

- **Model Import and Object Creation:**
  Users are created by instantiating the User class and calling save() to persist them.

- **Querying:**
  The User.objects.all() method retrieves all user records, and User.objects.filter(age__lt=30) filters users with age less than 30.
- **Django ORM:**
  Provides a clean and Pythonic way to interact with the database without writing raw SQL.

**4. Best Practices for Using ORMs**

- **Abstract Database Logic:**
  Encapsulate database access within models and use the ORM's query methods instead of raw SQL whenever possible.
- **Optimize Queries:**
  Use features like select_related() and prefetch_related() in Django ORM or SQLAlchemy's eager loading options to optimize performance.
- **Handle Exceptions:**
  Always handle potential exceptions (e.g., DoesNotExist, IntegrityError) that may arise during database operations.
- **Maintain Migrations:**
  Keep your database schema in sync with your models using migrations, and document changes thoroughly.
- **Use Virtual Environments:**
  Isolate your project dependencies using virtual environments to ensure consistent behavior across different development and production systems.

**In Summary**

Both SQLAlchemy and Django ORM provide powerful abstractions for interacting with databases in Python:

- **SQLAlchemy:**
  - A flexible, powerful ORM that supports both high-level ORM queries and low-level SQL expression language.
  - Suitable for projects where fine-grained control over SQL is necessary.
- **Django ORM:**
  - Integrated with the Django web framework, offering a high-level and intuitive interface for model management.
  - Provides automatic migrations and a robust query system out-of-the-box.

By mastering these ORMs, you can develop applications that interact with databases in a more maintainable, secure, and efficient manner.

## Example Exercises

Storing and retrieving records from a database is a common task in many applications, from web development to data analysis. Python's built-in sqlite3 module provides an easy and efficient way to work with a lightweight, file-based SQLite database.

### 1. Creating the Database and Table

The first step is to create a database file and define a table structure. In our example, we will create a table named students with columns for an auto-incrementing ID, name, age, and grade.

**Code: Creating the Table**

```
import sqlite3

def create_table():
    """
    Create a 'students' table in the database if it does not already exist.
```

```
    """

    # Connect to the SQLite database (creates the file if it doesn't exist)

    with sqlite3.connect("records.db") as conn:

        cursor = conn.cursor()

        # SQL statement to create the 'students' table

        cursor.execute("""

            CREATE TABLE IF NOT EXISTS students (

                id INTEGER PRIMARY KEY AUTOINCREMENT,

                name TEXT NOT NULL,

                age INTEGER,

                grade TEXT

            )

        """)

        conn.commit()

    print("Table 'students' created successfully.")


# Call the function to create the table

create_table()
```

**Explanation:**

- The create_table() function connects to (or creates) a database file named records.db.

- It executes a SQL CREATE TABLE IF NOT EXISTS command to create the students table with the specified columns.
- The use of with ensures the connection is properly closed after the operations.

## 2. Inserting Records into the Table

Next, we will insert multiple student records into the students table using the executemany() method to efficiently handle multiple inserts.

**Code: Inserting Records**

```
def insert_records():
    """
    Insert multiple student records into the 'students' table.
    """
    # Sample data: list of tuples representing students (name, age,
grade)
    students = [
        ("Alice", 20, "A"),
        ("Bob", 22, "B"),
        ("Charlie", 19, "A"),
        ("Diana", 21, "C")
    ]
    with sqlite3.connect("records.db") as conn:
        cursor = conn.cursor()
        # Use parameterized query to insert data safely
        cursor.executemany("""
```

```
        INSERT INTO students (name, age, grade)
        VALUES (?, ?, ?)
    """, students)
    conn.commit()
  print("Student records inserted successfully.")
# Call the function to insert records
insert_records()
```

**Explanation:**

- The insert_records() function defines a list of student tuples.
- The cursor.executemany() method inserts each tuple into the students table using a parameterized query, which helps prevent SQL injection.
- Changes are committed to persist the data.

### 3. Retrieving Records from the Table

Retrieving records involves executing SQL SELECT statements to query the data. We will demonstrate how to retrieve all records and filter records based on specific criteria.

#### 3.1 Retrieving All Records

```
def retrieve_all_records():
    """
    Retrieve all records from the 'students' table.
    Returns:
        list: A list of tuples representing all student records.
    """
```

```
    with sqlite3.connect("records.db") as conn:
        cursor = conn.cursor()
        cursor.execute("SELECT id, name, age, grade FROM students")
        rows = cursor.fetchall()
    return rows

# Fetch and display all student records
all_students = retrieve_all_records()
print("All Student Records:")
for student in all_students:
    print(student)
```

**Explanation:**

- The retrieve_all_records() function executes a SELECT query to fetch all columns from the students table.
- fetchall() returns a list of tuples, with each tuple representing a record.
- The retrieved records are printed in a loop.

### 3.2 Retrieving Filtered Records

We can also retrieve records that meet certain conditions. For example, let's filter students with a grade of "A".

```
def retrieve_by_grade(target_grade):
    """
    Retrieve student records with a specific grade.
    Parameters:
```

```
        target_grade (str): The grade to filter by.
    Returns:
        list: A list of tuples representing the filtered student records.
    """
    with sqlite3.connect("records.db") as conn:
        cursor = conn.cursor()
        cursor.execute("SELECT id, name, age, grade FROM students
WHERE grade = ?", (target_grade,))
        rows = cursor.fetchall()
    return rows
# Fetch and display students with grade 'A'
grade_a_students = retrieve_by_grade("A")
print("\nStudents with Grade A:")
for student in grade_a_students:
    print(student)
```

**Explanation:**

- The retrieve_by_grade() function accepts a grade as a parameter and uses it to filter records.
- A parameterized query (?) is used to safely insert the target grade into the SQL statement.
- The filtered records are fetched and printed.

**4. Best Practices for File I/O and Database Operations**

- **Use Context Managers:**
  Always use the with statement when connecting to the database

to ensure that connections are closed properly, even if an error occurs.

- **Parameterized Queries:**
  Always use parameterized queries (?) to prevent SQL injection and ensure safe insertion of data.

- **Commit Changes:**
  Remember to call conn.commit() after executing INSERT, UPDATE, or DELETE operations to persist the changes.

- **Error Handling:**
  Consider wrapping your database operations in try/except blocks to handle exceptions gracefully and log errors for debugging.

- **Modular Code:**
  Organize database operations into functions or classes to promote code reuse and maintainability.

**In Summary**

In this exercise, we built a simple data processing tool that demonstrates how to:

- **Create a Database and Table:**
  Use sqlite3 to connect to a database file and create a table with SQL.

- **Insert Records:**
  Insert multiple records into the table using parameterized queries and executemany().

- **Retrieve Records:**
  Query the database to retrieve all records or filter records based on specific criteria.

- **Best Practices:**
  Use context managers, parameterized queries, proper commit

operations, and error handling to create robust and maintainable code.

By mastering these techniques, you can build applications that efficiently store, retrieve, and process data using SQLite, forming a solid foundation for more advanced database interactions in your Python projects.

# Section IX: Advanced Topics
# Chapter 21: Concurrent and Parallel Programming

## Threads and the Global Interpreter Lock (GIL)

Concurrency and parallelism are essential concepts in modern programming, enabling your applications to perform multiple tasks simultaneously. In Python, one common approach to concurrency is through the use of threads. However, Python's threading model is unique due to the Global Interpreter Lock (GIL), which affects how threads execute in a multi-core environment.

### 1. Understanding Threads in Python

#### 1.1 What Are Threads?

- **Definition:**
  Threads are lightweight units of execution within a process. They allow a program to perform multiple operations concurrently.
- **Use Cases:**
  Threads are ideal for I/O-bound tasks (such as network operations, file I/O, or waiting for user input) because they allow the program to continue processing while waiting for external events.

#### 1.2 Creating and Running Threads

Python provides the threading module to work with threads. You can create a new thread by instantiating threading.Thread and specifying a target function that the thread will execute.

**Example: Simple Thread Example**

```
import threading

import time

def print_numbers():
```

```
    for i in range(1, 6):
        print(f"Number: {i}")
        time.sleep(1)
# Create a thread that runs the print_numbers function
number_thread = threading.Thread(target=print_numbers)
# Start the thread
number_thread.start()
# Main thread continues executing while the new thread runs
print("Main thread continues to run concurrently.")
number_thread.join()  # Wait for the thread to finish before exiting
print("Thread has finished execution.")
```

**Explanation:**

- A new thread is created to run the print_numbers function.
- The start() method begins thread execution.
- The main thread prints a message and then waits for the number_thread to finish using join().

**2. The Global Interpreter Lock (GIL)**

**2.1 What is the GIL?**

- **Definition:**
  The Global Interpreter Lock (GIL) is a mutex that protects access to Python objects, preventing multiple threads from executing Python bytecode concurrently. This lock is necessary because Python's memory management is not thread-safe.

- **Implications:**
  - **Concurrency vs. Parallelism:**
    While threads allow for concurrent I/O-bound operations, the GIL means that CPU-bound tasks do not run in true parallel on multi-core processors. Only one thread executes Python code at a time, limiting performance improvements for CPU-bound programs.
- **Example Scenario:**
  A program performing heavy numerical computations might not benefit from Python threads due to the GIL, whereas a program waiting for network responses can see improvements by using threads.

## 2.2 Demonstrating the GIL with a CPU-bound Task

Consider a CPU-bound task like calculating a large Fibonacci number. Using threads in this scenario will not result in significant speed improvements due to the GIL.

**Example: CPU-bound Task with Threads**

```
import threading

import time

def fibonacci(n):

    """Calculate the nth Fibonacci number (inefficient recursive implementation)."""

    if n <= 1:

        return n

    else:

        return fibonacci(n - 1) + fibonacci(n - 2)
```

```
def worker(task_id, n):
    start_time = time.time()
    result = fibonacci(n)
    end_time = time.time()
    print(f"Task {task_id}: Fibonacci({n}) = {result} computed in
{end_time - start_time:.2f} seconds.")
# Create threads for CPU-bound tasks
n = 30  # Relatively high to demonstrate CPU-bound work
threads = []
for i in range(2):
    thread = threading.Thread(target=worker, args=(i+1, n))
    threads.append(thread)
    thread.start()
# Wait for all threads to complete
for thread in threads:
    thread.join()
```

**Explanation:**

- Two threads are created to calculate the 30th Fibonacci number.
- Due to the GIL, these threads do not truly run in parallel for this CPU-bound task. They compete for the GIL, so the total execution time may be similar to running the task sequentially.
- This example illustrates that while threads are useful for I/O-bound tasks, they may not provide performance benefits for CPU-bound tasks.

### 3. Overcoming the GIL for CPU-bound Tasks

For CPU-bound tasks that require true parallelism, consider alternatives such as:

- **Multiprocessing:**
  The multiprocessing module creates separate processes that have their own Python interpreter and memory space, bypassing the GIL.

- **C Extensions:**
  Writing performance-critical code in C or using libraries like NumPy can help mitigate GIL limitations.

- **Asyncio:**
  Although not a solution for CPU-bound tasks, asyncio can improve concurrency in I/O-bound applications.

### 4. Best Practices for Using Threads in Python

- **Use Threads for I/O-bound Operations:**
  Threads are best suited for tasks that wait for external events, such as network I/O or file operations.

- **Avoid CPU-bound Tasks with Threads:**
  For tasks that require heavy computation, use the multiprocessing module or optimize the code using C extensions.

- **Keep Threading Code Simple:**
  Debugging multithreaded applications can be challenging. Keep your threading logic as simple as possible and use thread-safe practices.

- **Leverage Thread Synchronization:**
  Use locks, semaphores, or other synchronization primitives provided by the threading module when threads need to access shared resources.

- **Monitor and Profile:**
  Use profiling tools to monitor the performance of multithreaded applications and understand the impact of the GIL on your specific workload.

**In Summary**

- **Threads in Python:**
  Threads allow for concurrent execution of code, particularly beneficial for I/O-bound tasks.
- **Global Interpreter Lock (GIL):**
  The GIL prevents multiple threads from executing Python bytecode simultaneously, which limits parallelism for CPU-bound tasks.
- **Practical Implications:**
  - For I/O-bound operations, threads can improve responsiveness.
  - For CPU-bound operations, consider using the multiprocessing module or other alternatives to achieve true parallelism.
- **Best Practices:**
  Use threads wisely, synchronize shared resources, and choose the right tool (threads vs. processes) based on the nature of your task.

Understanding the role of the GIL and how to work effectively with threads is crucial for designing concurrent applications in Python. While threads provide a convenient way to manage I/O-bound tasks, knowing their limitations helps you choose the right approach for CPU-intensive operations.

## Multiprocessing

Multiprocessing is a powerful technique in Python that enables true parallelism by utilizing multiple processes, each with its own Python interpreter and memory space. Unlike threads - which are constrained by the Global Interpreter Lock (GIL) and thus primarily beneficial for I/O-bound tasks - multiprocessing is especially useful for CPU-bound tasks.

### 1. Introduction to Multiprocessing

**Key Points:**

- **True Parallelism:**
  Each process runs independently in its own memory space and interpreter, bypassing the GIL. This allows CPU-bound tasks to run concurrently on multiple cores.
- **Isolation:**
  Processes are isolated from each other, which can improve stability because an error in one process does not affect others.
- **Communication Overhead:**
  Inter-process communication (IPC) is more expensive than intra-thread communication. Use IPC mechanisms (like Queue or Pipe) only when necessary.

### 2. Basic Usage with multiprocessing.Process

The multiprocessing.Process class allows you to create and manage individual processes. Here's a simple example that demonstrates how to create a process to perform a task concurrently.

**Example: Creating and Running Processes**

```
import multiprocessing

import time

def worker(num):

    """

    A simple worker function that simulates a task by sleeping.
```

```
    Parameters:
        num (int): An identifier for the worker.
    """
    print(f"Worker {num} started.")
    time.sleep(2)
    print(f"Worker {num} finished.")
if __name__ == '__main__':
    # Create a list to hold process objects
    processes = []
    # Create and start 5 processes
    for i in range(5):
        p = multiprocessing.Process(target=worker, args=(i,))
        p.start()
        processes.append(p)
    # Wait for all processes to finish
    for p in processes:
        p.join()
    print("All processes have completed.")
```

**Explanation:**

- **Process Creation:**
  Each Process is created with the target function worker and an argument representing its identifier.

- **Starting Processes:**
  The start() method initiates the process, and they run concurrently.
- **Joining Processes:**
  The join() method ensures that the main program waits for all processes to complete before continuing.
- **Simulated Task:**
  The worker function sleeps for 2 seconds to simulate a CPU-bound task.

### 3. Using multiprocessing.Pool for Parallel Processing

For tasks that require applying the same function to multiple inputs, the multiprocessing.Pool class provides a convenient way to distribute work across multiple processes.

**Example: Calculating Squares Using a Pool**

```
from multiprocessing import Pool

def square(x):

    """

    Calculate the square of a number.

    Parameters:

        x (int): A number.

    Returns:

        int: The square of the number.

    """

    return x * x
```

```
if __name__ == '__main__':
    # Create a pool of 4 worker processes
    with Pool(4) as pool:
        # Map the square function to a range of numbers from 0 to 9
        results = pool.map(square, range(10))
    print("Squares:", results)
```

**Explanation:**

- **Pool Creation:**
  A pool of 4 processes is created, which allows up to 4 tasks to be executed concurrently.
- **Mapping Function:**
  The map() method applies the square function to each number in the given range. The pool distributes these tasks across the available processes.
- **Result Collection:**
  The results are gathered into a list, which is printed after all processes complete.

### 4. Inter-Process Communication

While processes do not share memory, you can communicate between them using IPC mechanisms provided by the multiprocessing module, such as Queue and Pipe. Below is a simple example using a Queue.

**Example: Using Queue for Communication**

```
import multiprocessing

def worker(queue, num):
    """
```

```
    Worker function that puts a computed value into the queue.
    Parameters:
        queue (multiprocessing.Queue): The queue to store the result.
        num (int): A number to process.
    """
    result = num * num
    queue.put(result)
    print(f"Worker {num} computed {result}")
if __name__ == '__main__':
    # Create a queue for inter-process communication
    result_queue = multiprocessing.Queue()
    processes = []
    # Start several worker processes
    for i in range(5):
        p = multiprocessing.Process(target=worker, args=(result_queue,
i))
        p.start()
        processes.append(p)
    # Wait for all processes to complete
    for p in processes:
        p.join()
    # Retrieve results from the queue
    results = [result_queue.get() for _ in range(5)]
```

```
print("Results from queue:", results)
```

**Explanation:**

- **Queue Creation:**
  A multiprocessing.Queue is used to collect results from multiple processes.
- **Worker Function:**
  Each worker computes the square of its input and puts the result into the queue.
- **Result Collection:**
  After all processes finish, the main process retrieves and prints the results from the queue.

**5. Best Practices for Multiprocessing**

- **Use if __name__ == '__main__':**
  Protect the entry point of your program to avoid unintended behavior when using multiprocessing on Windows.
- **Minimize Shared State:**
  Keep data shared between processes to a minimum to avoid the complexities of synchronization.
- **Monitor Resource Usage:**
  Creating too many processes can overwhelm the system. Use process pools and limit the number of concurrent processes.
- **Handle Exceptions in Worker Functions:**
  Ensure that worker functions catch and handle exceptions, and use queues or logs to report errors back to the main process.
- **Profile Performance:**
  Use profiling tools to monitor the performance gains from parallelism and to identify potential bottlenecks.

### In Summary

Multiprocessing in Python provides a robust way to achieve true parallelism for CPU-bound tasks by running code in separate processes. Key takeaways include:

- **Multiprocessing vs. Threads:**
  Multiprocessing overcomes the limitations imposed by the GIL, enabling true parallel execution on multiple CPU cores.
- **Creating Processes:**
  Use multiprocessing.Process to create individual processes and join() to wait for their completion.
- **Process Pools:**
  The multiprocessing.Pool class simplifies applying functions concurrently to multiple inputs.
- **Inter-Process Communication:**
  Use queues or pipes to exchange data between processes.
- **Best Practices:**
  Protect the entry point, minimize shared state, handle exceptions, and monitor resource usage.

By mastering the multiprocessing module, you can design and implement applications that efficiently leverage multiple CPU cores, significantly enhancing performance for CPU-intensive tasks.

## Asyncio for Asynchronous Programming

Asynchronous programming enables your application to perform tasks concurrently without the need for multiple threads or processes. In Python, the asyncio module provides a framework for writing asynchronous code using the async/await syntax. This approach is particularly effective for I/O-bound and high-level structured network code.

## 1. Introduction to Asynchronous Programming

Asynchronous programming is designed to handle operations that may involve waiting (such as network requests, file I/O, or time delays) without blocking the execution of your program. Instead of waiting for an operation to complete, your program can continue executing other tasks. The key benefits include:

- **Improved Responsiveness:**
  Your application remains responsive while waiting for I/O operations to finish.
- **Efficient Resource Usage:**
  Avoids the overhead of threading or multiprocessing for I/O-bound tasks.
- **Scalability:**
  Easily handles many simultaneous operations without creating a large number of threads or processes.

## 2. Getting Started with Asyncio

### 2.1 Basic Concepts

- **async def:**
  Declares an asynchronous function (also called a coroutine). These functions can pause their execution using the await keyword.
- **await:**
  Used within an async def function to suspend execution until an awaitable (such as another coroutine, a Task, or a Future) completes.
- **Event Loop:**
  The core of the asyncio framework that schedules and runs asynchronous tasks.

## 2.2 A Simple Asynchronous Function

Below is an example of a basic asynchronous function that simulates a delay using asyncio.sleep().

```
import asyncio

async def say_hello():

    print("Hello...")

    await asyncio.sleep(1)  # Simulate an I/O-bound operation (non-blocking sleep)

    print("...World!")

# Running the coroutine using asyncio.run (available in Python 3.7+)

asyncio.run(say_hello())
```

**Explanation:**

- The async def say_hello() function is a coroutine that prints "Hello...", waits asynchronously for 1 second using await asyncio.sleep(1), then prints "...World!".
- asyncio.run() starts the event loop, runs the coroutine until it completes, and then closes the loop.

### 3. Managing Multiple Asynchronous Tasks

One of the strengths of asyncio is its ability to run multiple coroutines concurrently. You can schedule multiple tasks and wait for them to complete using functions like asyncio.gather().

**Example: Running Multiple Coroutines Concurrently**

```
import asyncio

async def fetch_data(task_id, delay):

    print(f"Task {task_id} starting...")
```

```
    await asyncio.sleep(delay)
    print(f"Task {task_id} completed after {delay} seconds.")
    return f"Data from task {task_id}"
async def main():
    # Schedule three tasks concurrently
    tasks = [
        fetch_data(1, 2),
        fetch_data(2, 3),
        fetch_data(3, 1)
    ]
    # Wait for all tasks to complete and collect results
    results = await asyncio.gather(*tasks)
    print("All tasks completed. Results:", results)
# Run the main coroutine
asyncio.run(main())
```

**Explanation:**

- The fetch_data coroutine simulates an I/O-bound operation by sleeping for a given delay.
- The main coroutine creates a list of tasks and runs them concurrently using asyncio.gather().
- asyncio.gather(*tasks) returns the results of all tasks once they have completed.

## 4. Advanced Features: Creating Tasks and Canceling

### 4.1 Creating Tasks Explicitly

Sometimes you might want to create tasks explicitly using asyncio.create_task(). This is useful when you want tasks to run concurrently while performing other operations.

```
import asyncio

async def periodic_task():

    for i in range(3):

        print(f"Periodic task iteration {i + 1}")

        await asyncio.sleep(1)

async def main():

    task = asyncio.create_task(periodic_task())

    print("Main coroutine continues to run concurrently.")

    await task

    print("Periodic task has finished.")

asyncio.run(main())
```

**Explanation:**

- asyncio.create_task(periodic_task()) schedules periodic_task() to run concurrently as a Task.
- The main coroutine continues executing while the task runs in the background.
- Awaiting the task ensures that the main coroutine waits for its completion.

### 4.2 Canceling Tasks

Tasks can be canceled if they are no longer needed, using the cancel() method.

```
import asyncio

async def long_running_task():
    try:
        for i in range(10):
            print(f"Working... {i}")
            await asyncio.sleep(1)
    except asyncio.CancelledError:
        print("Long-running task was cancelled.")
        raise

async def main():
    task = asyncio.create_task(long_running_task())
    await asyncio.sleep(3)  # Let the task run for 3 seconds
    print("Cancelling the long-running task.")
    task.cancel()
    try:
        await task
    except asyncio.CancelledError:
        print("Task has been successfully cancelled.")

asyncio.run(main())
```

**Explanation:**

- The long_running_task() function runs in a loop and can be canceled.
- In main(), the task is allowed to run for 3 seconds before calling cancel().
- The task catches the asyncio.CancelledError and performs cleanup if necessary.
- The cancellation is confirmed by handling the exception.

**5. Best Practices for Asynchronous Programming with Asyncio**

- **Use asyncio.run():**
  In Python 3.7+, prefer asyncio.run() to start and manage the event loop.
- **Keep Coroutines Focused:**
  Each coroutine should have a single responsibility. This makes them easier to test, reuse, and maintain.
- **Avoid Blocking Calls:**
  Do not use blocking I/O operations in asynchronous functions. Use asynchronous libraries and methods instead.
- **Handle Exceptions in Coroutines:**
  Always handle exceptions in your asynchronous code, especially in long-running or background tasks.
- **Use asyncio.gather() for Concurrent Execution:**
  To run multiple tasks concurrently and wait for all of them, use asyncio.gather(). It provides a simple way to manage a group of coroutines.
- **Measure Performance:**
  Use tools like asyncio.run() in combination with logging or

profiling to understand and optimize the performance of your asynchronous code.

**In Summary**

Asyncio is a powerful framework in Python for writing asynchronous, non-blocking code. Key points include:

- **Coroutines:**
  Defined using async def and paused/resumed with await.
- **Event Loop:**
  The core mechanism that schedules and runs asynchronous tasks.
- **Concurrent Execution:**
  Use asyncio.gather() and asyncio.create_task() to run multiple coroutines concurrently.
- **Task Management:**
  Tasks can be explicitly created, awaited, and canceled to manage long-running operations.
- **Best Practices:**
  Avoid blocking operations, handle exceptions gracefully, and ensure your asynchronous code is modular and focused.

By mastering asyncio, you can build highly concurrent applications that handle I/O-bound tasks efficiently and scale to handle many simultaneous operations.

**Example Exercises**

A concurrent downloader is a practical application that demonstrates how to leverage asynchronous programming to perform multiple network I/O operations simultaneously. In contrast to sequential downloads that wait for each HTTP request to complete before starting the next, a concurrent downloader initiates multiple downloads in parallel. This approach is particularly useful for I/O-bound tasks, such as fetching data from multiple URLs, as it can significantly reduce total download time.

In Python, the asyncio module in combination with an asynchronous HTTP client library like aiohttp enables you to build such concurrent applications efficiently. In this exercise, we will build a concurrent downloader that fetches content from a list of URLs concurrently and processes the results.

### 1. Setting Up the Environment

Before we begin, you need to install the aiohttp library. You can install it via pip:

```
pip install aiohttp
```

### 2. Building the Concurrent Downloader

Below is a comprehensive example that demonstrates how to build a concurrent downloader using asyncio and aiohttp.

### 2.1 Code Example: Concurrent Downloader

```
import asyncio

import aiohttp

async def fetch(session, url):

    """

    Asynchronously fetch the content from a URL using the provided session.

    Parameters:

        session (aiohttp.ClientSession): The HTTP session to use for making the request.

        url (str): The URL to fetch.
```

```
    Returns:
        tuple: A tuple containing the URL and the fetched content as
text.
    """
    try:
        async with session.get(url) as response:
            # Check for HTTP errors
            response.raise_for_status()
            # Read the response content as text
            content = await response.text()
            print(f"Successfully fetched {url}")
            return url, content
    except Exception as e:
        print(f"Error fetching {url}: {e}")
        return url, None
async def download_all(urls):
    """
    Create an aiohttp session and concurrently fetch all URLs.
    Parameters:
        urls (list): A list of URLs to fetch.
    Returns:
        dict: A dictionary mapping each URL to its fetched content.
    """
```

```
    results = {}
    async with aiohttp.ClientSession() as session:
        # Schedule a fetch task for each URL
        tasks = [fetch(session, url) for url in urls]
        # Wait for all tasks to complete
        responses = await asyncio.gather(*tasks)
        # Map the responses to the results dictionary
        for url, content in responses:
            results[url] = content
    return results
def main():
    # Define a list of URLs to download (for demonstration, using
example URLs)
    urls = [
        "https://www.example.com",
        "https://httpbin.org/get",
        "https://jsonplaceholder.typicode.com/posts/1",
        "https://api.github.com"
    ]
    # Run the asynchronous download_all function
    results = asyncio.run(download_all(urls))
    # Process and display results
    for url, content in results.items():
```

```
    if content:
        print(f"\nContent from {url} (first 200 characters):\n{content[:200]}...\n")
    else:
        print(f"\nNo content fetched from {url}.\n")

if __name__ == "__main__":
    main()
```

### 3. Explanation of the Code

### 3.1 The fetch Coroutine

- **Purpose:**
  The fetch function is an asynchronous coroutine that takes an aiohttp session and a URL. It performs an HTTP GET request and returns the URL along with the fetched content.
- **Error Handling:**
  A try/except block catches and reports any errors (e.g., network issues, HTTP errors) during the fetch operation. If an error occurs, it returns None as the content.
- **Usage of async with:**
  The async with session.get(url) statement ensures that the HTTP connection is properly managed and closed after the request completes.

### 3.2 The download_all Coroutine

- **Purpose:**
  This coroutine creates an aiohttp.ClientSession and uses list comprehension to schedule concurrent fetch tasks for all provided URLs.

- **Concurrency:**
  asyncio.gather(*tasks) concurrently runs all the fetch tasks and waits until they are all complete.

- **Result Aggregation:**
  The responses (each a tuple of URL and content) are processed and stored in a dictionary, mapping each URL to its corresponding content.

### 3.3 The main Function

- **Purpose:**
  The main function defines a list of URLs and uses asyncio.run() to execute the download_all coroutine.

- **Processing Results:**
  The returned dictionary of results is iterated over, and for each URL, a snippet (first 200 characters) of the fetched content is printed. If no content was fetched, it notifies the user accordingly.

## 4. Best Practices for Concurrent Downloading

- **Use Asynchronous I/O for I/O-bound Tasks:**
  Asynchronous programming with asyncio and aiohttp is ideal for network operations where the program waits for external responses.

- **Handle Exceptions Gracefully:**
  Implement error handling in each asynchronous task to catch issues without crashing the entire application.

- **Resource Management:**
  Use context managers (e.g., async with) to ensure that network resources (HTTP sessions) are properly closed after use.

- **Limit Concurrency if Needed:**
  In real-world applications, consider using semaphores or limiting

the number of concurrent connections to avoid overwhelming the server or network.

- **Monitor Performance:**
  Use logging and profiling tools to monitor the performance of your concurrent downloads and adjust parameters (like timeouts and concurrency limits) accordingly.

**In Summary**

This exercise demonstrates how to build a concurrent downloader using Python's asynchronous programming capabilities:

- **Asyncio and Aiohttp:**
  Together, they allow you to send multiple HTTP requests concurrently, significantly improving the efficiency of I/O-bound operations.

- **Concurrent Execution:**
  By scheduling tasks with asyncio.gather(), you can fetch data from multiple URLs simultaneously.

- **Error Handling:**
  Each fetch operation is wrapped in error handling to ensure that issues with one URL do not disrupt the overall process.

- **Best Practices:**
  Use context managers, limit concurrency appropriately, and handle exceptions to create robust networked applications.

By mastering these techniques, you can build efficient, scalable applications that interact with web services and process data concurrently.

# Chapter 22: Functional Programming Techniques

## Map, Filter, and Reduce

Functional programming techniques allow you to write code that is more concise, declarative, and often easier to reason about. In Python, three core functions facilitate functional programming on iterables: **map**, **filter**, and **reduce**. These functions allow you to transform, filter, and aggregate data, respectively, in a functional style.

### 1. The map() Function

The map() function applies a given function to each item in an iterable (such as a list) and returns an iterator yielding the results.

**Basic Syntax**

```
map(function, iterable)
```

Example: Squaring Numbers

```
def square(x):
    return x * x
numbers = [1, 2, 3, 4, 5]
squared_numbers = list(map(square, numbers))
print("Squared Numbers:", squared_numbers)
```

**Explanation:**

- The square function is applied to every element in the numbers list.
- map() returns an iterator, which is converted to a list with list().

**Example: Using Lambda with map**

```
numbers = [1, 2, 3, 4, 5]
```

```
squared_numbers = list(map(lambda x: x ** 2, numbers))

print("Squared Numbers (Lambda):", squared_numbers)
```

**Explanation:**

A lambda function is used to square each number, making the code more concise.

**2. The filter() Function**

The filter() function creates an iterator from elements of an iterable for which a given function returns True.

**Basic Syntax**

```
filter(function, iterable)
```

Example: Filtering Even Numbers

```
def is_even(x):

    return x % 2 == 0

numbers = [1, 2, 3, 4, 5, 6, 7, 8, 9, 10]

even_numbers = list(filter(is_even, numbers))

print("Even Numbers:", even_numbers)
```

**Explanation:**

- The is_even function returns True for even numbers.
- filter() applies this function to each element, and only those that return True are included in the resulting iterator.

**Example: Using Lambda with filter**

```
numbers = [1, 2, 3, 4, 5, 6, 7, 8, 9, 10]

even_numbers = list(filter(lambda x: x % 2 == 0, numbers))
```

```
print("Even Numbers (Lambda):", even_numbers)
```

**Explanation:**

A lambda function is used to check for even numbers in a concise way.

### 3. The reduce() Function

The reduce() function applies a binary function cumulatively to the items of an iterable, reducing it to a single value. In Python 3, reduce() is available in the functools module.

**Basic Syntax**

```
from functools import reduce

reduce(function, iterable[, initializer])
```

Example: Calculating the Product of a List

```
from functools import reduce

def multiply(a, b):
    return a * b

numbers = [1, 2, 3, 4, 5]

product = reduce(multiply, numbers)

print("Product of Numbers:", product)
```

**Explanation:**

- The multiply function multiplies two numbers.
- reduce() applies multiply() cumulatively across the numbers list, resulting in the product of all numbers.

**Example: Using Lambda with reduce**

```
from functools import reduce
```

```
numbers = [1, 2, 3, 4, 5]

product = reduce(lambda a, b: a * b, numbers)

print("Product of Numbers (Lambda):", product)
```

**Explanation:**

A lambda function is used to multiply the numbers in a concise manner.

### 4. Combining Map, Filter, and Reduce

These functions can be combined to perform complex data transformations in a functional style.

**Example: Processing a List of Numbers**

Suppose you have a list of numbers and you want to:

- Filter out the even numbers.
- Square the remaining numbers.
- Compute the sum of the squared values.

```
from functools import reduce

numbers = [1, 2, 3, 4, 5, 6, 7, 8, 9, 10]

# Step 1: Filter out odd numbers (i.e., keep only odd numbers)

odd_numbers = list(filter(lambda x: x % 2 != 0, numbers))

print("Odd Numbers:", odd_numbers)

# Step 2: Square the odd numbers

squared_odds = list(map(lambda x: x ** 2, odd_numbers))

print("Squared Odd Numbers:", squared_odds)
```

```
# Step 3: Sum the squared odd numbers using reduce
sum_of_squares = reduce(lambda a, b: a + b, squared_odds)
print("Sum of Squared Odd Numbers:", sum_of_squares)
```

**Explanation:**

- **Filtering:**
  filter(lambda x: x % 2 != 0, numbers) selects odd numbers.
- **Mapping:**
  map(lambda x: x ** 2, odd_numbers) squares each odd number.
- **Reducing:**
  reduce(lambda a, b: a + b, squared_odds) sums the squared values.
- This demonstrates how to use map, filter, and reduce in combination for multi-step data processing.

**5. Best Practices for Functional Programming in Python**

- **Keep Functions Simple:**
  Ensure that the functions used with map, filter, and reduce are simple and focused. Overly complex lambda expressions can reduce readability.
- **Use Built-in Functions Where Appropriate:**
  Consider using list comprehensions or generator expressions for simpler transformations, as they are often more readable.
- **Leverage Readability:**
  Even though functional programming promotes conciseness, prioritize clear and understandable code over overly terse expressions.

- **Test Thoroughly:**
  Functional constructs can sometimes obscure control flow. Write unit tests to ensure that your transformations yield the expected results.

### In Summary

Functional programming techniques using map, filter, and reduce allow for elegant and efficient data processing in Python:

- **map():**
  Applies a function to every element in an iterable.
- **filter():**
  Selects elements from an iterable that meet a specified condition.
- **reduce():**
  Aggregates elements in an iterable into a single value by cumulatively applying a binary function.

By combining these functions, you can build concise and expressive data processing pipelines. Mastering these techniques can lead to cleaner, more modular, and efficient code.

## Iterators and Generators

Iterators and generators are fundamental concepts in Python's functional programming paradigm that enable efficient, lazy evaluation of data. They allow you to work with potentially large or even infinite sequences without the overhead of storing all items in memory at once.

### 1. Iterators

### 1.1 What Is an Iterator?

An **iterator** is an object that represents a stream of data; it returns one element at a time when iterated over, typically using a loop. In Python, an iterator must implement two methods:

- __iter__(): Returns the iterator object itself.
- __next__(): Returns the next element in the sequence; raises StopIteration when no more elements are available.

Python's built-in functions like iter() and next() facilitate working with iterators.

### 1.2 Built-in Iterators

Many built-in types (e.g., lists, tuples, dictionaries, and sets) are iterable, meaning you can obtain an iterator from them:

```
numbers = [1, 2, 3, 4, 5]

iterator = iter(numbers)

print(next(iterator))  # Output: 1

print(next(iterator))  # Output: 2

# ... and so on until StopIteration is raised
```

### 1.3 Creating a Custom Iterator

You can create your own iterator by defining a class that implements the __iter__() and __next__() methods. For example, let's create an iterator that generates even numbers up to a given limit:

```
class EvenNumbers:

    def __init__(self, limit):

        self.limit = limit

        self.current = 0

    def __iter__(self):

        # The iterator object is returned by __iter__()

        return self
```

```
    def __next__(self):
        # Compute the next even number
        self.current += 2
        if self.current > self.limit:
            # No more items: raise StopIteration
            raise StopIteration
        return self.current
# Using the custom iterator
even_iter = EvenNumbers(10)
for num in even_iter:
    print("Even Number:", num)
# Output:
# Even Number: 2
# Even Number: 4
# Even Number: 6
# Even Number: 8
# Even Number: 10
```

**Explanation:**

- The EvenNumbers class initializes with a limit and starts from 0.
- The __next__() method increments the current number by 2 each time and raises StopIteration once the limit is exceeded.
- The class is its own iterator, as returned by the __iter__() method.

## 2. Generators

### 2.1 What Is a Generator?

A **generator** is a special type of iterator defined by a function that uses the yield keyword. Generators produce items one at a time and only when requested, which is known as lazy evaluation. This approach is memory efficient and ideal for handling large datasets or infinite sequences.

### 2.2 Creating a Generator Function

Generator functions are defined like normal functions but use yield to return values one at a time:

```
def even_numbers_generator(limit):
    """
    Generator function that yields even numbers up to the specified limit.
    Parameters:
        limit (int): The upper bound for even numbers.
    Yields:
        int: The next even number.
    """
    current = 0
    while current < limit:
        current += 2
        yield current
# Using the generator function
```

```
for num in even_numbers_generator(10):
    print("Even Number (Generator):", num)
# Output:
# Even Number (Generator): 2
# Even Number (Generator): 4
# Even Number (Generator): 6
# Even Number (Generator): 8
# Even Number (Generator): 10
```

**Explanation:**

- The function even_numbers_generator() uses a while loop to generate even numbers.
- The yield keyword returns a value and suspends the function's state, allowing it to resume where it left off on subsequent iterations.
- This lazy evaluation means numbers are generated on-the-fly rather than stored in memory all at once.

### 2.3 Generator Expressions

Generator expressions provide a concise way to create generators without defining a full function. They are similar to list comprehensions but use parentheses instead of square brackets.

**Example: Generator Expression for Squaring Numbers**

```
numbers = [1, 2, 3, 4, 5]
squares = (x ** 2 for x in numbers)
# Iterate over the generator expression
```

```
for square in squares:
    print("Square:", square)
# Output:
# Square: 1
# Square: 4
# Square: 9
# Square: 16
# Square: 25
```

**Explanation:**

- The generator expression (x ** 2 for x in numbers) creates a generator that yields the square of each number in the list.
- Unlike list comprehensions, generator expressions do not immediately compute all values, making them more memory efficient.

**3. Advantages of Using Generators and Iterators**

- **Memory Efficiency:**
  Generators produce items on-the-fly without storing the entire sequence in memory.
- **Lazy Evaluation:**
  Values are computed as needed, which is beneficial for large datasets or infinite sequences.
- **Improved Performance:**
  They can lead to performance gains in I/O-bound or data processing tasks by reducing memory usage and overhead.

- **Simplicity:**
  Custom iterators and generators offer a clear and concise way to encapsulate iteration logic.

**4. Best Practices**

- **Use Generators for Large Datasets:**
  When working with large amounts of data, prefer generators over lists to avoid high memory consumption.
- **Keep Generator Functions Simple:**
  Ensure that your generator functions are easy to understand. Avoid overly complex logic that could hinder readability.
- **Leverage Generator Expressions:**
  Use generator expressions for simple transformations where a full function definition would be unnecessarily verbose.
- **Graceful Termination:**
  Ensure that your custom iterators and generators properly raise StopIteration to signal the end of the sequence.
- **Document Your Code:**
  Provide clear docstrings for your custom iterators and generators, explaining what they yield and how they behave.

**In Summary**

Iterators and generators are powerful constructs in Python for handling sequences efficiently and elegantly:

- **Iterators:**
  - Define custom iteration behavior by implementing __iter__() and __next__().
  - Allow sequential access to items one at a time.
- **Generators:**

- Use the yield keyword to produce values lazily.
- Provide memory-efficient solutions for handling large or infinite sequences.
- Can be defined as functions or expressions.

By leveraging these functional programming techniques, you can write more efficient, readable, and maintainable code that handles data streams and large datasets effectively.

## Example Exercises

When dealing with large amounts of data - such as log files, sensor outputs, or real-time data feeds - it's crucial to process the data efficiently to avoid exhausting system memory. Python's functional programming techniques, particularly generators and iterators, enable lazy evaluation, meaning data is processed on-the-fly rather than loaded entirely into memory.

### 1. Why Use Generators and Functional Techniques for Large Data Streams?

- **Memory Efficiency:**
  Generators yield items one at a time and only when requested, making them ideal for processing large or infinite sequences.
- **Lazy Evaluation:**
  Operations such as filtering, mapping, and reducing can be applied lazily, ensuring that only necessary data is in memory at any time.
- **Modularity and Readability:**
  Functional constructs like map(), filter(), and generator expressions allow you to write concise, declarative code that is easier to reason about.

### 2. Example Exercise: Filtering Error Logs from a Large File

Suppose you have a large log file (server.log) containing millions of lines, and you want to filter out and count the lines that contain the word "ERROR". Loading the entire file into memory is impractical, so we'll use a generator to read the file line-by-line.

**Step 2.1: Create a Generator to Read the File**

```
def read_log_file(filename):
    """
    A generator function that reads a log file line by line.
    Parameters:
        filename (str): The path to the log file.
    Yields:
        str: The next line from the file.
    """
    with open(filename, "r", encoding="utf-8") as file:
        for line in file:
            yield line
# Usage example (assuming 'server.log' exists):
# for log_line in read_log_file("server.log"):
#     process(log_line)
```

**Explanation:**

- The read_log_file generator opens the file and yields one line at a time.
- Using a generator avoids loading the entire file into memory.

### Step 2.2: Filter for Error Lines and Count Them

We can combine the generator with a filter() to extract only lines containing "ERROR" and then count them.

```
def count_error_logs(filename):
    """
    Count the number of lines in a log file that contain the word
'ERROR'.
    Parameters:
        filename (str): The path to the log file.
    Returns:
        int: The count of error lines.
    """
    # Create a generator for the log file
    log_lines = read_log_file(filename)
    # Filter lines that contain the word "ERROR"
    error_lines = filter(lambda line: "ERROR" in line, log_lines)
    # Count the number of error lines
    error_count = sum(1 for _ in error_lines)
    return error_count
# Example usage:
# error_count = count_error_logs("server.log")
# print("Number of error logs:", error_count)
```

**Explanation:**

- The filter() function applies a lambda that checks if "ERROR" is present in each line.
- A generator expression sum(1 for _ in error_lines) iterates through the filtered lines and counts them.
- This approach is memory efficient because each line is processed and discarded.

### 3. Example Exercise: Aggregating Values from a Large CSV File

Imagine you have a large CSV file (sales.csv) containing sales data with columns such as "date", "product", and "amount". You need to calculate the total sales amount without loading the entire file into memory.

**Step 3.1: Reading the CSV File with a Generator**

```
import csv

def read_csv_file(filename):

    """

    A generator function that reads a CSV file row by row.

    Parameters:

        filename (str): The path to the CSV file.

    Yields:

        dict: Each row of the CSV file as a dictionary.

    """

    with open(filename, "r", encoding="utf-8") as csvfile:

        reader = csv.DictReader(csvfile)
```

```
        for row in reader:
            yield row
# Usage example (assuming 'sales.csv' exists):
# for row in read_csv_file("sales.csv"):
#     process(row)
```

**Explanation:**

- The read_csv_file generator uses csv.DictReader to convert each row into a dictionary.
- Each row is yielded one at a time, making the approach scalable for large files.

**Step 3.2: Aggregating Sales Data**

We then filter rows based on criteria (e.g., a specific product or date range) and aggregate the "amount" values.

```
def total_sales_amount(filename, product_filter=None):
    """
    Calculate the total sales amount from a CSV file.
    Parameters:
        filename (str): The path to the CSV file.
        product_filter (str, optional): Filter sales by product name.
    Returns:
        float: The total sales amount.
    """
    total_amount = 0.0
```

```
    for row in read_csv_file(filename):
        if product_filter is None or row["product"] == product_filter:
            try:
                total_amount += float(row["amount"])
            except ValueError:
                print(f"Warning: Skipping row with invalid amount:
{row['amount']}")
    return total_amount
# Example usage:
# total_amount = total_sales_amount("sales.csv",
product_filter="Widget")
# print("Total Sales Amount for Widget:", total_amount)
```

**Explanation:**

- The function iterates over rows from the CSV generator.
- It optionally filters rows based on a product name.
- The sales amounts are converted to floats and summed to compute the total sales.
- Errors in conversion (e.g., non-numeric values) are handled gracefully with a warning message.

**4. Best Practices for Processing Large Data Streams**

- **Use Generators:**
  Generators help process data lazily, reducing memory overhead.
- **Chain Functional Operations:**
  Combine generators with filter(), map(), and generator expressions to create efficient data pipelines.

- **Handle Exceptions Gracefully:**
  Validate and sanitize input data (e.g., using try/except when converting values).
- **Modularize Your Code:**
  Break down your data processing tasks into small, reusable functions for reading, filtering, and aggregating data.
- **Profile and Optimize:**
  For very large datasets, use profiling tools to identify bottlenecks and optimize performance.

### In Summary

Processing large data streams efficiently is critical for applications that deal with substantial volumes of data. By leveraging Python's generators and functional programming techniques, you can:

- **Read Data Lazily:**
  Process files (text, CSV, JSON) one item at a time to minimize memory usage.
- **Filter and Transform Data:**
  Use functional constructs such as filter(), map(), and generator expressions for on-the-fly data transformation.
- **Aggregate Results:**
  Compute summaries and perform data aggregation efficiently.
- **Build Robust Tools:**
  Create modular and maintainable data processing pipelines that handle large datasets with ease.

By mastering these techniques, you can build applications that efficiently store, process, and analyze large volumes of data.

# Chapter 23: Decorators and Context Managers

## Function Decorators and Their Uses

Function decorators are a powerful feature in Python that allow you to modify, extend, or enhance the behavior of functions and methods without permanently altering their source code. By "wrapping" a function with another function, decorators let you inject additional processing - such as logging, timing, caching, authentication, and more - before or after the original function executes. This modular approach promotes code reuse and separation of concerns.

In this section, we'll cover the following:

- **What Are Function Decorators?**
- **Basic Decorator Syntax and Examples**
- **Parameterized Decorators**
- **Best Practices and Considerations**

### 1. What Are Function Decorators?

A **decorator** is a higher-order function that takes another function (or method) as its argument, wraps it with additional behavior, and returns a new function with that enhanced behavior. In Python, decorators are typically applied to functions using the @decorator_name syntax placed above the function definition.

**Key Concepts:**

- **Separation of Concerns:** Decorators help separate cross-cutting concerns (e.g., logging, authentication) from core business logic.
- **Code Reusability:** A single decorator can be applied to multiple functions, avoiding code duplication.

- **Higher-Order Functions:** Decorators are functions that accept functions as arguments and return modified functions.

## 2. Basic Decorator Syntax and Example

The simplest decorator wraps a function to add behavior before and after its execution.

### 2.1 Basic Logging Decorator Example

Below is an example of a decorator that logs function calls along with their arguments and return values.

```
def log_decorator(func):
    """
    A simple decorator that logs function call details.
    """
    def wrapper(*args, **kwargs):
        print(f"[LOG] Calling function '{func.__name__}' with arguments {args} {kwargs}")
        result = func(*args, **kwargs)
        print(f"[LOG] Function '{func.__name__}' returned {result}")
        return result
    return wrapper
@log_decorator
def add(a, b):
    """Return the sum of a and b."""
    return a + b
# Example usage
```

```
result = add(3, 5)

print("Final Result:", result)
```

**Explanation:**

- **Decorator Function (log_decorator):**
  Accepts a function func and returns a new function wrapper that logs the function call details.
- **Wrapper Function:**
  Uses *args and **kwargs to accept any number of positional and keyword arguments. It prints the function's name and arguments before calling func, then logs the return value.
- **Application:**
  The @log_decorator syntax applies this behavior to the add function, so every call to add is logged automatically.

### 3. Parameterized Decorators

Sometimes you want a decorator to accept its own parameters. This is achieved by creating a decorator factory—a function that returns a decorator.

### 3.1 Example: Repeat Decorator

This decorator repeats the execution of the decorated function a specified number of times.

```
def repeat(num_times):

    """

    A decorator factory that repeats the execution of the decorated function.

    Parameters:

        num_times (int): Number of times to execute the function.
```

```
    """
    def decorator(func):
        def wrapper(*args, **kwargs):
            result = None
            for i in range(num_times):
                print(f"[LOG] Execution {i + 1} of {num_times}")
                result = func(*args, **kwargs)
            return result
        return wrapper
    return decorator
@repeat(3)
def greet(name):
    """Print a greeting message."""
    print(f"Hello, {name}!")
# Example usage
greet("Alice")
```

**Explanation:**

- **Decorator Factory (repeat):**
  Takes num_times as an argument and returns a decorator.
- **Decorator (decorator):**
  Wraps the function and repeats its execution num_times.
- **Application:**
  The @repeat(3) syntax causes greet("Alice") to be executed three times, with logging for each execution.

## 4. Preserving Metadata with functools.wraps

When you decorate a function, the metadata (such as its name, docstring, etc.) of the original function is lost unless you use functools.wraps. This is important for debugging, documentation, and introspection.

### 4.1 Example: Using functools.wraps

```
import functools

def log_decorator(func):
    """
    A decorator that logs function calls and preserves the original
function's metadata.
    """
    @functools.wraps(func)
    def wrapper(*args, **kwargs):
        print(f"[LOG] Calling function '{func.__name__}' with
arguments {args} {kwargs}")
        result = func(*args, **kwargs)
        print(f"[LOG] Function '{func.__name__}' returned {result}")
        return result
    return wrapper

@log_decorator
def multiply(a, b):
    """Return the product of a and b."""
    return a * b
```

```
# Checking metadata
print("Function Name:", multiply.__name__)      # Output: multiply
print("Function Docstring:", multiply.__doc__)   # Output: Return the product of a and b.
```

**Explanation:**

- **functools.wraps:**
  This decorator copies the metadata from func to wrapper, ensuring that attributes like __name__ and __doc__ remain unchanged.

**5. Use Cases for Function Decorators**

Decorators can be used in a wide variety of scenarios, including but not limited to:

- **Logging and Monitoring:**
  Automatically log function calls, arguments, and return values.
- **Authentication and Authorization:**
  Check user credentials before allowing access to a function.
- **Caching/Memoization:**
  Cache the results of function calls to avoid repeated computations.
- **Performance Measurement:**
  Measure the execution time of functions for optimization purposes.
- **Input Validation:**
  Validate function arguments before executing the function logic.

**Example: Timing Decorator**

```
import time
```

```
import functools

def timer(func):

    """

    A decorator that measures the execution time of the decorated
function.

    """

    @functools.wraps(func)

    def wrapper(*args, **kwargs):

        start_time = time.time()

        result = func(*args, **kwargs)

        end_time = time.time()

        print(f"[TIMER] {func.__name__} executed in {end_time -
start_time:.4f} seconds.")

        return result

    return wrapper

@timer

def compute_sum(n):

    """Compute the sum of numbers from 1 to n."""

    return sum(range(1, n + 1))


# Example usage

total = compute_sum(1000000)

print("Total Sum:", total)
```

### Explanation:

- The timer decorator measures how long the compute_sum function takes to execute.
- It prints the elapsed time after the function completes, allowing you to monitor performance.

### 6. Best Practices for Function Decorators

- **Keep Decorators Focused:**
  Each decorator should address a single concern. Avoid creating decorators that try to do too much.
- **Use functools.wraps:**
  Always use functools.wraps in your decorator definitions to preserve the original function's metadata.
- **Test Decorators Thoroughly:**
  Since decorators can alter behavior in non-obvious ways, ensure that you write tests to validate their functionality.
- **Be Mindful of Order:**
  When stacking multiple decorators, the order in which they are applied matters. Test the combined effects to ensure the desired behavior.
- **Document Decorators:**
  Provide clear docstrings for decorators to explain their purpose, usage, and any parameters they might accept.

### In Summary

Function decorators are a powerful mechanism in Python that enable you to extend or modify the behavior of functions in a reusable and expressive manner. Key takeaways include:

- **What They Are:**
  Higher-order functions that wrap another function to add additional behavior.
- **Basic Syntax:**
  Use the @decorator syntax to apply a decorator to a function.
- **Parameterized Decorators:**
  Create decorator factories to accept parameters and customize behavior.
- **Metadata Preservation:**
  Utilize functools.wraps to ensure the original function's metadata is retained.
- **Common Use Cases:**
  Logging, authentication, caching, performance measurement, and input validation.

By mastering function decorators, you can write cleaner, more modular code that separates concerns and enhances functionality without modifying the underlying functions.

## Class Decorators

Class decorators provide a powerful mechanism to modify or enhance classes without altering their source code. Like function decorators, class decorators are higher-order functions that take a class as input and return either the same class with additional functionality or a new class altogether. They are useful for adding cross-cutting concerns such as logging, enforcing design patterns, registering classes, or modifying class attributes and methods.

### 1. What Are Class Decorators?

A **class decorator** is a function (or callable) that accepts a class as its argument and returns a class. They are applied using the

@decorator_name syntax just like function decorators. However, rather than wrapping a function, they wrap a class definition.

**Use Cases for Class Decorators:**

- **Registration:** Automatically register classes for later use (e.g., plugin systems or factory patterns).
- **Modification:** Add or modify class attributes or methods without changing the original source.
- **Enforcing Constraints:** Ensure that classes meet certain criteria or implement specific interfaces.
- **Logging and Debugging:** Automatically inject logging into class methods.

**2. Basic Class Decorator Example**

Below is a simple example of a class decorator that adds a logging mechanism to a class. This decorator logs a message when an instance of the decorated class is created.

**Code Example: Logging Class Decorator**

```
def log_class_creation(cls):
    """
    A class decorator that logs the creation of an instance.
    Parameters:
        cls (type): The class being decorated.
    Returns:
        type: The original class with modified __init__.
    """
    # Save the original __init__ method
```

```
    original_init = cls.__init__
    # Define a new __init__ method
    def new_init(self, *args, **kwargs):
        print(f"[LOG] Creating instance of {cls.__name__} with args:
{args} kwargs: {kwargs}")
        original_init(self, *args, **kwargs)
    # Replace the class's __init__ with the new one
    cls.__init__ = new_init
    return cls
@log_class_creation
class MyClass:
    def __init__(self, value):
        self.value = value
    def display(self):
        print(f"MyClass with value: {self.value}")
# Using the decorated class
obj = MyClass(10)
obj.display()
```

**Explanation:**

- **Decorator Definition:**
  - log_class_creation is defined as a function that takes a class cls as its argument.
  - The original __init__ method is stored in original_init.

- A new __init__ method, new_init, is defined, which logs a message before calling the original initializer.
- The original __init__ is replaced by new_init, and the class is returned.

- **Decorator Application:**
  - The @log_class_creation syntax applies the decorator to MyClass.
  - When an instance of MyClass is created, the new __init__ logs the creation details before executing the original initialization logic.

**3. More Advanced Use: Automatic Class Registration**

A common use of class decorators is to automatically register classes in a central registry. This is especially useful in plugin architectures or factory patterns.

**Code Example: Registration Decorator**

```
# Global registry for plugins

plugin_registry = {}

def register_plugin(cls):

    """

    A class decorator that registers the decorated class in a global
plugin registry.

    Parameters:

        cls (type): The class to register.

    Returns:

        type: The original class.
```

```
    """
    plugin_registry[cls.__name__] = cls
    return cls
@register_plugin
class PluginA:
    def run(self):
        print("PluginA is running.")
@register_plugin
class PluginB:
    def run(self):
        print("PluginB is running.")
# Using the registry to instantiate and run plugins
def run_plugins():
    for name, plugin_class in plugin_registry.items():
        print(f"Running {name}:")
        plugin = plugin_class()
        plugin.run()
run_plugins()
```

**Explanation:**

- **Registration Decorator (register_plugin):**
  - This decorator registers the class in a global dictionary plugin_registry using the class's name as the key.
  - The class is returned unmodified.

- **Applying the Decorator:**
  - PluginA and PluginB are decorated with @register_plugin, so they are automatically added to plugin_registry.
- **Utilizing the Registry:**
  - The run_plugins() function iterates over the registered plugins, instantiates them, and calls their run() method.
  - This pattern enables a flexible plugin system where new plugins can be added simply by decorating them.

**4. Best Practices for Class Decorators**

- **Simplicity:**
  Keep class decorators focused on a single responsibility. Avoid mixing multiple concerns in one decorator.
- **Preserve Class Metadata:**
  When modifying class methods (such as __init__), consider using tools like functools.wraps (or manually copying metadata) to preserve the original class's documentation and attributes.
- **Document Decorators:**
  Provide clear docstrings and comments explaining what the decorator does, which parameters it accepts (if any), and its intended use.
- **Test Thoroughly:**
  Because decorators modify class behavior, write tests to ensure that decorated classes behave as expected in different scenarios.
- **Avoid Unnecessary Complexity:**
  Use class decorators when they provide clear benefits, but avoid over-engineering. Sometimes, simple composition or explicit method calls may be more appropriate.

## In Summary

Class decorators offer a powerful mechanism to enhance or modify class behavior without altering the original source code. They are particularly useful for:

- **Logging and Debugging:**
  Automatically log class instantiation and method calls.
- **Registration:**
  Automatically register classes for plugin systems or factories.
- **Enhancement:**
  Modify class methods (like __init__) to inject additional behavior.

By mastering class decorators, you can write more modular, reusable, and maintainable code, and cleanly implement cross-cutting concerns in your object-oriented design.

## Writing Custom Context Managers

Context managers in Python provide a convenient way to allocate and release resources precisely when you want to. They allow you to wrap the execution of a block of code with methods that set up a context and ensure that cleanup is performed regardless of how the block exits (normally or via an exception). The most common way to work with context managers is using the with statement.

You can create custom context managers in two primary ways:

1. **By defining a class with __enter__ and __exit__ methods.**
2. **By using the @contextmanager decorator from the contextlib module.**

Both methods allow you to control resource management, error handling, and cleanup. Let's explore each approach with detailed examples.

### 1. Creating a Custom Context Manager Using a Class

When you define a class-based context manager, you implement two special methods:

- **__enter__(self)**: This method is called at the beginning of the with block. It can perform setup operations and return an object that will be assigned to the variable after the as clause (if present).
- **__exit__(self, exc_type, exc_value, traceback)**: This method is called when the with block is exited. It handles cleanup actions, and its parameters provide information about any exception that occurred in the block.

#### Example: A Custom Context Manager for Timing Code Execution

Below is an example of a custom context manager that measures the execution time of a block of code:

```
import time

class Timer:

    """

    A simple context manager for timing code execution.

    """

    def __enter__(self):

        # Record the start time when entering the context.

        self.start_time = time.time()

        return self  # Optionally, return self if you need to access
attributes later.

    def __exit__(self, exc_type, exc_value, traceback):
```

```
        # Calculate and print the elapsed time when exiting the context.
        self.end_time = time.time()
        elapsed_time = self.end_time - self.start_time
        print(f"Elapsed time: {elapsed_time:.4f} seconds")
        # Returning False (or nothing) allows exceptions to propagate if
any occur.
        return False
# Using the Timer context manager
with Timer() as timer:
    # Code block to be timed
    total = sum(i * i for i in range(1000000))
    print("Computation result:", total)
```

**Explanation:**

- When the with Timer() as timer: statement is executed, the __enter__ method is called, starting the timer.
- The code within the with block runs, and when it completes (or if an exception occurs), the __exit__ method is called.
- The __exit__ method computes the elapsed time and prints it.
- Any exception that occurs inside the block will propagate because __exit__ returns False.

**2. Creating a Custom Context Manager Using contextlib.contextmanager**

The @contextmanager decorator from the contextlib module offers a more concise way to create context managers. Instead of defining a class with __enter__ and __exit__, you write a generator function that yields control back to the with block.

**Example: A Custom Context Manager for File Handling**

Let's write a custom context manager that opens a file, yields the file object for processing, and then ensures the file is properly closed.

```
from contextlib import contextmanager

@contextmanager

def open_file(file_path, mode="r", encoding="utf-8"):

    """

    A context manager for opening and closing a file.

    Parameters:

        file_path (str): The path to the file.

        mode (str): The mode in which to open the file (default is 'r').

        encoding (str): The file encoding (default is 'utf-8').

    Yields:

        file: The file object.

    """

    file = open(file_path, mode, encoding=encoding)

    try:

        yield file  # Provide the file object to the caller.

    finally:

        file.close()

        print(f"File '{file_path}' closed.")
```

```
# Using the custom file context manager
with open_file("example.txt", "w") as f:
    f.write("Hello, World!\n")
    f.write("This file is managed by a custom context manager.\n")
```

**Explanation:**

- The open_file function is decorated with @contextmanager, turning it into a context manager.
- The function opens the file and then yields the file object to the with block.
- After the block completes (or if an exception occurs), the code in the finally clause executes, ensuring that the file is closed.
- This pattern is especially useful for resource management, such as file I/O, network connections, or locking mechanisms.

### 3. Best Practices for Writing Custom Context Managers

- **Resource Cleanup:**
  Always ensure that resources (files, connections, locks, etc.) are properly released in the __exit__ method or the finally block of a context manager function.
- **Error Propagation:**
  Design your context managers so that exceptions are either handled appropriately or allowed to propagate. Returning False from __exit__ (or not catching exceptions in a @contextmanager function) will let exceptions pass through.
- **Use contextlib When Appropriate:**
  For simple context managers, prefer the @contextmanager decorator for its simplicity and readability.

- **Document Behavior:**
  Clearly document what your context manager does, what resources it manages, and any exceptions it might handle.

- **Test Thoroughly:**
  Ensure that your context managers behave as expected, particularly in error scenarios. Write tests to simulate exceptions and verify that resources are correctly released.

**In Summary**

Custom context managers in Python are invaluable tools for managing resources and ensuring proper cleanup, especially in the presence of errors. They can be created in two main ways:

- **Class-Based Context Managers:**
  Implement the __enter__ and __exit__ methods to manage resource allocation and cleanup.

- **Function-Based Context Managers:**
  Use the @contextmanager decorator from the contextlib module to write concise context managers using generator functions.

By mastering custom context managers, you can write more reliable and maintainable code that gracefully handles resource management, making your applications robust and easier to debug.

**Example Exercises**

Efficient resource management is a critical aspect of robust software development. Resources - such as file handles, network connections, or locks - must be properly acquired and released to avoid resource leaks and ensure system stability. Python provides powerful constructs to manage resources elegantly: **context managers** (commonly used with the with statement) and **decorators**.

## 1. Using Context Managers for Resource Management

Context managers are ideal for managing resources that require setup and cleanup actions. The with statement ensures that resources are released properly, even if errors occur. We can create custom context managers either by defining a class with __enter__ and __exit__ methods or by using the @contextmanager decorator from the contextlib module.

### 1.1 Exercise: Creating a Custom Context Manager for File Handling

In this exercise, we create a context manager that opens a file, yields the file object for processing, and then guarantees the file is closed once the block exits.

```
from contextlib import contextmanager

@contextmanager

def managed_file(filename, mode="r", encoding="utf-8"):

    """

    A context manager for opening and closing a file.

    Parameters:

        filename (str): The path to the file.

        mode (str): The mode in which to open the file (default is 'r').

        encoding (str): The encoding to use (default is 'utf-8').

    Yields:

        file: The file object.

    """

    file = open(filename, mode, encoding=encoding)
```

```
    try:
        yield file  # Provide the file object to the caller.
    finally:
        file.close()
        print(f"File '{filename}' closed.")
# Example usage:
with managed_file("example.txt", "w") as f:
    f.write("Hello, Resource Management with Context Managers!\n")
```

**Explanation:**

- The managed_file function is decorated with @contextmanager, converting it into a context manager.
- It opens the file and yields the file object so that it can be used within the with block.
- The finally block ensures that the file is closed after the block, regardless of whether an error occurred.

### 2. Using Decorators for Resource Management

Decorators can also be used for resource management by wrapping function calls with setup and teardown logic. This approach is particularly useful when you want to enforce resource management across multiple functions without repeating boilerplate code.

#### 2.1 Exercise: A Decorator for Acquiring and Releasing a Lock

Consider a scenario where multiple functions need to execute in a thread-safe manner by acquiring a lock before execution and releasing it afterward. We can write a decorator that handles this automatically.

```
import threading
import functools
# Create a global lock
global_lock = threading.Lock()
def synchronized(func):
    """
    A decorator that acquires a lock before executing the function and
releases it afterward.
    """
    @functools.wraps(func)
    def wrapper(*args, **kwargs):
        with global_lock:
            print(f"[LOCK] {func.__name__} has acquired the lock.")
            result = func(*args, **kwargs)
            print(f"[LOCK] {func.__name__} is releasing the lock.")
            return result
    return wrapper
@synchronized
def critical_section(task_id):
    """
    A function that simulates work in a critical section.
    Parameters:
        task_id (int): An identifier for the task.
```

```
    """
    print(f"Task {task_id} is running in a critical section.")
# Example usage:
critical_section(1)
critical_section(2)
```

**Explanation:**

- **Decorator Definition (synchronized):**
  The synchronized decorator wraps a function so that it always runs within the context of global_lock. The lock is automatically acquired and released by the with statement.
- **Preserving Metadata:**
  functools.wraps is used to preserve the original function's metadata.
- **Usage:**
  When critical_section is called, it prints messages indicating that the lock is acquired and then released, ensuring that the function's execution is thread-safe.

**3. Combining Context Managers and Decorators**

In some cases, you may want to use both techniques together. For example, you might have a function that performs both file I/O and requires synchronization.

**3.1 Exercise: A Combined Approach**

Suppose we need to write to a log file from multiple threads safely. We can combine a context manager for file I/O and a decorator for thread synchronization.

```
import threading
```

```
from contextlib import contextmanager
import functools
# Global lock for synchronizing file access
file_lock = threading.Lock()
@contextmanager
def open_log(filename, mode="a", encoding="utf-8"):
    """
    A context manager for safely opening a log file.
    Parameters:
        filename (str): The log file path.
        mode (str): Mode for opening the file (default 'a' for append).
        encoding (str): File encoding (default 'utf-8').
    Yields:
        file: The opened file object.
    """
    file = open(filename, mode, encoding=encoding)
    try:
        yield file
    finally:
        file.close()
        print(f"Log file '{filename}' closed.")
def synchronized(func):
```

```
    """
    A decorator that synchronizes function execution using a lock.
    """
    @functools.wraps(func)
    def wrapper(*args, **kwargs):
        with file_lock:
            return func(*args, **kwargs)
    return wrapper
@synchronized
def write_log(message, filename="log.txt"):
    """
    Write a message to a log file safely.
    Parameters:
        message (str): The log message.
        filename (str): The path to the log file.
    """
    with open_log(filename, "a") as log_file:
        log_file.write(message + "\n")
    print("Log message written.")
# Example usage:
write_log("This is a test log message.")
write_log("Another log message.")
```

**Explanation:**

- The open_log context manager ensures that the log file is opened and closed safely.
- The synchronized decorator wraps write_log so that file writes are synchronized with file_lock, preventing concurrent writes from multiple threads.
- The write_log function writes a message to the log file and then prints a confirmation message.
- Combining these techniques ensures both resource management (file I/O) and safe concurrency (synchronized access).

**In Summary**

Function decorators and context managers are powerful tools for resource management in Python:

- **Context Managers:**
  Provide a clean way to allocate and release resources using the with statement. They are ideal for tasks like file I/O, network connections, and resource cleanup.
- **Decorators:**
  Enable you to wrap functions with additional behavior, such as logging, synchronization, or error handling, without modifying the function's code.
- **Combining Techniques:**
  You can integrate context managers and decorators to handle complex resource management scenarios, such as synchronized file access from multiple threads.

By mastering these techniques, you can write robust, maintainable code that gracefully manages resources and ensures that cleanup actions are always performed, even in the face of errors.

# Section X: Specialized Libraries and Frameworks
# Chapter 24: Data Analysis and Visualization

## NumPy for Numerical Computing

NumPy is the fundamental package for numerical computing in Python. It provides a high-performance multidimensional array object, along with tools for working with these arrays. NumPy forms the foundation of many data analysis and visualization libraries such as Pandas, SciPy, and Matplotlib. In this section, we'll explore the key features of NumPy, illustrate how to create and manipulate arrays, and demonstrate how its vectorized operations lead to efficient numerical computations.

### 1. Why Use NumPy?

- **Efficient Array Operations:**
  NumPy arrays (ndarray) are implemented in C, making them much faster than Python lists for numerical operations.
- **Vectorization:**
  Operations on NumPy arrays are vectorized, meaning they are applied element-wise without explicit loops, which improves performance and code readability.
- **Broadcasting:**
  NumPy supports broadcasting, which allows operations on arrays of different shapes.
- **Rich Mathematical Functions:**
  NumPy provides a wide range of functions for linear algebra, statistics, Fourier analysis, and more.
- **Memory Efficiency:**
  NumPy arrays use less memory and provide convenient mechanisms for manipulating numerical data.

## 2. Creating and Manipulating Arrays

### 2.1 Creating NumPy Arrays

You can create NumPy arrays from Python lists or tuples using np.array(). NumPy also provides functions for generating arrays with predefined values, such as np.zeros(), np.ones(), and np.arange().

**Example: Creating Arrays**

```
import numpy as np

# Creating a 1D array from a list

array_1d = np.array([1, 2, 3, 4, 5])

print("1D Array:", array_1d)

# Creating a 2D array (matrix) from a list of lists

array_2d = np.array([[1, 2, 3], [4, 5, 6], [7, 8, 9]])

print("2D Array:\n", array_2d)

# Creating arrays with predefined values

zeros = np.zeros((2, 3))

ones = np.ones((2, 3))

range_array = np.arange(10)  # 0 through 9

print("Zeros:\n", zeros)

print("Ones:\n", ones)

print("Range Array:", range_array)
```

**Explanation:**

- np.array() converts Python lists into NumPy arrays.

- Functions like np.zeros(), np.ones(), and np.arange() allow you to generate arrays quickly with specified shapes and values.

### 3. Vectorized Operations and Broadcasting

NumPy allows you to perform arithmetic operations on arrays in a vectorized manner. This means that operations are applied element-wise without the need for explicit loops.

### 3.1 Vectorized Arithmetic Operations

**Example: Adding and Multiplying Arrays**

```
import numpy as np

a = np.array([1, 2, 3, 4, 5])

b = np.array([10, 20, 30, 40, 50])

# Element-wise addition

sum_result = a + b

print("Element-wise Sum:", sum_result)

# Element-wise multiplication

product_result = a * b

print("Element-wise Product:", product_result)
```

**Explanation:**

- Operations such as addition and multiplication are performed on corresponding elements of arrays a and b.
- This vectorized approach is highly efficient compared to looping through each element in Python.

### 3.2 Broadcasting

Broadcasting allows operations on arrays of different shapes by automatically expanding their dimensions to be compatible.

**Example: Broadcasting in Action**

```
import numpy as np

# 2D array (matrix)

matrix = np.array([[1, 2, 3], [4, 5, 6]])

# 1D array (vector)

vector = np.array([10, 20, 30])

# Broadcasting: Adding the 1D array to each row of the 2D array

broadcasted_sum = matrix + vector

print("Broadcasted Sum:\n", broadcasted_sum)
```

**Explanation:**

- The 1D array vector is broadcasted to match the shape of the 2D array matrix, allowing element-wise addition.
- Broadcasting simplifies operations and eliminates the need for manual reshaping or looping.

### 4. Aggregation and Statistical Operations

NumPy provides a suite of functions to perform aggregate and statistical operations on arrays.

**Example: Calculating Aggregates**

```
import numpy as np

data = np.array([1, 2, 3, 4, 5, 6, 7, 8, 9, 10])

# Compute sum, mean, min, and max
```

```
total_sum = np.sum(data)
mean_value = np.mean(data)
min_value = np.min(data)
max_value = np.max(data)
print("Sum:", total_sum)
print("Mean:", mean_value)
print("Min:", min_value)
print("Max:", max_value)
```

**Explanation:**

- Functions like np.sum(), np.mean(), np.min(), and np.max() quickly compute aggregate values on the array data.

**5. Reshaping and Slicing Arrays**

Manipulating array shapes and slicing data are common tasks in data processing.

**Example: Reshaping and Slicing**

```
import numpy as np
# Create a 1D array
data = np.arange(12)
print("Original 1D Array:", data)
# Reshape the array into a 3x4 matrix
matrix = data.reshape((3, 4))
print("Reshaped to 3x4 Matrix:\n", matrix)
# Slicing: Extract the first two rows and the first two columns
```

```
sub_matrix = matrix[:2, :2]

print("Sliced Sub-matrix:\n", sub_matrix)
```

**Explanation:**

- The reshape() method changes the shape of an array without altering its data.
- Slicing allows you to extract specific parts of an array using index ranges.

**6. Best Practices for Using NumPy**

- **Use Vectorized Operations:**
  Always favor vectorized operations over explicit loops to leverage NumPy's performance benefits.
- **Leverage Broadcasting:**
  Use broadcasting to perform operations on arrays of different shapes without complex reshaping.
- **Profile Your Code:**
  Use profiling tools to ensure that your NumPy operations are efficient, especially when working with large datasets.
- **Understand Array Memory Layout:**
  Familiarize yourself with concepts like array strides and memory order (C vs. Fortran) to optimize performance.
- **Keep Code Readable:**
  Although vectorized code is compact, strive for clarity by breaking complex expressions into simpler, well-documented steps.

### In Summary

NumPy is a cornerstone of numerical computing in Python, offering:

- **Efficient Data Structures:**
  The ndarray is optimized for numerical operations and memory efficiency.
- **Vectorized Operations and Broadcasting:**
  These features allow you to perform operations on entire arrays without explicit loops, significantly enhancing performance.
- **Aggregation and Statistical Functions:**
  Built-in functions enable quick computation of aggregate values and statistical measures.
- **Reshaping and Slicing:**
  Flexible tools for modifying array shapes and accessing subsets of data.

By mastering NumPy, you can perform complex numerical computations and data analysis tasks efficiently, making it a vital tool in the realm of data analysis and visualization.

## Pandas for Data Wrangling

Pandas is one of the most popular libraries in Python for data analysis and manipulation. It provides powerful, flexible, and easy-to-use data structures - primarily the DataFrame and Series - that are well-suited for cleaning, transforming, and analyzing structured data. Data wrangling, the process of cleaning and transforming raw data into a useful format, is made much simpler with pandas.

### 1. Introduction to Pandas Data Structures

#### 1.1 Series

A **Series** is a one-dimensional labeled array capable of holding any data type. It is similar to a column in a spreadsheet or a database table.

```
import pandas as pd

# Creating a Series from a list

s = pd.Series([10, 20, 30, 40, 50])

print("Series:")

print(s)
```

### 1.2 DataFrame

A **DataFrame** is a two-dimensional, size-mutable, and potentially heterogeneous tabular data structure with labeled axes (rows and columns). It is the core data structure for data analysis in pandas.

```
# Creating a DataFrame from a dictionary

data = {

    "Name": ["Alice", "Bob", "Charlie", "David"],

    "Age": [25, 30, 35, 40],

    "Department": ["HR", "Engineering", "Marketing", "Finance"]

}

df = pd.DataFrame(data)

print("\nDataFrame:")

print(df)
```

**Explanation:**

- A Series is useful for one-dimensional data.

- A DataFrame organizes data in rows and columns, making it ideal for representing tabular data.

## 2. Reading and Writing Data

Pandas makes it easy to load data from various file formats and export data back to files.

### 2.1 Reading CSV Files

```
# Read data from a CSV file into a DataFrame

df_csv = pd.read_csv("employees.csv")

print("\nCSV Data:")

print(df_csv.head())
```

2.2 Writing Data to CSV Files

```
# Write the DataFrame to a new CSV file

df_csv.to_csv("employees_cleaned.csv", index=False)

print("\nData written to 'employees_cleaned.csv'")
```

2.3 Reading and Writing Excel Files

```
# Reading from an Excel file

df_excel = pd.read_excel("data.xlsx", sheet_name="Sheet1")

print("\nExcel Data:")

print(df_excel.head())

# Writing to an Excel file

df_excel.to_excel("data_processed.xlsx", index=False)

print("\nData written to 'data_processed.xlsx'")
```

**Explanation:**

- read_csv() and read_excel() load data into DataFrames.
- to_csv() and to_excel() export DataFrames to the corresponding file formats.

### 3. Data Cleaning and Transformation

Data wrangling often involves cleaning data, handling missing values, and transforming data into a more usable format.

#### 3.1 Handling Missing Data

```
# Create a sample DataFrame with missing values
data = {
    "Name": ["Alice", "Bob", "Charlie", None],
    "Age": [25, None, 35, 40],
    "Department": ["HR", "Engineering", None, "Finance"]
}
df_missing = pd.DataFrame(data)
print("\nOriginal Data with Missing Values:")
print(df_missing)
# Drop rows with any missing values
df_dropped = df_missing.dropna()
print("\nData after Dropping Missing Values:")
print(df_dropped)
# Fill missing values with specified values
```

```
df_filled = df_missing.fillna({"Name": "Unknown", "Age": df_missing["Age"].mean(), "Department": "Unknown"})

print("\nData after Filling Missing Values:")

print(df_filled)
```

**Explanation:**

- dropna() removes rows that contain any missing values.
- fillna() replaces missing values with specified defaults (e.g., a constant or the mean of a column).

**3.2 Filtering and Selecting Data**

```
# Filtering rows based on a condition

df_filtered = df_filled[df_filled["Age"] > 30]

print("\nFiltered Data (Age > 30):")

print(df_filtered)

# Selecting specific columns

df_selected = df_filled[["Name", "Department"]]

print("\nSelected Columns:")

print(df_selected)
```

**Explanation:**

- Filtering is performed by applying boolean conditions to the DataFrame.
- Column selection is done using a list of column names.

**3.3 Grouping and Aggregation**

```
# Create a sample DataFrame for grouping
```

```
data = {
    "Department": ["HR", "Engineering", "HR", "Engineering", "Marketing"],
    "Salary": [50000, 80000, 55000, 90000, 60000]
}
df_group = pd.DataFrame(data)
print("\nData for Grouping:")
print(df_group)
# Group by Department and calculate the average salary
grouped = df_group.groupby("Department")["Salary"].mean().reset_index()
print("\nAverage Salary by Department:")
print(grouped)
```

**Explanation:**

- groupby() groups data based on one or more columns.
- Aggregation functions (e.g., mean()) are applied to grouped data.
- reset_index() is used to convert the grouped result back to a DataFrame.

### 3.4 Merging and Joining DataFrames

```
# Sample DataFrames for merging
df1 = pd.DataFrame({
    "EmployeeID": [1, 2, 3],
    "Name": ["Alice", "Bob", "Charlie"]
```

```
})
df2 = pd.DataFrame({
    "EmployeeID": [1, 2, 4],
    "Department": ["HR", "Engineering", "Marketing"]
})
# Merge the DataFrames on EmployeeID
merged_df = pd.merge(df1, df2, on="EmployeeID", how="inner")
print("\nMerged DataFrame:")
print(merged_df)
```

**Explanation:**

- pd.merge() combines two DataFrames based on a common key.
- The how="inner" parameter specifies an inner join, meaning only matching rows are included.

### 4. Data Visualization with Pandas

While pandas is primarily a data manipulation library, it has built-in plotting capabilities that leverage Matplotlib for quick visualizations.

#### 4.1 Example: Plotting a Bar Chart

```
import matplotlib.pyplot as plt
# Use the grouped DataFrame from the previous example
plt.figure(figsize=(8, 4))
plt.bar(grouped["Department"], grouped["Salary"], color='skyblue')
plt.xlabel("Department")
plt.ylabel("Average Salary")
```

```
plt.title("Average Salary by Department")

plt.show()
```

**Explanation:**

- A bar chart is created using plt.bar() with departments on the x-axis and average salaries on the y-axis.
- The grouped DataFrame (result of a groupby operation) provides the data for the chart.
- This integration of pandas with Matplotlib allows for quick and effective data visualization.

**5. Best Practices for Data Wrangling with Pandas**

- **Leverage Vectorized Operations:**
  Use pandas' built-in vectorized operations for efficient data processing instead of Python loops.
- **Handle Missing Data Thoughtfully:**
  Decide whether to drop or fill missing values based on the context of your analysis.
- **Chain Methods for Clarity:**
  Use method chaining to write concise, readable code. For example:

```
df_clean =
df.dropna().groupby("Department")["Salary"].mean().reset_index()
```

- **Use Context Managers for File I/O:**
  When reading from or writing to files, use the with statement to ensure proper resource management.
- **Visualize Data Early:**
  Create visualizations early in your analysis to gain insights into your data's distribution and potential issues.

### In Summary

Pandas is an essential tool for data wrangling and analysis in Python. It provides powerful functionalities to:

- **Read and Write Data:**
  Easily load data from CSV, Excel, JSON, and other formats.
- **Clean and Transform Data:**
  Handle missing values, filter, select, group, and merge data efficiently.
- **Visualize Data:**
  Generate quick visualizations to explore data patterns and insights.
- **Process Large Datasets:**
  Leverage vectorized operations and method chaining to work efficiently with large datasets.

By mastering pandas for data wrangling, you can build robust data analysis pipelines that streamline your workflow and facilitate insightful data visualizations.

## Matplotlib and Seaborn for Plotting

Visualizing data is essential for understanding trends, patterns, and insights hidden within datasets. Python offers a variety of powerful libraries for creating static, interactive, and publication-quality visualizations. Two of the most widely used libraries in this domain are **Matplotlib** and **Seaborn**. Matplotlib provides a flexible, low-level API for creating detailed visualizations, while Seaborn builds on top of Matplotlib to offer a high-level, aesthetically pleasing interface for statistical graphics.

### 1. Introduction to Matplotlib

Matplotlib is the foundational plotting library in Python. It allows you to create a wide range of plots, such as line charts, scatter plots, bar charts, histograms, and more. Its core object is pyplot, a module that provides a MATLAB-like interface.

### 1.1 Basic Line Plot

**Example: Plotting a Simple Line Chart**

```
import matplotlib.pyplot as plt

import numpy as np

# Generate sample data

x = np.linspace(0, 10, 100)

y = np.sin(x)

# Create a line plot

plt.plot(x, y, label="sin(x)", color="blue", linewidth=2)

plt.title("Line Plot of sin(x)")

plt.xlabel("x-axis")

plt.ylabel("sin(x)")

plt.legend()

plt.grid(True)

plt.show()
```

**Explanation:**

- **Data Generation:**
  np.linspace(0, 10, 100) creates an array of 100 points between 0 and 10. The sine of these values is computed using np.sin(x).
- **Plotting:**
  plt.plot() plots the line with a label, color, and line width.

- **Customization:**
  The plot is enhanced with a title, axis labels, a legend, and a grid.
- **Display:**
  plt.show() renders the plot.

## 2. Introduction to Seaborn

Seaborn is a statistical data visualization library built on top of Matplotlib. It simplifies the process of creating attractive plots by providing a high-level interface for drawing common types of statistical graphics. Seaborn comes with several built-in datasets and themes that make it easy to create polished visualizations.

### 2.1 Scatter Plot with Seaborn

**Example: Creating a Scatter Plot**

```
import seaborn as sns

import matplotlib.pyplot as plt

# Load an example dataset

tips = sns.load_dataset("tips")

# Create a scatter plot

sns.scatterplot(x="total_bill", y="tip", data=tips, hue="time",
style="sex")

plt.title("Scatter Plot: Total Bill vs. Tip")

plt.xlabel("Total Bill ($)")

plt.ylabel("Tip ($)")

plt.show()
```

**Explanation:**

- **Dataset Loading:**
  sns.load_dataset("tips") loads a sample dataset about restaurant tips.
- **Scatter Plot:**
  sns.scatterplot() creates a scatter plot with total_bill on the x-axis and tip on the y-axis. The plot uses color (hue) to differentiate time of day and marker style (style) to distinguish gender.
- **Customization:**
  The plot includes a title and axis labels for clarity.

### 2.2 Bar Plot and Box Plot with Seaborn

**Example: Bar Plot for Average Total Bill by Day**

```
import seaborn as sns

import matplotlib.pyplot as plt

# Create a bar plot

sns.barplot(x="day", y="total_bill", data=tips, palette="muted", ci=None)

plt.title("Average Total Bill by Day")

plt.xlabel("Day of the Week")

plt.ylabel("Average Total Bill ($)")

plt.show()
```

Example: Box Plot for Total Bill Distribution by Day

```
sns.boxplot(x="day", y="total_bill", data=tips, palette="cool")

plt.title("Box Plot of Total Bill by Day")

plt.xlabel("Day")
```

```
plt.ylabel("Total Bill ($)")

plt.show()
```

**Explanation:**

- **Bar Plot:**
  sns.barplot() aggregates data to display the average total bill for each day. The ci=None parameter disables confidence intervals for simplicity.
- **Box Plot:**
  sns.boxplot() displays the distribution of total bill values by day, including medians and quartiles.
- **Themes and Colors:**
  Seaborn's built-in palettes ("muted", "cool") help create visually appealing plots.

### 3. Combining Matplotlib and Seaborn

Seaborn is built on top of Matplotlib, so you can mix and match functionality from both libraries to fine-tune your visualizations.

**Example: Customizing a Seaborn Plot with Matplotlib**

```
import seaborn as sns

import matplotlib.pyplot as plt

# Load dataset

tips = sns.load_dataset("tips")

# Create a scatter plot using Seaborn

sns.scatterplot(x="total_bill", y="tip", data=tips, hue="time",
style="sex")
```

```
# Customize the plot using Matplotlib
plt.title("Enhanced Scatter Plot: Total Bill vs. Tip")
plt.xlabel("Total Bill ($)")
plt.ylabel("Tip ($)")
plt.xlim(0, 60)  # Set x-axis limits
plt.ylim(0, 15)  # Set y-axis limits
plt.grid(True)
plt.show()
```

**Explanation:**

- The base plot is created using Seaborn's scatterplot().
- Matplotlib's functions (plt.title(), plt.xlabel(), plt.xlim(), etc.) are used to further customize the plot.
- This combination leverages Seaborn's ease of use with Matplotlib's detailed customization capabilities.

### 4. Best Practices for Data Visualization

- **Keep Visualizations Clear:**
  Ensure your plots have appropriate titles, labels, and legends to make them easy to interpret.
- **Choose the Right Plot Type:**
  Select a plot type that best represents your data and the insights you wish to convey. For example, use scatter plots for relationships, bar plots for comparisons, and box plots for distributions.
- **Utilize Color Wisely:**
  Use color palettes consistently to enhance readability without overwhelming the viewer.

- **Optimize for Performance:**
  When working with large datasets, consider downsampling or using efficient plotting techniques to avoid performance issues.
- **Iterate and Refine:**
  Data visualization is an iterative process. Use feedback to refine your plots for clarity and impact.

**In Summary**

Matplotlib and Seaborn are powerful libraries for data visualization in Python:

- **Matplotlib:**
  Offers granular control over every aspect of your plot, making it ideal for customized visualizations.
- **Seaborn:**
  Provides a high-level interface for creating attractive, statistical graphics with minimal effort.
- **Combining Tools:**
  You can use Seaborn for rapid visualization and then leverage Matplotlib's customization features to fine-tune the final output.

By mastering these libraries, you can create clear, informative, and aesthetically pleasing visualizations that help communicate data insights effectively.

# Chapter 25: Web Development

## Flask vs. Django: Basic Comparison

Flask and Django are two of the most popular web frameworks in Python, each offering distinct philosophies and feature sets that cater to different project needs. Understanding the strengths and trade-offs of each can help you choose the best framework for your project.

### 1. Overview

#### Flask

- **Microframework:**
  Flask is a lightweight "microframework" that provides the essentials for web development. It is highly flexible and allows you to add only the components you need.
- **Flexibility:**
  Flask gives you fine-grained control over your application's structure and components. You can choose your own database, form library, and template engine.
- **Simplicity:**
  Flask's minimalistic design makes it easy to learn and use, which is ideal for small to medium-sized projects, prototypes, and microservices.

#### Django

- **Full-Featured Framework:**
  Django is a high-level web framework that includes many built-in features, such as an ORM (Object-Relational Mapping), an admin interface, authentication, and more.
- **Convention Over Configuration:**
  Django follows a "batteries-included" approach and enforces a

standard project structure, which can speed up development by reducing the need for boilerplate code.

- **Rapid Development:**
  With many built-in tools and an emphasis on best practices, Django is well-suited for large-scale applications that require rapid development and robust security.

## 2. Architectural Differences

### Flask

- **Lightweight and Modular:**
  Flask's core is minimal, and additional functionality is provided by extensions. This modularity allows you to build an application tailored exactly to your needs.
- **Routing and Views:**
  Flask uses decorators to map URLs to Python functions (views). Each view is responsible for handling a particular route.

### Flask Example: Minimal Application

```
from flask import Flask, jsonify

app = Flask(__name__)

@app.route("/")

def home():

    return "Welcome to Flask!"

@app.route("/api/data")

def get_data():

    # Return a JSON response

    data = {"message": "Hello from Flask API"}
```

```
    return jsonify(data)

if __name__ == "__main__":

    app.run(debug=True)
```

**Explanation:**

- The example creates a simple Flask app with two routes: a home page and an API endpoint that returns JSON data.
- The @app.route() decorator maps URLs to view functions.
- Running this app starts a lightweight development server.

**Django**

- **Monolithic and Convention-Driven:**
  Django provides a complete, integrated solution that includes an ORM, templating system, authentication, and an admin interface. This "all-in-one" approach enforces a standard structure.
- **MVC Pattern (MVT in Django):**
  Django follows the Model-View-Template (MVT) pattern. Models represent the data layer, views handle business logic, and templates are used for presentation.

**Django Example: Minimal Application Structure**

1. **Project Setup:**

```
django-admin startproject myproject

cd myproject

python manage.py startapp myapp
```

2. Defining a View in myapp/views.py:

```
from django.http import HttpResponse, JsonResponse
```

```
def home(request):
    return HttpResponse("Welcome to Django!")
def get_data(request):
    data = {"message": "Hello from Django API"}
    return JsonResponse(data)
```

3. Mapping URLs in myapp/urls.py:

```
from django.urls import path
from .views import home, get_data
urlpatterns = [
    path("", home, name="home"),
    path("api/data/", get_data, name="get_data"),
]
```

4. Including the App URLs in myproject/urls.py

```
from django.contrib import admin
from django.urls import path, include
urlpatterns = [
    path('admin/', admin.site.urls),
    path('', include('myapp.urls')),
]
```

5. Running the Development Server:

```
python manage.py runserver
```

**Explanation:**

- The Django example demonstrates setting up a project and an app, defining views, and mapping URLs.
- Django's built-in development server serves your application, and the URL configuration routes requests to the appropriate view functions.
- The structure enforces a clear separation of concerns, with models, views, and templates organized in distinct files and directories.

**3. Key Comparison Points**

- **Learning Curve:**
  - *Flask:*
    Easier to learn due to its minimalistic nature. Ideal for beginners or small projects.
  - *Django:*
    Has a steeper learning curve because of its many built-in features and conventions but offers more structure for large projects.
- **Flexibility vs. Convention:**
  - *Flask:*
    Offers greater flexibility, allowing you to choose libraries and project structure.
  - *Django:*
    Emphasizes convention over configuration, which can accelerate development but may be less flexible for unconventional requirements.

- **Built-in Features:**
  - *Flask:*
    Provides a basic core with minimal features. Functionality is extended through third-party extensions.
  - *Django:*
    Comes with a rich set of built-in features (ORM, admin panel, authentication, form handling, etc.) that cater to full-stack web development.
- **Scalability and Maintenance:**
  - *Flask:*
    Suitable for smaller applications or microservices. Scalability can be achieved with careful design.
  - *Django:*
    Designed for larger applications with robust security and scalability features built-in.

**4. When to Choose Flask vs. Django**

- **Flask:**
  - Use Flask for small to medium-sized applications, prototypes, or microservices where you want full control over the components.
  - Ideal when you need a simple, flexible solution without many predefined conventions.
- **Django:**
  - Choose Django for large, complex applications where rapid development and built-in features (like the admin interface and ORM) are beneficial.
  - Best when you prefer a framework that enforces a standard project structure and includes many out-of-the-box tools.

### In Summary

Both Flask and Django are powerful web frameworks, each with its own strengths:

- **Flask:**
  - Minimalistic and highly flexible.
  - Provides the essentials, with the ability to extend functionality using third-party extensions.
  - Best suited for smaller applications and microservices.
- **Django:**
  - A full-featured, batteries-included framework.
  - Enforces a robust project structure with many built-in tools for database handling, authentication, and more.
  - Ideal for large-scale applications requiring rapid development and comprehensive functionality.

Understanding these differences helps you choose the right framework based on your project requirements, development speed, and long-term maintenance considerations.

## Building a Simple Web App with Flask

Flask is a lightweight, micro web framework for Python that makes it easy to build web applications quickly and with minimal overhead. It provides the essential tools to route HTTP requests, render responses, and integrate with templates and databases, while allowing you the flexibility to structure your project as you see fit.

### 1. Introduction to Flask

Flask is designed to be simple yet extensible. It doesn't enforce a particular project structure, making it ideal for small to medium-sized projects, prototypes, and microservices. Flask's core functionality includes:

- **Routing:** Mapping URLs to Python functions.
- **Templating:** Using Jinja2 for dynamic HTML generation.
- **Request Handling:** Managing GET and POST requests.
- **Development Server:** A built-in server for testing your application locally.

### 2. Setting Up a Basic Flask Application

A basic Flask application involves creating an instance of the Flask class, defining route handlers (view functions), and running the development server.

**Example: Minimal Flask App**

```
from flask import Flask

# Create a Flask application instance

app = Flask(__name__)

# Define a route for the home page

@app.route("/")

def home():

    return "<h1>Welcome to my Flask Web App!</h1><p>This is the home page.</p>"

# Define another route for the About page

@app.route("/about")

def about():
```

```
    return "<h1>About</h1><p>This is a simple web app built with Flask.</p>"

if __name__ == "__main__":
    # Run the app in debug mode for development
    app.run(debug=True)
```

**Explanation:**

- **Creating the App:**
  The application instance is created with app = Flask(__name__). The __name__ variable helps Flask determine the root path of the application.
- **Routing:**
  The @app.route("/") decorator maps the URL path / to the home function. Similarly, /about is mapped to the about function.
- **Running the Server:**
  The app.run(debug=True) command starts the development server in debug mode. Debug mode provides detailed error messages and automatically reloads the server when code changes.

3. Handling GET and POST Requests

Web applications often need to process form data or other user inputs. Flask simplifies this by allowing you to specify the HTTP methods a route should accept.

Example: A Greeting Form

```
from flask import Flask, request, redirect, url_for, render_template_string
```

```
app = Flask(__name__)
# Define a route that handles both GET and POST requests
@app.route("/greet", methods=["GET", "POST"])
def greet():
    if request.method == "POST":
        # Retrieve the name from the submitted form data
        name = request.form.get("name", "Guest")
        # Return a personalized greeting
        return f"<h1>Hello, {name}!</h1><p><a
href='{url_for('greet')}'>Greet another</a></p>"
    else:
        # Display the form for the user to input their name
        form_html = """
        <h1>Greeting Form</h1>
        <form method="post">
            <label for="name">Enter your name:</label>
            <input type="text" id="name" name="name"
placeholder="Your name">
            <input type="submit" value="Greet me!">
        </form>
        """
        return render_template_string(form_html)
```

```
if __name__ == "__main__":
    app.run(debug=True)
```

**Explanation:**

- **Route Handling Both Methods:**
  The /greet route accepts both GET and POST requests.
- **Processing Form Data:**
  If the request method is POST, the function retrieves the submitted name using request.form.get() and returns a personalized greeting.
- **Rendering a Form:**
  For GET requests, a simple HTML form is rendered using render_template_string().
- **Redirection:**
  The example includes a link to allow the user to return to the form for additional greetings.

## 4. Using Templates for Better Organization

For more complex applications, separating HTML into template files is preferred over embedding HTML in your Python code. Flask uses the Jinja2 templating engine, which allows for dynamic content rendering.

### Example: Using a Template File

1. **Project Structure:**

```
my_flask_app/
├── app.py
└── templates/
    └── greet.html
```

2. Template File: templates/greet.html

```
<!DOCTYPE html>
<html>
<head>
  <title>Greeting Form</title>
</head>
<body>
  <h1>Greeting Form</h1>
  {% if name %}
    <h2>Hello, {{ name }}!</h2>
    <p><a href="{{ url_for('greet') }}">Greet again</a></p>
  {% else %}
    <form method="post">
      <label for="name">Enter your name:</label>
      <input type="text" id="name" name="name"
placeholder="Your name">
      <input type="submit" value="Greet me!">
    </form>
  {% endif %}
</body>
</html>
```

3. Flask Application: app.py

```
from flask import Flask, request, render_template, redirect, url_for
```

```
app = Flask(__name__)
@app.route("/greet", methods=["GET", "POST"])
def greet():
    if request.method == "POST":
        name = request.form.get("name", "Guest")
        return render_template("greet.html", name=name)
    return render_template("greet.html", name=None)
if __name__ == "__main__":
    app.run(debug=True)
```

**Explanation:**

- **Template Directory:**
  Flask automatically looks for templates in a folder named templates.
- **Template Rendering:**
  The render_template() function is used to render the HTML template and pass variables (like name) to it.
- **Dynamic Content:**
  The template uses Jinja2 syntax to conditionally display content based on whether the name variable is provided.

**5. Best Practices for Building a Simple Flask Web App**

- **Keep Routes Organized:**
  Define clear and concise routes that map directly to specific functionalities.

- **Use Templates for HTML:**
  Separate presentation logic from application logic by using templates.
- **Implement Error Handling:**
  Use error handlers to manage HTTP errors (e.g., 404, 500) gracefully.
- **Enable Debug Mode During Development:**
  Use debug=True in app.run() to automatically reload your server and provide detailed error reports. However, disable debug mode in production.
- **Modularize Your Code:**
  For larger applications, consider structuring your project into blueprints or packages to organize routes, models, and templates.

**In Summary**

Building a simple web app with Flask involves:

- **Creating a Flask Application:**
  Instantiate a Flask object and define routes using decorators.
- **Handling Requests:**
  Manage GET and POST requests to interact with users.
- **Rendering Templates:**
  Use Jinja2 templates to separate HTML from Python code, promoting a clean codebase.
- **Running the Application:**
  Use the built-in development server with debug mode for rapid development and troubleshooting.

By mastering these fundamental concepts, you can build scalable and maintainable web applications using Flask, taking full advantage of Python's simplicity and flexibility.

## Templates and Routing

Templates and routing are fundamental components of modern web development frameworks. They work together to determine how an application responds to user requests and presents dynamic content. Routing maps URLs to Python functions (view functions), while templates allow you to separate the presentation layer from your business logic by generating dynamic HTML pages.

### 1. Routing

**Routing** is the process of defining URL patterns and linking them to corresponding functions in your application. When a user visits a URL, the framework determines which function to call based on these routes.

**Key Concepts:**

- **URL Mapping:**
  Routes associate specific URL patterns with view functions.
- **HTTP Methods:**
  Routes can handle different HTTP methods (e.g., GET, POST) to determine the behavior for a given endpoint.
- **Dynamic Routing:**
  Routes can include variable parts (e.g., <int:id>) to handle dynamic content.

**Example: Basic Routing with Flask**

```
from flask import Flask, request

app = Flask(__name__)

# Route for the home page

@app.route("/")

def home():
```

```
    return "<h1>Welcome to the Home Page</h1>"
# Route with dynamic URL parameter
@app.route("/user/<username>")
def user_profile(username):
    return f"<h1>User Profile: {username}</h1>"
# Route handling both GET and POST requests
@app.route("/submit", methods=["GET", "POST"])
def submit():
    if request.method == "POST":
        data = request.form.get("data", "No data provided")
        return f"<h1>Data Received: {data}</h1>"
    return '''
        <form method="post">
            <input type="text" name="data" placeholder="Enter some data">
            <input type="submit" value="Submit">
        </form>
    '''
if __name__ == "__main__":
    app.run(debug=True)
```

**Explanation:**

- **Static Routes:**
  The / route returns a simple welcome message.

- **Dynamic Routes:**
  The /user/<username> route extracts the username from the URL and uses it in the response.
- **Handling Methods:**
  The /submit route handles both GET (displaying the form) and POST (processing form data) requests.

**2. Templates**

**Templates** enable you to generate dynamic HTML content by separating the presentation layer from your application logic. Flask uses the Jinja2 templating engine, which supports template inheritance, variable interpolation, and control structures.

**Key Concepts:**

- **Template Files:**
  HTML files with placeholders for dynamic content, stored in a dedicated templates directory.
- **Variable Interpolation:**
  Insert variables into the HTML using Jinja2 syntax ({{ variable }}).
- **Control Structures:**
  Use loops and conditional statements in templates with {% %} syntax.
- **Template Inheritance:**
  Create a base template that defines the common structure, which other templates can extend.

**Example: Basic Template**

1. **Project Structure:**

```
my_flask_app/
├── app.py
└── templates/
    ├── base.html
    └── home.html
```

2. **Base Template (templates/base.html):**

```
<!DOCTYPE html>
<html>
<head>
    <title>{% block title %}My Web App{% endblock %}</title>
</head>
<body>
    <header>
        <h1>Welcome to My Web App</h1>
    </header>
    <main>
        {% block content %}
        {% endblock %}
    </main>
    <footer>
        <p>&copy; 2024 My Web App</p>
    </footer>
```

```
</body>
</html>
```

3. Home Template (templates/home.html):

```
{% extends "base.html" %}
% block title %}
Home - My Web App
{% endblock %}
{% block content %}
<p>This is the home page content, dynamically rendered using a template.</p>
{% endblock %}
```

4. Flask Application (app.py):

```
from flask import Flask, render_template
app = Flask(__name__)
@app.route("/")
def home():
    # Render the home template, which extends the base template
    return render_template("home.html")
if __name__ == "__main__":
    app.run(debug=True)
```

**Explanation:**

- **Template Inheritance:**
  The home.html template extends base.html and fills in the title and content blocks.

- **render_template():**
  The render_template function in Flask loads the specified template and renders it with any passed variables.

- **Separation of Concerns:**
  By separating the HTML structure (templates) from the application logic (Flask routes), the code becomes easier to manage and maintain.

### 3. Combining Templates and Routing

Templates and routing work together to create dynamic web applications. Routes determine what content is displayed, while templates define how the content is structured and styled.

**Example: Dynamic User Profile Page**

1. **User Profile Template (templates/user_profile.html):**

```
{% extends "base.html" %}

{% block title %}

Profile - {{ username }}

{% endblock %}

{% block content %}

<h2>User Profile for {{ username }}</h2>

<p>Welcome, {{ username }}! This is your profile page.</p>

{% endblock %}
```

2. **Flask Application with Dynamic Route (app.py):**

```
from flask import Flask, render_template
app = Flask(__name__)
@app.route("/")
def home():
    return render_template("home.html")
@app.route("/user/<username>")
def user_profile(username):
    # Pass the username to the template
    return render_template("user_profile.html", username=username)
if __name__ == "__main__":
    app.run(debug=True)
```

**Explanation:**

- **Dynamic Routing:**
  The /user/<username> route dynamically captures the username from the URL.
- **Template Variables:**
  The captured username is passed to the user_profile.html template, where it is used to dynamically populate the page content.
- **User Experience:**
  This approach allows the application to render personalized pages for different users without duplicating code.

## 4. Best Practices for Templates and Routing

- **Keep Business Logic Out of Templates:**
  Templates should focus solely on presentation. Use view functions (routes) to handle business logic and pass the processed data to templates.
- **Use Template Inheritance:**
  Create a base template that contains common layout elements (header, footer, navigation) and extend it in child templates. This promotes consistency and reduces code duplication.
- **Design Clear Routes:**
  Define routes that are intuitive and consistent. Use meaningful URL patterns that reflect the content they serve.
- **Organize Templates:**
  Store templates in a dedicated directory (usually named templates) and organize them logically based on the application structure.
- **Utilize URL Building:**
  Use functions like url_for() in Flask to generate URLs dynamically, which helps avoid hardcoding and facilitates maintenance.

### In Summary

Templates and routing are the backbone of web development in frameworks like Flask:

- **Routing:**
  Determines how URLs map to view functions, which process requests and return responses.
- **Templates:**
  Define the structure and layout of your web pages, allowing you to render dynamic content.

- **Integration:**
  Together, they enable the creation of dynamic, data-driven web applications that separate business logic from presentation.
- **Best Practices:**
  Keep business logic in view functions, use template inheritance for consistency, and maintain clear and organized project structures.

By mastering templates and routing, you can build robust, scalable, and maintainable web applications that deliver dynamic content and an engaging user experience.

## Example Exercises: Building a Mini Blog

Building a mini blog is an excellent exercise to learn how to combine various web development concepts such as routing, templating, form handling, and data persistence into a single, cohesive application. In this exercise, we'll build a simple blog using Flask - a lightweight web framework in Python. This mini blog will allow users to view a list of blog posts, view individual post details, and create new posts using a web form.

### 1. Project Structure

A well-organized project structure is key to maintainability. For our mini blog, we can use a structure similar to the following:

```
mini_blog/
│
├── app.py
├── posts.py          # (Optional) For managing blog posts (data storage)
├── templates/
│   ├── base.html
│   ├── index.html
│   ├── post.html
│   └── new_post.html
└── static/           # (Optional) For CSS, images, JavaScript
    └── style.css
```

- **app.py:** The main application file containing route definitions and application logic.
- **posts.py:** A module to manage blog post data (for simplicity, we will use an in-memory list).
- **templates/:** Contains HTML templates for different pages.
- **static/:** Holds static files like CSS (optional for basic functionality).

### 2. Creating the Mini Blog Application

Below, we provide comprehensive code examples for each part of the mini blog.

### 2.1 Managing Blog Posts (posts.py)

For demonstration purposes, we'll use an in-memory list to store blog posts. In a production app, you would likely use a database.

```
# posts.py

# This module manages blog post data.

posts = []  # List to store blog posts as dictionaries

def add_post(title, content):
    """
    Add a new post to the posts list.
    Parameters:
        title (str): The title of the post.
        content (str): The content of the post.
    """
    post_id = len(posts) + 1  # Simple auto-incrementing ID
    post = {
        "id": post_id,
        "title": title,
        "content": content
    }
    posts.append(post)


def get_all_posts():
    """Return all blog posts."""
```

```
    return posts
def get_post(post_id):
    """
    Retrieve a post by its ID.
    Parameters:
        post_id (int): The ID of the post.
    Returns:
        dict or None: The post dictionary if found, else None.
    """
    for post in posts:
        if post["id"] == post_id:
            return post
    return None
```

**Explanation:**

- add_post adds a new blog post with a unique ID.
- get_all_posts returns all posts.
- get_post retrieves a single post by its ID.

**2.2 Flask Application (app.py)**

The Flask application will define routes to display the list of posts, view an individual post, and create new posts via a form.

```
# app.py
from flask import Flask, render_template, request, redirect, url_for
import posts  # Import our simple posts management module
```

```
app = Flask(__name__)
# Home route: Display all blog posts
@app.route("/")
def index():
    all_posts = posts.get_all_posts()
    return render_template("index.html", posts=all_posts)
# Route to display a single blog post by ID
@app.route("/post/<int:post_id>")
def post_detail(post_id):
    post = posts.get_post(post_id)
    if post:
        return render_template("post.html", post=post)
    else:
        return "Post not found", 404
# Route to create a new post (handles both GET and POST
requests)
@app.route("/new", methods=["GET", "POST"])
def new_post():
    if request.method == "POST":
        title = request.form.get("title")
        content = request.form.get("content")
        if title and content:
```

```
            posts.add_post(title, content)
            return redirect(url_for("index"))
        else:
            error = "Title and content are required."
            return render_template("new_post.html", error=error)
    return render_template("new_post.html")


if __name__ == "__main__":
    app.run(debug=True)
```

**Explanation:**

- **Index Route ("/"):**
  Retrieves all posts using posts.get_all_posts() and passes them to the index.html template.
- **Post Detail Route ("/post/<int:post_id>"):**
  Displays details for a specific post based on the dynamic URL parameter.
- **New Post Route ("/new"):**
  Handles both GET (rendering the form) and POST (processing form submission) methods. If the post data is valid, it adds the post and redirects to the index; otherwise, it displays an error.

### 2.3 HTML Templates

Create a directory named templates and add the following HTML files:

**base.html**

```
<!-- templates/base.html -->
```

```
<!DOCTYPE html>
<html>
<head>
    <meta charset="UTF-8">
    <title>{% block title %}Mini Blog{% endblock %}</title>
    <link rel="stylesheet" href="{{ url_for('static',
filename='style.css') }}">
</head>
<body>
    <header>
        <h1>Mini Blog</h1>
        <nav>
            <a href="{{ url_for('index') }}">Home</a> |
            <a href="{{ url_for('new_post') }}">New Post</a>
        </nav>
    </header>
    <main>
        {% block content %}{% endblock %}
    </main>
    <footer>
        <p>&copy; 2024 Mini Blog</p>
    </footer>
</body>
```

```
</html>
```

index.html

```
<!-- templates/index.html -->
{% extends "base.html" %}
{% block title %}Home - Mini Blog{% endblock %}
{% block content %}
<h2>All Posts</h2>
{% if posts %}
   <ul>
      {% for post in posts %}
      <li>
         <a href="{{ url_for('post_detail', post_id=post.id) }}">{{ post.title }}</a>
      </li>
      {% endfor %}
   </ul>
{% else %}
   <p>No posts available.</p>
{% endif %}
{% endblock %}
```

post.html

```
<!-- templates/post.html -->
{% extends "base.html" %}
```

```
{% block title %}{{ post.title }} - Mini Blog{% endblock %}
{% block content %}
<article>
    <h2>{{ post.title }}</h2>
    <p>{{ post.content }}</p>
    <a href="{{ url_for('index') }}">Back to Home</a>
</article>
{% endblock %}
```

new_post.html

```
<!-- templates/new_post.html -->
{% extends "base.html" %}
{% block title %}New Post - Mini Blog{% endblock %}
{% block content %}
<h2>Create a New Post</h2>
{% if error %}
    <p style="color:red;">{{ error }}</p>
{% endif %}
<form method="post">
    <label for="title">Title:</label><br>
    <input type="text" id="title" name="title"><br><br>
    <label for="content">Content:</label><br>
```

```
    <textarea id="content" name="content" rows="5"
cols="30"></textarea><br><br>

    <input type="submit" value="Submit">

</form>

{% endblock %}
```

**Explanation:**

- **Base Template (base.html):**
  Defines the overall structure of the web pages (header, navigation, footer) and includes a placeholder for content using {% block content %}.
- **Index Template (index.html):**
  Extends base.html and displays a list of posts with links to individual post details.
- **Post Detail Template (post.html):**
  Displays the title and content of a single post.
- **New Post Template (new_post.html):**
  Provides a form for creating a new post. If there is an error (e.g., missing title or content), it displays an error message.

**4. Running the Mini Blog**

To run your mini blog:

1. Ensure your project structure is as described.
2. Execute python app.py from the project root.
3. Open a web browser and navigate to http://127.0.0.1:5000/ to view your blog.

## 5. Best Practices for Web Development with Flask

- **Separate Concerns:**
  Keep your routing logic, business logic, and presentation (templates) separate.
- **Use URL Building:**
  Use url_for() to generate URLs dynamically, which prevents hardcoding and makes your code more maintainable.
- **Form Handling:**
  Validate and sanitize form inputs to avoid issues such as injection attacks.
- **Debug Mode:**
  Use debug=True only during development; disable it in production for security.
- **Modularize Your Application:**
  For larger applications, consider using Flask blueprints to organize your routes and views into separate modules.

### In Summary

Building a mini blog with Flask involves:

- **Defining Routes:**
  Map URLs to view functions that handle different aspects of the blog (home page, post details, new post form).
- **Using Templates:**
  Render dynamic HTML pages using Jinja2 templates that extend a base layout for consistency.
- **Handling Forms:**
  Process GET and POST requests to allow users to submit new blog posts.

- **Data Persistence:**
  For this simple example, blog posts are stored in memory. In a real application, consider using a database for persistent storage.

This exercise demonstrates how to integrate routing, templates, and form handling to build a functional and scalable web application using Flask. By mastering these concepts, you can create dynamic web applications tailored to your specific needs.

# Section XI: Project Deployment and Best Practices
## Chapter 26: Packaging and Distribution

### Using setuptools and pip for Installation

Packaging and distributing your Python projects allows others to install and use your code easily, whether for personal use, open-source contributions, or commercial applications. The most common tools for packaging Python projects are **setuptools** for building distribution packages and **pip** for installing them.

#### 1. Overview of Packaging and Distribution

- **Packaging:**
  Packaging involves organizing your code, metadata, and resources in a standard format so that it can be easily shared and installed. Python packages typically include a directory structure with modules, an optional README, license files, and a setup script.
- **Distribution:**
  Once packaged, your project can be distributed via the Python Package Index (PyPI) or other channels. Users can install your package using pip.
- **setuptools:**
  Setuptools is the de facto tool for building and distributing Python packages. It extends Python's standard library with utilities for packaging.
- **pip:**
  pip is the standard package installer for Python, which installs packages from PyPI and other package repositories.

#### 2. Structuring Your Project

A typical Python project structure for packaging might look like this:

```
my_project/
├── my_package/
│   ├── __init__.py
│   ├── module1.py
│   └── module2.py
├── tests/
│   └── test_module1.py
├── README.md
├── LICENSE
└── setup.py
```

- **my_package/**: Contains your package's modules.
- **tests/**: Contains test scripts.
- **README.md**: Provides an overview and usage instructions.
- **LICENSE**: Contains licensing information.
- **setup.py**: The build script for setuptools, which defines package metadata and dependencies.

### 3. Creating a setup.py File

The setup.py file is the heart of your package distribution. It defines metadata about your project (name, version, description, etc.), its dependencies, and which modules to include.

**Example: A Basic setup.py File**

```
from setuptools import setup, find_packages

setup(
```

```
    name="my_project",
    version="0.1.0",
    author="Your Name",
    author_email="your.email@example.com",
    description="A short description of your project.",
    long_description=open("README.md").read(),
    long_description_content_type="text/markdown",
    url="https://github.com/yourusername/my_project",
    packages=find_packages(),  # Automatically find packages in the
project directory
    classifiers=[
        "Programming Language :: Python :: 3",
        "License :: OSI Approved :: MIT License",
        "Operating System :: OS Independent",
    ],
    python_requires=">=3.6",
    install_requires=[
        # List your project's dependencies here, e.g.:
        # "requests>=2.25.1",
    ],
)
```

**Explanation:**

- **Metadata:**
  Fields such as name, version, author, and description provide essential information about your package.
- **long_description:**
  Reads the contents of README.md for a detailed description on PyPI.
- **find_packages():**
  Automatically discovers all packages and sub-packages in your project.
- **classifiers:**
  Provide standardized metadata about your package, such as supported Python versions and license.
- **python_requires:**
  Specifies the Python version requirement.
- **install_requires:**
  Lists the package dependencies that pip will install automatically.

### 4. Building the Distribution Package

Once your setup.py is ready, you can build your package into a distributable format using setuptools. The common formats are:

- **Source Distribution (sdist):**
  A tarball containing your source code.
- **Built Distribution (wheel):**
  A pre-built package that is faster to install.

**Steps to Build:**

1. **Install build tools (if not already installed):**

```
pip install setuptools wheel
```

2. Build the package:

```
python setup.py sdist bdist_wheel
```

1. This command generates distribution files in a new dist/ directory.

**Explanation:**

- The sdist command creates a source distribution.
- The bdist_wheel command creates a wheel distribution, which is the preferred format for installation.

**5. Installing Your Package with pip**

After building your package, you can install it using pip. This is useful for testing the installation process or distributing your package to other environments.

**Example: Installing from a Local Distribution**

```
pip install dist/my_project-0.1.0-py3-none-any.whl
```

**Explanation:**

- Replace my_project-0.1.0-py3-none-any.whl with the actual filename generated in the dist/ directory.
- pip installs the package along with any dependencies specified in install_requires.

**Example: Upgrading an Installed Package**

```
pip install --upgrade dist/my_project-0.1.0-py3-none-any.whl
```

**Explanation:**

- The --upgrade flag tells pip to upgrade the package if an older version is already installed.

**6. Publishing Your Package to PyPI**

Once your package is ready and thoroughly tested, you can publish it to the Python Package Index (PyPI) so that others can install it via pip.

**Steps to Publish:**

1. **Install Twine:**

```
pip install twine
```

2. Upload Your Package:

```
twine upload dist/*
```

Follow the prompts to authenticate with your PyPI credentials.

**Explanation:**

- Twine is a utility for securely uploading Python packages to PyPI.
- After a successful upload, your package becomes publicly available for installation via pip.

**7. Best Practices for Packaging and Distribution**

- **Organize Your Code:**
  Use a clear directory structure for your project with separate directories for your package, tests, documentation, and configuration files.
- **Write Comprehensive Documentation:**
  Include a detailed README.md, a changelog, and inline documentation to help users understand and use your package.
- **Automate Testing:**
  Integrate automated tests to ensure that your package works as expected before distribution.

- **Versioning:**
  Follow semantic versioning (e.g., MAJOR.MINOR.PATCH) to clearly indicate changes and compatibility.
- **Use Virtual Environments:**
  Develop and test your package in isolated virtual environments to avoid dependency conflicts.

**In Summary**

Packaging and distributing your Python projects using setuptools and pip offers many benefits:

- **Modularity and Reusability:**
  Packaging allows you to structure your code into reusable modules.
- **Ease of Distribution:**
  Creating source and wheel distributions enables easy installation with pip.
- **Community Sharing:**
  Publishing your package to PyPI makes it accessible to a global community of developers.
- **Best Practices:**
  Following best practices in organization, documentation, versioning, and testing helps maintain a high-quality, maintainable project.

By mastering these packaging and distribution techniques, you can ensure that your Python projects are easy to install, use, and maintain, fostering a smoother development workflow and broader collaboration.

## Structuring a Python Project for Distribution

A well-organized project structure is essential for packaging, distributing, and maintaining a Python project. By following established conventions, you ensure that your project is easy to navigate, test, and share with other developers.

### 1. Recommended Project Structure

```
my_project/
├── my_package/            # Main package directory
│   ├── __init__.py        # Package initialization file
│   ├── module1.py         # Module containing core functionality
│   ├── module2.py         # Additional module(s)
│   └── subpackage/        # Subpackage (optional)
│       ├── __init__.py
│       └── module3.py
├── tests/                 # Test suite for your project
│   ├── __init__.py        # Optional: Makes tests a package
│   └── test_module1.py    # Test file for module1
├── docs/                  # Documentation files (optional)
│   └── index.md
├── setup.py               # Build script for setuptools
├── requirements.txt       # List of runtime dependencies
├── MANIFEST.in            # Instructions for including non-
code files
├── README.md              # Project description and usage
instructions
└── LICENSE                # License file
```

# Section XI: Project Deployment and Best Practices
# Chapter 27: Packaging and Distribution

## Using setuptools and pip for Installation

Packaging and distributing your Python projects allows others to install and use your code easily, whether for personal use, open-source contributions, or commercial applications. The most common tools for packaging Python projects are **setuptools** for building distribution packages and **pip** for installing them. In this section, we'll explore how to package a Python project using setuptools and how to distribute and install it via pip.

### 1. Overview of Packaging and Distribution

- **Packaging:**
  Packaging involves organizing your code, metadata, and resources in a standard format so that it can be easily shared and installed. Python packages typically include a directory structure with modules, an optional README, license files, and a setup script.
- **Distribution:**
  Once packaged, your project can be distributed via the Python Package Index (PyPI) or other channels. Users can install your package using pip.
- **setuptools:**
  Setuptools is the de facto tool for building and distributing Python packages. It extends Python's standard library with utilities for packaging.
- **pip:**
  pip is the standard package installer for Python, which installs packages from PyPI and other package repositories.

## 2. Structuring Your Project

A typical Python project structure for packaging might look like this:

```
my_project/
├── my_package/
│   ├── __init__.py
│   ├── module1.py
│   └── module2.py
├── tests/
│   └── test_module1.py
├── README.md
├── LICENSE
└── setup.py
```

- **my_package/**: Contains your package's modules.
- **tests/**: Contains test scripts.
- **README.md**: Provides an overview and usage instructions.
- **LICENSE**: Contains licensing information.
- **setup.py**: The build script for setuptools, which defines package metadata and dependencies.

## 3. Creating a setup.py File

The setup.py file is the heart of your package distribution. It defines metadata about your project (name, version, description, etc.), its dependencies, and which modules to include.

**Example: A Basic setup.py File**

```
from setuptools import setup, find_packages

setup(
    name="my_project",
    version="0.1.0",
    author="Your Name",
    author_email="your.email@example.com",
    description="A short description of your project.",
    long_description=open("README.md").read(),
    long_description_content_type="text/markdown",
    url="https://github.com/yourusername/my_project",
    packages=find_packages(),  # Automatically find packages in the
project directory
    classifiers=[
        "Programming Language :: Python :: 3",
        "License :: OSI Approved :: MIT License",
        "Operating System :: OS Independent",
    ],
    python_requires=">=3.6",
    install_requires=[
        # List your project's dependencies here, e.g.:
        # "requests>=2.25.1",
    ],
)
```

**Explanation:**

- **Metadata:**
  Fields such as name, version, author, and description provide essential information about your package.
- **long_description:**
  Reads the contents of README.md for a detailed description on PyPI.
- **find_packages():**
  Automatically discovers all packages and sub-packages in your project.
- **classifiers:**
  Provide standardized metadata about your package, such as supported Python versions and license.
- **python_requires:**
  Specifies the Python version requirement.
- **install_requires:**
  Lists the package dependencies that pip will install automatically.

**4. Building the Distribution Package**

Once your setup.py is ready, you can build your package into a distributable format using setuptools. The common formats are:

- **Source Distribution (sdist):**
  A tarball containing your source code.
- **Built Distribution (wheel):**
  A pre-built package that is faster to install.

**Steps to Build:**

1. **Install build tools (if not already installed):**

```
pip install setuptools wheel
```

2. Build the package:

```
python setup.py sdist bdist_wheel
```

This command generates distribution files in a new dist/ directory.

**Explanation:**

- The sdist command creates a source distribution.
- The bdist_wheel command creates a wheel distribution, which is the preferred format for installation.

### 5. Installing Your Package with pip

After building your package, you can install it using pip. This is useful for testing the installation process or distributing your package to other environments.

**Example: Installing from a Local Distribution**

```
pip install dist/my_project-0.1.0-py3-none-any.whl
```

**Explanation:**

- Replace my_project-0.1.0-py3-none-any.whl with the actual filename generated in the dist/ directory.
- pip installs the package along with any dependencies specified in install_requires.

**Example: Upgrading an Installed Package**

```
pip install --upgrade dist/my_project-0.1.0-py3-none-any.whl
```

**Explanation:**

- The --upgrade flag tells pip to upgrade the package if an older version is already installed.

## 6. Publishing Your Package to PyPI

Once your package is ready and thoroughly tested, you can publish it to the Python Package Index (PyPI) so that others can install it via pip.

**Steps to Publish:**

1. **Install Twine:**

```
pip install twine
```

2. Upload Your Package:

```
twine upload dist/*
```

Follow the prompts to authenticate with your PyPI credentials.

**Explanation:**

- Twine is a utility for securely uploading Python packages to PyPI.
- After a successful upload, your package becomes publicly available for installation via pip.

## 7. Best Practices for Packaging and Distribution

- **Organize Your Code:**
  Use a clear directory structure for your project with separate directories for your package, tests, documentation, and configuration files.
- **Write Comprehensive Documentation:**
  Include a detailed README.md, a changelog, and inline documentation to help users understand and use your package.
- **Automate Testing:**
  Integrate automated tests to ensure that your package works as expected before distribution.

- **Versioning:**
  Follow semantic versioning (e.g., MAJOR.MINOR.PATCH) to clearly indicate changes and compatibility.
- **Use Virtual Environments:**
  Develop and test your package in isolated virtual environments to avoid dependency conflicts.

**In Summary**

Packaging and distributing your Python projects using setuptools and pip offers many benefits:

- **Modularity and Reusability:**
  Packaging allows you to structure your code into reusable modules.
- **Ease of Distribution:**
  Creating source and wheel distributions enables easy installation with pip.
- **Community Sharing:**
  Publishing your package to PyPI makes it accessible to a global community of developers.
- **Best Practices:**
  Following best practices in organization, documentation, versioning, and testing helps maintain a high-quality, maintainable project.

By mastering these packaging and distribution techniques, you can ensure that your Python projects are easy to install, use, and maintain, fostering a smoother development workflow and broader collaboration.

## Structuring a Python Project for Distribution

A well-organized project structure is essential for packaging, distributing, and maintaining a Python project. By following established conventions, you ensure that your project is easy to navigate, test, and share with other developers.

**1. Recommended Project Structure**

```
my_project/
├── my_package/           # Main package directory
│   ├── __init__.py       # Package initialization file
│   ├── module1.py        # Module containing core functionality
│   ├── module2.py        # Additional module(s)
│   └── subpackage/       # Subpackage (optional)
│       ├── __init__.py
│       └── module3.py
├── tests/                # Test suite for your project
│   ├── __init__.py       # Optional: Makes tests a package
│   └── test_module1.py   # Test file for module1
├── docs/                 # Documentation files (optional)
│   └── index.md
├── setup.py              # Build script for setuptools
├── requirements.txt      # List of runtime dependencies
├── MANIFEST.in           # Instructions for including non-
code files
├── README.md             # Project description and usage
instructions
└── LICENSE               # License file
```

**Explanation:**

- **my_package/**:
  Contains your package's source code. The __init__.py file makes this directory a Python package, and additional modules and subpackages are organized here.
- **tests/**:
  Holds all your test files. Keeping tests in a separate directory encourages a clear separation between production code and test code.
- **docs/**:
  Optional directory for documentation. This can include Markdown files, Sphinx documentation, or other resources.
- **setup.py**:
  The build script for your project. It contains metadata and configuration for packaging your project.
- **requirements.txt**:
  Lists the dependencies required to run your project, making it easier for users to install the necessary packages.
- **MANIFEST.in**:
  Specifies additional files to include in the package (such as documentation, configuration files, or data files) that are not automatically included.
- **README.md**:
  Provides an overview, installation instructions, usage examples, and other important information about your project.
- **LICENSE**:
  Specifies the licensing under which your project is distributed.

### 2. Creating the setup.py File

The setup.py file is the centerpiece of your project's packaging configuration. It uses setuptools to define metadata, dependencies, and package structure.

**Example: A Basic setup.py File**

```
from setuptools import setup, find_packages

setup(
    name="my_project",
    version="0.1.0",
    author="Your Name",
    author_email="your.email@example.com",
    description="A short description of your project.",
    long_description=open("README.md", encoding="utf-8").read(),
    long_description_content_type="text/markdown",
    url="https://github.com/yourusername/my_project",
    packages=find_packages(),  # Automatically find all packages in the directory
    classifiers=[
        "Programming Language :: Python :: 3",
        "License :: OSI Approved :: MIT License",
        "Operating System :: OS Independent",
    ],
    python_requires=">=3.6",
```

```
    install_requires=[
        # List your project's dependencies here
        # e.g., "requests>=2.25.1",
    ],
)
```

**Explanation:**

- **Metadata:**
  Fields like name, version, author, and description provide essential information about your package.
- **long_description:**
  Reads your README.md to provide a detailed package description on PyPI.
- **find_packages():**
  Automatically discovers all packages and subpackages within your project.
- **classifiers:**
  Standardized metadata for PyPI.
- **python_requires:**
  Specifies the Python version compatibility.
- **install_requires:**
  Lists runtime dependencies that pip will install automatically.

**3. Additional Files for Packaging**

**requirements.txt**

List all the packages your project depends on, one per line. For example:

```
requests>=2.25.1
```

```
numpy>=1.19.5
```

This file helps users install the necessary dependencies using:

```
pip install -r requirements.txt
```

**MANIFEST.in**

This file tells setuptools which non-code files to include in your distribution. For example:

```
include README.md LICENSE
recursive-include docs *
```

This ensures that your README, license, and documentation files are included in the packaged distribution.

**4. Building and Distributing Your Package**

**Building the Distribution**

Before distributing your package, build the distribution files:

1. **Install setuptools and wheel:**

```
pip install setuptools wheel
```

2. Build the package:

```
python setup.py sdist bdist_wheel
```

This creates source distributions (.tar.gz) and wheels (.whl) in the dist/ directory.

**Uploading to PyPI**

To upload your package to PyPI:

1. **Install Twine:**

```
pip install twine
```

2. Upload the package:

```
twine upload dist/*
```

Follow the prompts to enter your PyPI credentials.

### 5. Best Practices for Structuring Your Python Project

- **Modular Design:**
  Organize your code into packages and modules based on functionality. This improves maintainability and reusability.
- **Clear Documentation:**
  Provide comprehensive documentation in your README and within your code via docstrings.
- **Version Control:**
  Use version control systems (like Git) to track changes and manage your project's evolution.
- **Automated Testing:**
  Include a robust test suite (e.g., in the tests/ directory) and integrate it with continuous integration (CI) systems.
- **Consistent Naming:**
  Follow Python's naming conventions (PEP 8) for modules, packages, classes, and functions to ensure consistency.
- **Environment Isolation:**
  Use virtual environments to manage dependencies and ensure consistent behavior across different systems.

### In Summary

Structuring a Python project for distribution is a crucial step in the development lifecycle. A well-organized project:

- Enhances **readability** and **maintainability**.

- Facilitates **packaging** and **distribution** using tools like setuptools and pip.
- Promotes **code reuse** and **collaboration** across different environments.

Key components include:

- A clear directory structure with separate folders for your package, tests, documentation, and configuration files.
- A comprehensive setup.py file that includes metadata, dependency information, and package discovery.
- Supporting files like requirements.txt and MANIFEST.in to manage dependencies and include additional resources.

By adhering to these best practices, you can ensure that your Python project is well-prepared for distribution, making it easier for others to install, use, and contribute to your code.

## PyPI and Private Repositories

Publishing your Python project for distribution is a key step in sharing your work with the world or within your organization. The two common avenues for distributing Python packages are the public Python Package Index (PyPI) and private repositories.

### 1. Publishing to PyPI

PyPI is the primary repository for Python packages, allowing developers to share their libraries with the global community. Once your package is published to PyPI, users can install it easily with pip.

### 1.1 Preparing Your Package

Ensure your project is organized with a clear directory structure. A common structure might be:

```
my_project/
├── my_package/
│   ├── __init__.py
│   └── module.py
├── tests/
│   └── test_module.py
├── README.md
├── LICENSE
├── setup.py
└── requirements.txt
```

### 1.2 Example setup.py File

Your setup.py file is critical for packaging. Here's a sample setup.py:

```
from setuptools import setup, find_packages

setup(
    name="my_project",
    version="0.1.0",
    author="Your Name",
    author_email="your.email@example.com",
    description="A short description of your project.",
    long_description=open("README.md", encoding="utf-
8").read(),
    long_description_content_type="text/markdown",
    url="https://github.com/yourusername/my_project",
```

```
    packages=find_packages(), # Automatically find packages in the directory
    classifiers=[
        "Programming Language :: Python :: 3",
        "License :: OSI Approved :: MIT License",
        "Operating System :: OS Independent",
    ],
    python_requires=">=3.6",
    install_requires=[
        # List your dependencies here, for example:
        # "requests>=2.25.1",
    ],
)
```

**Explanation:**

- **Metadata:** Provides necessary details about your package such as name, version, author, and description.
- **find_packages():** Automatically discovers all packages and subpackages.
- **install_requires:** Lists the dependencies that pip will install along with your package.
- **long_description:** Reads the README for a detailed package description on PyPI.

### 1.3 Building Your Distribution Package

To build your package, run the following commands from your project root:

1. **Install Build Tools:**

```
pip install setuptools wheel
```

2. Build the Package:

```
python setup.py sdist bdist_wheel
```

This command creates distribution files (a source distribution and a wheel) in a new dist/ directory.

### 1.4 Uploading to PyPI Using Twine

Twine is the recommended tool for securely uploading your package to PyPI.

1. **Install Twine:**

```
pip install twine
```

2. Upload Your Package:

```
twine upload dist/*
```

You will be prompted for your PyPI username and password. After a successful upload, your package will be available on PyPI for installation with pip.

**Example: Installing Your Package via pip**

```
pip install my_project
```

## 2. Using Private Repositories

For organizations or private projects where you do not wish to publish your code publicly, private repositories offer a controlled way to distribute Python packages. Private repositories can be hosted on internal servers or through third-party services such as Artifactory, Nexus, or GitHub Packages.

### 2.1 Configuring pip to Use a Private Repository

To install packages from a private repository, you can configure pip to use a custom index URL. Create or modify the pip.conf (Linux/Mac) or pip.ini (Windows) file.

**Example pip.conf (Linux/Mac):**

```
[global]

index-url = https://your-private-repo.example.com/simple/
```

Example pip.ini (Windows):

```
[global]

index-url = https://your-private-repo.example.com/simple/
```

Alternatively, you can specify the index URL directly when installing a package:

```
pip install my_project --index-url https://your-private-repo.example.com/simple/
```

### 2.2 Uploading to a Private Repository

Many private repositories support standard PyPI tools like Twine. The process is similar to uploading to PyPI, but you need to specify the repository URL.

**Example: Uploading with Twine to a Private Repository**

```
twine upload --repository-url https://your-private-repo.example.com/simple/ dist/*
```

**Explanation:**

- The --repository-url flag tells Twine where to upload your package.
- Ensure that your private repository is properly configured to accept package uploads.

### 3. Best Practices for Packaging and Distribution

- **Organize Your Project:**
  Use a clear, modular directory structure. Separate your source code, tests, documentation, and configuration files.
- **Versioning:**
  Follow semantic versioning (e.g., MAJOR.MINOR.PATCH) to indicate changes and maintain compatibility.
- **Documentation:**
  Provide comprehensive documentation (README, changelog, and inline comments) to help users understand and use your package.
- **Automate Testing:**
  Incorporate a robust test suite and consider integrating continuous integration (CI) tools to run tests automatically.
- **Security:**
  Use secure methods for uploading and installing packages. Ensure credentials for private repositories are stored securely.
- **Use Virtual Environments:**
  Develop and test your package in isolated environments to avoid dependency conflicts.

### In Summary

Packaging and distributing your Python project is a critical step in sharing your work and ensuring maintainability. Key points include:

- **PyPI Distribution:**
  - Use setuptools to define your package structure and metadata.
  - Build source and wheel distributions using python setup.py sdist bdist_wheel.
  - Upload your package to PyPI using Twine for global distribution.
- **Private Repositories:**
  - Configure pip to use a private repository for internal or private projects.
  - Upload packages to your private repository similarly to PyPI, using the appropriate repository URL.
- **Best Practices:**
  - Maintain a clear project structure, follow semantic versioning, provide thorough documentation, and use CI tools to automate testing.

By following these guidelines and leveraging the available tools, you can create Python packages that are easy to distribute, install, and maintain, whether for public use via PyPI or for internal distribution through private repositories.

# Section XII: Putting It All Together
## Chapter 28: Capstone Projects

### Project 1: Building a CLI Task Manager

A capstone project is an excellent opportunity to integrate multiple programming concepts into a cohesive application. In this project, we'll build a Command-Line Interface (CLI) Task Manager in Python. This project will cover several core areas, including:

- **Modular Design:** Organizing code into functions and modules.
- **File I/O and Data Serialization:** Persisting tasks in a JSON file.
- **Error Handling:** Managing errors gracefully.
- **Argument Parsing:** Creating a user-friendly CLI using the argparse module.
- **Best Practices:** Clean code structure, documentation, and usability.

The CLI Task Manager will allow users to add tasks, list all tasks, mark tasks as complete, and remove tasks. The tasks will be stored in a JSON file for persistence between sessions.

**1. Project Overview**

**Features:**

- **Add Task:** Create a new task with a description.
- **List Tasks:** Display all tasks, indicating which tasks are completed.
- **Mark Task as Complete:** Update a task's status to completed.
- **Remove Task:** Delete a task from the list.

- **Data Persistence:** All tasks are stored in a JSON file (tasks.json), ensuring that the task list is maintained between runs.

**Project Structure:**

```
cli_task_manager/
├── task_manager.py        # Main application logic
├── tasks.json            # Data file for storing tasks (created
automatically)
└── README.md             # Project documentation (optional)
```

## 2. Implementation Details

### 2.1 Data Model

We'll represent each task as a dictionary with the following keys:

- id: A unique identifier for the task.
- description: A string describing the task.
- completed: A boolean indicating whether the task is complete.

Tasks will be stored in a list and persisted as JSON.

### 2.2 File I/O for Task Persistence

We'll write functions to load tasks from tasks.json and save tasks back to it. Using the with statement ensures that the file is properly closed after each operation.

```
import json
import os
TASKS_FILE = "tasks.json"
def load_tasks():
    """
```

```
    Load tasks from the JSON file. If the file doesn't exist, return an
empty list.

    Returns:

        list: A list of task dictionaries.

    """

    if not os.path.exists(TASKS_FILE):

        return []

    try:

        with open(TASKS_FILE, "r", encoding="utf-8") as file:

            tasks = json.load(file)

            return tasks

    except json.JSONDecodeError:

        print("Error: Corrupted tasks file. Starting with an empty task
list.")

        return []

def save_tasks(tasks):

    """

    Save tasks to the JSON file.

    Parameters:

        tasks (list): The list of task dictionaries to be saved.

    """

    with open(TASKS_FILE, "w", encoding="utf-8") as file:

        json.dump(tasks, file, indent=4)
```

## 2.3 Task Management Functions

Next, we define functions for adding, listing, completing, and removing tasks.

```
def add_task(description):
    """
    Add a new task with the given description.
    Parameters:
        description (str): The task description.
    """
    tasks = load_tasks()
    task_id = max([task["id"] for task in tasks], default=0) + 1
    new_task = {
        "id": task_id,
        "description": description,
        "completed": False
    }
    tasks.append(new_task)
    save_tasks(tasks)
    print(f"Task added with ID {task_id}.")
def list_tasks():
    """
    List all tasks.
    """
```

```
    tasks = load_tasks()
    if not tasks:
        print("No tasks available.")
        return
    for task in tasks:
        status = "Done" if task["completed"] else "Pending"
        print(f"ID: {task['id']} | {task['description']} [{status}]")
def complete_task(task_id):
    """
    Mark a task as completed.
    Parameters:
        task_id (int): The ID of the task to mark as completed.
    """
    tasks = load_tasks()
    for task in tasks:
        if task["id"] == task_id:
            if task["completed"]:
                print(f"Task {task_id} is already completed.")
            else:
                task["completed"] = True
                print(f"Task {task_id} marked as completed.")
            save_tasks(tasks)
```

```
            return
    print(f"Task with ID {task_id} not found.")
def remove_task(task_id):
    """
    Remove a task from the list.
    Parameters:
        task_id (int): The ID of the task to remove.
    """
    tasks = load_tasks()
    new_tasks = [task for task in tasks if task["id"] != task_id]
    if len(new_tasks) == len(tasks):
        print(f"Task with ID {task_id} not found.")
    else:
        save_tasks(new_tasks)
        print(f"Task {task_id} removed successfully.")
```

### 2.4 Command-Line Interface with argparse

We use the argparse module to create a simple CLI that allows users to interact with our Task Manager.

```
import argparse
def main():
    parser = argparse.ArgumentParser(description="CLI Task
Manager")
```

```
    subparsers = parser.add_subparsers(dest="command",
required=True, help="Available commands")

    # Add task command

    add_parser = subparsers.add_parser("add", help="Add a new
task")

    add_parser.add_argument("description", type=str,
help="Description of the task")

    # List tasks command

    subparsers.add_parser("list", help="List all tasks")

    # Complete task command

    complete_parser = subparsers.add_parser("complete",
help="Mark a task as complete")

    complete_parser.add_argument("id", type=int, help="ID of the
task to complete")

    # Remove task command

    remove_parser = subparsers.add_parser("remove", help="Remove
a task")

    remove_parser.add_argument("id", type=int, help="ID of the task
to remove")

    args = parser.parse_args()

    if args.command == "add":

        add_task(args.description)

    elif args.command == "list":

        list_tasks()

    elif args.command == "complete":
```

```
        complete_task(args.id)
    elif args.command == "remove":
        remove_task(args.id)
    else:
        parser.print_help()
if __name__ == "__main__":
    main()
```

**Explanation:**

- **Argument Parsing:**
  - argparse.ArgumentParser is used to create a CLI with subcommands for different operations (add, list, complete, remove).
  - Each subcommand is associated with specific arguments.
- **Command Handling:**
  Based on the command, the appropriate function is called.
- **User Experience:**
  Users can interact with the Task Manager via the command line, for example:

```
python task_manager.py add "Finish the project report"
python task_manager.py list
python task_manager.py complete 1
python task_manager.py remove 1
```

### 3. Best Practices for CLI Projects

- **Modular Code:**
  Separate concerns by organizing your code into functions (e.g., task operations) and modules (e.g., a module for file I/O).
- **Error Handling:**
  Validate user inputs and handle errors gracefully to provide informative feedback.
- **Documentation:**
  Include a README file that explains how to install and use your CLI Task Manager.
- **Testing:**
  Develop tests for individual functions to ensure your Task Manager behaves as expected.
- **User-Friendly CLI:**
  Use descriptive help messages and subcommands to create an intuitive command-line interface.

### In Summary

The CLI Task Manager capstone project brings together various advanced topics:

- **File I/O and Data Serialization:**
  Tasks are persisted in a JSON file for long-term storage.
- **Functional Decomposition:**
  The application is structured into functions for adding, listing, completing, and removing tasks.
- **Command-Line Interface:**
  The argparse module is used to parse command-line arguments, making the application user-friendly.

- **Error Handling and Best Practices:**
  The project includes error handling for missing tasks and invalid inputs, ensuring robustness.

By completing this project, you integrate essential programming concepts - such as modularity, data persistence, CLI development, and error handling - into a cohesive application. This capstone project not only reinforces your understanding of these topics but also provides a solid foundation for more complex software development tasks.

## Project 2: Creating a Data Analysis Pipeline

A data analysis pipeline is an end-to-end system that ingests, cleans, transforms, analyzes, and visualizes data. This capstone project integrates multiple advanced topics - file I/O, data wrangling, data visualization, error handling, and modular design - into one cohesive application. In this project, you'll build a pipeline that processes raw CSV data, performs analysis using pandas, and produces visual insights with Matplotlib/Seaborn.

### 1. Project Overview

In this project, we will create a data analysis pipeline that:

- **Ingests Data:** Reads raw data from a CSV file.
- **Cleans and Transforms Data:** Handles missing values, filters records, and aggregates key metrics.
- **Performs Analysis:** Computes summary statistics and extracts meaningful insights.
- **Visualizes Data:** Generates plots to visualize trends and distributions.
- **Handles Errors Gracefully:** Incorporates error handling to manage issues during file I/O or data processing.

- **Is Modular:** Organizes code into reusable functions for each stage of the pipeline.

For demonstration, let's assume we have a CSV file called sales_data.csv with the following columns:

- **Date:** Date of the sale.
- **Product:** Product name.
- **Region:** Sales region.
- **Sales:** Sales amount.
- **Profit:** Profit amount.

Our goal is to calculate the total sales and profit by region and then visualize these metrics.

## 2. Implementation Details

### 2.1 Data Ingestion

We use pandas to read the CSV file efficiently. The read_csv() function loads the data into a DataFrame, which provides powerful data manipulation capabilities.

```
import pandas as pd

def load_data(file_path):
    """
    Load data from a CSV file into a pandas DataFrame.

    Parameters:
        file_path (str): The path to the CSV file.

    Returns:
        pd.DataFrame: The loaded data.
```

```
    """
    try:
        df = pd.read_csv(file_path, encoding="utf-8")
        print("Data loaded successfully.")
        return df
    except FileNotFoundError:
        print(f"Error: File '{file_path}' not found.")
        return pd.DataFrame()
    except pd.errors.ParserError:
        print("Error: Could not parse the CSV file.")
        return pd.DataFrame()
# Example usage:
df_sales = load_data("sales_data.csv")
```

**Explanation:**

- The load_data function reads a CSV file into a DataFrame and includes error handling for missing or malformed files.

### 2.2 Data Cleaning and Transformation

After loading the data, we clean it by handling missing values and converting data types as necessary. Then, we transform the data by aggregating sales and profit metrics by region.

```
def clean_and_transform(df):
    """
    Clean and transform the sales DataFrame.
```

```
    Parameters:
        df (pd.DataFrame): The raw sales data.
    Returns:
        pd.DataFrame: The transformed data with aggregated metrics.
    """
    # Remove duplicate rows if any
    df = df.drop_duplicates()
    # Fill missing values for Sales and Profit with 0
    df['Sales'] = pd.to_numeric(df['Sales'], errors='coerce').fillna(0)
    df['Profit'] = pd.to_numeric(df['Profit'], errors='coerce').fillna(0)
    # Optionally, convert Date column to datetime
    if 'Date' in df.columns:
        df['Date'] = pd.to_datetime(df['Date'], errors='coerce')
    # Group data by Region and calculate total sales and profit
    aggregated = df.groupby("Region").agg({
        "Sales": "sum",
        "Profit": "sum"
    }).reset_index()
    print("Data cleaning and transformation complete.")
    return aggregated
# Example usage:
df_transformed = clean_and_transform(df_sales)
```

```
print(df_transformed)
```

**Explanation:**

- Duplicate rows are removed with drop_duplicates().
- Sales and profit columns are converted to numeric types, with missing values filled with 0.
- The Date column is optionally converted to a datetime object.
- Data is aggregated by the "Region" column to compute total sales and profit.

## 2.3 Data Visualization

Using Matplotlib or Seaborn, we can create visualizations to represent the aggregated data. Below is an example of a bar chart to display total sales and profit by region.

```
import matplotlib.pyplot as plt

import seaborn as sns

def visualize_data(df):

    """

    Visualize the aggregated sales data using a bar chart.

    Parameters:

        df (pd.DataFrame): The transformed DataFrame with
aggregated data.

    """

    sns.set(style="whitegrid")

   # Create a figure with two subplots: one for Sales and one for
Profit
```

```
    fig, ax = plt.subplots(1, 2, figsize=(14, 6))

    # Bar plot for total sales by region

    sns.barplot(x="Region", y="Sales", data=df, palette="Blues_d",
ax=ax[0])

    ax[0].set_title("Total Sales by Region")

    ax[0].set_xlabel("Region")

    ax[0].set_ylabel("Total Sales")

    # Bar plot for total profit by region

    sns.barplot(x="Region", y="Profit", data=df, palette="Greens_d",
ax=ax[1])

    ax[1].set_title("Total Profit by Region")

    ax[1].set_xlabel("Region")

    ax[1].set_ylabel("Total Profit")

    plt.tight_layout()

    plt.show()

# Example usage:

visualize_data(df_transformed)
```

**Explanation:**

- Seaborn is configured with a white grid style for clear visualization.
- Two bar charts are created: one for total sales and one for total profit, each in its own subplot.
- The charts are customized with titles, axis labels, and color palettes.

- plt.tight_layout() adjusts subplot spacing for a neat presentation.

### 3. Bringing It All Together: The Data Analysis Pipeline

We can combine the individual components into a single function that executes the entire pipeline—from data loading to visualization.

```
def run_data_pipeline(file_path):
    """
    Execute the full data analysis pipeline:
    1. Load data from a CSV file.
    2. Clean and transform the data.
    3. Visualize the aggregated results.
        Parameters:
        file_path (str): The path to the CSV file containing raw sales
data.
    """
    # Load the data
    df_raw = load_data(file_path)
    if df_raw.empty:
        print("No data to process.")
        return
    # Clean and transform the data
    df_aggregated = clean_and_transform(df_raw)
    # Visualize the data
    visualize_data(df_aggregated)
```

```
# Run the data pipeline (ensure 'sales_data.csv' exists in your working directory)

run_data_pipeline("sales_data.csv")
```

**Explanation:**

- The run_data_pipeline function orchestrates the entire process: loading data, cleaning and transforming it, and visualizing the results.
- This modular approach allows each component of the pipeline to be tested and maintained independently.
- The pipeline provides a clear, end-to-end workflow for data analysis.

**4. Best Practices for Data Analysis Pipelines**

- **Modularity:**
  Break down the pipeline into distinct functions (data ingestion, cleaning, transformation, and visualization) for easier maintenance and testing.
- **Error Handling:**
  Incorporate error handling in each function to manage issues such as missing files or malformed data.
- **Documentation:**
  Provide clear docstrings and comments to explain the purpose and usage of each function.
- **Reusability:**
  Design functions to be reusable across different projects or datasets.
- **Automation:**
  Integrate your pipeline into automated workflows (e.g., scheduled scripts or CI/CD pipelines) for regular data processing.

## In Summary

Building a data analysis pipeline is a comprehensive capstone project that integrates multiple advanced topics:

- **Data Ingestion:**
  Efficiently load data from files (e.g., CSV) using pandas.
- **Data Cleaning and Transformation:**
  Clean, filter, and aggregate data to extract meaningful insights.
- **Data Visualization:**
  Use libraries like Matplotlib and Seaborn to create informative visualizations.
- **Modularity and Reusability:**
  Structure the pipeline into well-defined functions to promote code reuse and maintainability.
- **Error Handling:**
  Implement robust error handling to ensure the pipeline can handle unexpected issues gracefully.

By mastering these techniques, you can build powerful data analysis pipelines that turn raw data into actionable insights.

## Project 3: Developing a Simple Web Application

Developing a web application is an excellent capstone project that integrates various programming concepts including routing, templating, form handling, and error management. In this project, you will build a simple web application using Flask - a lightweight and flexible Python web framework. The application will demonstrate the following features:

- **Dynamic Routing:** Map URLs to view functions.
- **Templating:** Render dynamic HTML pages using Jinja2 templates.

- **Form Handling:** Process user input from web forms.
- **Error Handling:** Gracefully manage potential errors.
- **Modular Design:** Organize code for maintainability and scalability.

For this project, we will create a basic "Simple Website" with the following pages:

- **Home:** A welcome page.
- **About:** A page describing the application.
- **Contact:** A page with a form where users can send a message (for demonstration purposes, the message will be printed to the console).

**1. Project Overview**

**Objective:**
Develop a simple web application that serves dynamic content and handles user inputs via forms. The application will have:

- A **Home** page to welcome visitors.
- An **About** page to describe the website.
- A **Contact** page where users can submit a message.

**Key Components:**

- **Routing:** Directing URLs to the appropriate view functions.
- **Templates:** HTML files with dynamic placeholders.
- **Form Processing:** Handling POST requests and validating form data.
- **Error Handling:** Managing errors gracefully to enhance user experience.

### 2. Project Structure

A recommended project structure for the application might look like this:

```
simple_web_app/
├── app.py                  # Main Flask application
├── templates/              # Directory for HTML templates
│   ├── base.html           # Base template for common layout
│   ├── home.html           # Home page template
│   ├── about.html          # About page template
│   └── contact.html        # Contact page template
└── static/                 # Directory for static files (optional)
    └── style.css           # CSS for styling (optional)
```

- **app.py:** Contains the Flask application, routes, and form handling logic.
- **templates/:** Stores HTML templates that define the structure and layout of the pages.
- **static/:** (Optional) Contains static assets like CSS, JavaScript, and images.

### 3. Implementation Details

#### 3.1 Main Application (app.py)

Below is the complete code for a simple Flask application:

```
from flask import Flask, render_template, request, redirect, url_for,
flash
```

```
app = Flask(__name__)
app.secret_key = "your_secret_key"  # Needed for flashing messages
# Home page route
@app.route("/")
def home():
    return render_template("home.html")


# About page route
@app.route("/about")
def about():
    return render_template("about.html")
# Contact page route (handles both GET and POST requests)
@app.route("/contact", methods=["GET", "POST"])
def contact():
    if request.method == "POST":
        # Retrieve form data
        name = request.form.get("name")
        email = request.form.get("email")
        message = request.form.get("message")
        # Simple validation
        if not name or not email or not message:
            flash("All fields are required.", "error")
```

```
        return render_template("contact.html", name=name,
email=email, message=message)


      # Process the contact form (e.g., save to a file or send an email)

      # For this example, we'll simply print the message to the
console.

      print(f"New Contact Message:\nName: {name}\nEmail:
{email}\nMessage: {message}\n")

      flash("Your message has been sent successfully!", "success")

      return redirect(url_for("contact"))

    # For GET request, render the contact form

    return render_template("contact.html")

if __name__ == "__main__":

    app.run(debug=True)
```

**Explanation:**

- **Application Setup:**
  An instance of Flask is created with a secret key for session management (required for flashing messages).
- **Routing:**
  - The / route renders the home page.
  - The /about route renders the about page.
  - The /contact route handles both GET (displaying the form) and POST (processing form submissions) requests.
- **Form Handling:**
  In the contact route, form data is retrieved using

request.form.get(). Basic validation ensures all fields are filled; otherwise, a flash message is shown.

- **Flashing Messages:**
  The flash() function provides feedback to the user, and redirect(url_for("contact")) ensures the form is cleared after a successful submission.
- **Debug Mode:**
  The app runs in debug mode for development purposes.

### 3.2 HTML Templates

Place the following templates in the templates directory.

**base.html**

```
<!DOCTYPE html>

<html lang="en">

<head>

    <meta charset="UTF-8">

    <title>{% block title %}Simple Web App{% endblock
%}</title>

    <link rel="stylesheet" href="{{ url_for('static',
filename='style.css') }}">

</head>

<body>

    <header>

        <h1>Simple Web App</h1>

        <nav>

            <a href="{{ url_for('home') }}">Home</a> |
```

```
        <a href="{{ url_for('about') }}">About</a> |
        <a href="{{ url_for('contact') }}">Contact</a>
      </nav>
    </header>
    <main>
      {% with messages =
get_flashed_messages(with_categories=true) %}
        {% if messages %}
          <ul class="flashes">
            {% for category, message in messages %}
              <li class="{{ category }}">{{ message }}</li>
            {% endfor %}
          </ul>
        {% endif %}
      {% endwith %}
      {% block content %}{% endblock %}
    </main>
    <footer>
      <p>&copy; 2024 Simple Web App</p>
    </footer>
  </body>
</html>
```

**Explanation:**

- **Template Inheritance:**
  The base template provides the overall structure, including header, navigation, and footer.
- **Dynamic Title and Content Blocks:**
  Child templates override {% block title %} and {% block content %} to provide page-specific content.
- **Flash Messages:**
  The template includes a section to display flashed messages, using categories for styling (e.g., error, success).

**home.html**

```
{% extends "base.html" %}

{% block title %}Home - Simple Web App{% endblock %}

{% block content %}

    <h2>Welcome to the Simple Web App</h2>

    <p>This is the home page of our capstone project.</p>

{% endblock %}
```

about.html

```
{% extends "base.html" %}

{% block title %}About - Simple Web App{% endblock %}

{% block content %}

    <h2>About</h2>

    <p>This web application is a simple demonstration of how to
build a dynamic website using Flask.</p>

{% endblock %}
```

contact.html

```
{% extends "base.html" %}


{% block title %}Contact - Simple Web App{% endblock %}

{% block content %}

  <h2>Contact Us</h2>

  <form method="post">

    <label for="name">Name:</label><br>

    <input type="text" id="name" name="name" value="{{ name | default('') }}"><br><br>

    <label for="email">Email:</label><br>

    <input type="email" id="email" name="email" value="{{ email | default('') }}"><br><br>

    <label for="message">Message:</label><br>

    <textarea id="message" name="message" rows="5" cols="40">{{ message | default('') }}</textarea><br><br>

    <input type="submit" value="Send Message">

  </form>

{% endblock %}
```

**Explanation:**

- **Dynamic Content:**
  The contact template renders a form for users to submit their name, email, and a message. It uses default filters to preserve form data if there is an error.

- **Template Inheritance:**
  Each template extends the base.html template to maintain a consistent look and feel.

### 4. Running the Web Application

To run your web application:

1. Navigate to your project directory in the terminal.
2. Execute the following command:

```
python app.py
```

3. Open your web browser and visit http://127.0.0.1:5000/ to view your application.

### 5. Best Practices for Web Development Projects

- **Modular Design:**
  Organize your code by separating business logic, routing, and templating. Use blueprints in Flask for larger projects.
- **Error Handling:**
  Implement error handlers and validations to manage unexpected inputs and server errors gracefully.
- **Version Control:**
  Use Git or another version control system to manage your code and collaborate effectively.
- **Testing:**
  Write tests for your routes and functions to ensure your application behaves as expected.
- **Documentation:**
  Provide clear documentation in a README file, detailing how to set up, run, and use your web application.

## In Summary

Building a simple web application with Flask is an excellent way to put together various web development concepts:

- **Routing:**
  Map URLs to Python functions that render dynamic content.
- **Templating:**
  Use Jinja2 templates to separate presentation from business logic.
- **Form Handling:**
  Process GET and POST requests to capture user input.
- **Data Persistence (Optional):**
  Extend the application with database integration for persistent data storage.
- **Error Handling:**
  Incorporate error messages and flash notifications to improve user experience.

This capstone project not only reinforces your understanding of Flask and web development but also provides a solid foundation for developing more complex, data-driven web applications.

www.ingramcontent.com/pod-product-compliance
Lightning Source LLC
LaVergne TN
LVHW052013200926
848481LV00005B/1478